CHARTERS OF SHERBORNE

ANGLO-SAXON CHARTERS · III

CHARTERS OF SHERBORNE

EDITED BY

M. A. O'DONOVAN

Published for THE BRITISH ACADEMY
by THE OXFORD UNIVERSITY PRESS
1988

Oxford University Press, Walton Street, Oxford OX2 6DP

*Oxford New York Toronto
Delhi Bombay Calcutta Madras Karachi
Petaling Jaya Singapore Hong Kong Tokyo
Nairobi Dar es Salaam Cape Town
Melbourne Auckland*

*and associated companies in
Beirut Berlin Ibadan Nicosia*

Oxford is a trade mark of Oxford University Press

*Published in the United States
by Oxford University Press, New York*

© *1988 The British Academy*

*All rights reserved. No part of this publication may be reproduced,
stored in a retrieval system, or transmitted, in any form or any means,
electronic, mechanical, photocopying, recording, or otherwise, without
the prior permission of The British Academy*

British Library Cataloguing in Publication Data

O'Donovan, Mary Anne
 Corpus of Anglo-Saxon charters.
 Vol. 3: The charters of Sherborne
 1. Cartularies 2. Church lands—England
 —History
 I. Title
 333.3'22'0932 HD604

ISBN 0-19-726051-9

*Printed and bound in Great Britain by
Latimer Trend & Company Ltd, Plymouth*

TO
THE MEMORY OF
DOROTHY WHITELOCK

FOREWORD

THE APPEARANCE of Dr M. A. O'Donovan's edition of the charters of Sherborne Abbey, the third volume in the Anglo-Saxon Charters series sponsored jointly by the British Academy and the Royal Historical Society, has been regrettably delayed, largely by factors beyond the control of the editor and of the editorial committee. The delay in publication has at least brought compensation in one important respect, namely that Dr O'Donovan, as she gladly acknowledges, has been able to benefit from the advice not only of Professor P. H. Sawyer while he was still Honorary Secretary of the joint committee but also of his successor Dr Simon Keynes and of a number of other scholars who are specialists in the various fields of palaeography, onomastics and early medieval Latin, notably Professor Julian Brown, Dr Margaret Gelling and Dr Michael Lapidge. Although the surviving corpus of Sherborne charters is small, the estates dealt with by the documents cited in this volume lay in the heartland of Wessex, and the collection carries us back to the earliest period of West Saxon Christianity and kingship. In the twelfth century Sherborne acquired control over the small Benedictine monastery of Horton, also in Dorset, and the earliest charters of this house, whose history dates from the tenth century, are included within the Sherborne collection.

Membership of the joint editorial committee has inevitably undergone some alteration over the years. The sadly untimely deaths of Dr Neil Ker and of Professor Julian Brown, and the resignation of Dr Pierre Chaplais, have deprived the committee of the counsel of three outstanding scholars of the Anglo-Saxon period, but the committee must count itself fortunate in having benefited from their expertise in palaeography and diplomatic over so many years. Professor Peter Sawyer, having borne the heavy duties of Honorary Secretary and, in effect, 'resident editor', since 1966, demitted office in 1982. A special word of thanks must go to him for so freely giving of his energy, enthusiasm and wide knowledge of all things Anglo-Saxon in furtherance of the committee's objectives. The committee has also been fortunate in securing the services of Dr Simon Keynes as Professor Sawyer's successor. Besides him and the Chairman, the committee now consists of Professor Nicholas Brooks, Dr David Dumville, Dr Margaret Gelling, Dr Michael Lapidge, Dr Michael Roper and Professor Eric Stanley. It is hoped that publication of the charters of Selsey will follow Sherborne after only a short interval, while the important collections for Canterbury and Exeter are well advanced.

This Foreword must conclude on a note of sadness but also of profound thankfulness. Professor Christopher Cheney died on 19 June 1987. He was a moving spirit at the inception of the idea of a planned edition of all the charters of the Anglo-Saxon period, bringing the influence of his opinions, always quietly but cogently expressed, to bear upon both the Royal Historical Society and the British Academy. When the joint editorial committee was set up in 1966, Christopher Cheney became its chairman and held this position until 1978, remaining on the committee for a few years as an ordinary member. The Anglo-Saxon Charters project is emphatically a co-operative and collaborative venture, in which a large number of scholars have played and (it is to be hoped) will play a part; but in so far as it has owed its motivation, cohesion and direction to the inspiration of one person, that person—as all would gladly acknowledge—has been Christopher Cheney.

G. W. S. BARROW

ACKNOWLEDGEMENTS

MY THANKS go to all the members of the Anglo-Saxon Charters committee who commented on the typescript, read the proofs, and thereby saved me from many errors. I am particularly grateful to Dr Michael Lapidge for his help in editing the Latin texts, and for compiling the Latin glossary; to Professor Eric Stanley for his advice on editing the Old English texts; to Dr Margaret Gelling for her generous help with the place-name and boundary marks indexes; and to Professor Nicholas Brooks and Dr Simon Keynes for much constructive criticism. The late Dr Neil Ker contributed most of the palaeographical notes on the manuscripts involved, and the late Professor Julian Brown supplied further details. I am also grateful to Dr David Mills and Mr Oliver Padel for their advice on the place-names of Dorset and Cornwall respectively. But above all I am indebted to the late Professor Dorothy Whitelock for her unfailing and invaluable criticism, advice and encouragement.

I am obliged to the British Library Board for permission to reproduce two photographs of pages from the Sherborne cartulary.

CONTENTS

INTRODUCTION
   1. The Abbeys of Sherborne and Horton   xiii
   2. The Archive   xiii
   3. The Manuscripts   xiv
   4. The Diplomatic of the Charters   xxi
   5. Sherborne Lands: Monastic and Episcopal   xxxii
   6. The Early History of Horton Abbey   lviii

ABBREVIATIONS   lxiii

LIST OF CHARTERS   lxix

CONCORDANCE   lxxi

NOTE ON THE METHOD OF EDITING   lxxiii

THE CHARTERS   1

APPENDIX 1   81

APPENDIX 2   83

INDEXES
   1. Index of Personal Names   89
   2. Index of Place-Names   94
   3. Words and Names used in Boundary Marks   97
   4. Latin Glossary   101
   5. Diplomatic Index   103

ILLUSTRATIONS

Plate I	BL Add. 46487, 10v	between
Plate II	BL Add. 46487, 17r	pp. lxxiv and 1

Figure 1	The Estates assigned to the Monastery of Sherborne in Various Sources	xxxiii
Figure 2	Map of Sherborne and Horton Estates	xxxiv
Figure 3	Map of Sherborne Episcopal Estates *c.* 900	xxxviii

INTRODUCTION

1. THE ABBEYS OF SHERBORNE AND HORTON

THE charters presented in this volume concern the estates of the two abbeys of Sherborne and Horton. Sherborne was chosen as the episcopal seat of Wessex 'west of the wood' in 705, according to the *Anglo-Saxon Chronicle*, and continued to administer this large area until the early tenth century, when a much-needed division was finally effected. Somerset was then allotted to a bishop seated at Wells, and Devon with Cornwall to one seated at Crediton; the bishop of Sherborne was thus left with Dorset alone. Presumably at this time Sherborne lost many estates in the areas removed from its jurisdiction (see below, pp. l–lvi). At the end of the tenth century, as part of his reorganization of the foundation at Sherborne as a Benedictine community, Bishop Wulfsige III appears to have consolidated and placed on a more formal footing those estates which supported the monastery, as opposed to those which belonged to the bishopric (see pp. xxxii–xxxiii; **11** and commentary), and it is with these monastic lands that the charters printed here are almost exclusively concerned.

Shortly after the Norman Conquest the decision was made to move the episcopal seat from Sherborne, by then a very insignificant centre, to Salisbury (Old Sarum). The move was begun by Bishop Hermann before his death in 1078, and completed by his successor, Bishop Osmund. Sherborne was left as a priory under the control of the bishops of Salisbury.

Horton was originally founded as a nunnery, perhaps during the tenth century, but fell into disuse and was refounded as a monastery in the last decades before the Norman Conquest. It was a small house, and by 1122 was so poor that it was demoted to a priory and amalgamated with Sherborne, which in turn was promoted to the status of abbey (see below, pp. xv–xvi). It must have been at this juncture that the Horton charters passed to the Sherborne archives, to be copied together with the Sherborne documents into the Sherborne cartulary a quarter of a century later.

2. THE ARCHIVE

Not one of the Sherborne or Horton charters printed here has survived in its original form, and only one (**13**) exists in a pre-

Conquest copy. The episcopal muniments at Sherborne would certainly have followed the bishop to Salisbury, and quite probably some of the monastic documents went with them, since the bishop retained control of the monastery.[1] But no traces of pre-Conquest documents appear in the later Salisbury records, and the compiler of the *Registrum Osmundi* found it sufficient simply to list the estates that belonged to the bishopric of Salisbury as of ancient right, by which he meant the lands inherited from the bishoprics of Sherborne and Ramsbury; charters are not even mentioned.[2] Other bishoprics that were moved at about the same time show a similar dearth of original pre-Conquest material: Selsey has only one original charter, surviving at Chichester (S 1184); Dorchester, moved to Lincoln, and Wells, moved to Bath, have one each (S 1379 and 677); Lichfield, transferred to Chester, has none.

However, the charters which remained at Sherborne did not fare any better. **11** (with its later appendage **12**), **14** and **17**, which were probably not taken to Salisbury, disappeared some time after the compilation of the cartulary, as did the Horton charters.

There are two charters recording grants to Sherborne which are not edited in this volume, since the estates concerned passed to other owners before the Conquest. One of these, a grant of land at Crediton to Forthhere, bishop of Sherborne, has survived in an eleventh-century single-sheet copy at Exeter (S 255, dated 739; see below, pp. xlvii–xlviii); the other, an exchange of estates in Somerset and Devon (S 380), survives only in a cartulary copy at Wells (see below, p. liv).

3. THE MANUSCRIPTS

(a) *The Sherborne cartulary*

All the texts in this volume have been taken, with one exception (**13**), from the Sherborne cartulary, BL Add. 46487. Only one charter, **11**, has survived (albeit partially) in a second copy, in the miscellaneous collection BL Cotton Otho A. xviii. Add. 46487 has been described in some detail by Francis Wormald.[3] It measures 270 × 180 mm, and has a written area of *c*. 192 × 115 mm, with twenty-eight lines to the page. In the seventeenth century it consisted of ninety-two leaves, not counting two parchment flyleaves at the beginning, to judge from a foliation of

---

[1] See below, pp. xv–xvi.
[2] *Registrum Osmundi*, i. 198–9. This part is in a hand of s. xii¹.
[3] Wormald 1957, pp. 101–19. The manuscript is calendared in Davis, *Cartularies*, no. 892. See also C. M. Kauffmann, *Romanesque Manuscripts 1066–1190*, A Survey of Manuscripts illuminated in the British Isles iii (London, 1975), no. 60.

that date. By the time the British Museum acquired the manuscript in 1947,[4] seven leaves (30, 64–5, 72–3 and 89–90) had apparently been lost, and all the leaves after fo. 31 were in a disturbed order. On acquisition the leaves were refoliated in the then existing order, including the two flyleaves as fos 1–2. In 1967 the disturbed order was corrected, and the leaves given their present numbers, fos 1–47 and 49–88[5]. Fortunately, the various foliations are hardly relevant here, since we are concerned only with fos 3–31, which were fos 3–31 when Wormald examined the manuscript, and fos 1–29 in the seventeenth century. These twenty-nine leaves are made up of two complete quires of eight leaves (fos 3–18), followed by two quires of eight leaves from which three have been removed, the last leaf in quire 3 (after fo. 25) and the last two leaves in quire 4 (after fo. 31). The first of the two leaves missing from quire 4 would have contained the last part of Edward the Confessor's grant of liberties to Horton (**22**), and appears still to have been present in the manuscript in the seventeenth century, since the old foliation passes at this point from 29 to 31. The other two leaves missing from quires 3 and 4 may well have been blanks: each comes after one of the sections described by Wormald (1957, pp. 103–4, and below).

Add. 46487 is an impressive product of the mid twelfth century, and had a dual purpose, combining the cartulary texts with liturgical material suitable for the use of an abbot during the church year. Its date and the reasons for its existence in this particular form have been examined and explained by Professor Wormald, who set out the contents under forty-four heads (1957, pp. 112–17), and showed that the non-liturgical part falls into three sections, the first (fos 3–25: arts 2–24) containing Sherborne land documents both pre- and post-Conquest, the second (fos 26–31: arts 26–31) dealing with Horton material, and the third (fos 32–8: arts 32–3 and 35–41) concerned with a serious dispute which took place in about 1145 between the community at Sherborne, by then an abbey, and Joscelin, bishop of Salisbury.

When the bishopric was moved to Salisbury in 1078, the community at Sherborne at first remained governed as before, by a prior under the formal abbacy of the bishop (see **11** and **17**). Then in 1122, while Thurstin was prior, Sherborne and the abbey of Horton were joined, and either at that time, or a few years later, Horton was demoted to a priory, and Sherborne was made a full abbey, with Thurstin as the first abbot.[6] Under the Benedictine

---

[4] *British Museum Quarterly* xv (1951), pp. 19, 21 and Pl. xi, a reduced facsimile of fo. 7.
[5] Fo. 48 is a stub. Photographs taken at this time are kept as Add. 46487*.
[6] See BL Cotton Faustina A. ii, fos 25–6; Add. 46487, art. 32; the Sherborne Missal, p. 388; *Mon. Angl.*, i. 333; and Knowles, *HRH*, p. 70.

xvi INTRODUCTION

Rule, which lays down that an abbot shall be freely elected from among the brethren, and by canon law, which forbade bishops to interfere with such elections, this should have meant that Sherborne was now free of Salisbury's direct rule. However, some time between 1142 and 1145, when Joscelin had succeeded to the bishopric, and when Thurstin's successor Roger had died, Joscelin forced on the abbey as its new abbot one Peter, then prior of Farley in Wiltshire. The Sherborne community appealed to Pope Eugenius III against this move, and won their case. Eugenius wrote to Joscelin in February 1146 forbidding him to interfere with the election of a new abbot – Peter evidently having already been deposed – and by November of that year a man called Henry was installed.[7]

Professor Wormald suggested (1957, p. 109) that the manuscript represents a juxtaposition of legal documents and liturgical material with the deliberate intent thereby to safeguard Sherborne independence and possessions with all possible religious sanctions. The book itself is written in a fine hand, with large coloured initials throughout, and two (once probably four) miniatures. It is beautifully bound in oak boards, which were originally covered with panels of Limoges enamel, only one of which survives.[8] It is very clearly designed as a precious book, for display and use at the altar on feasts and ceremonial occasions.

It was common practice in the Anglo-Saxon and early Norman periods to copy important documents into gospel books, because the innate sanctity of the book would lend weight to the document, and also preserve it from alteration, since 'to tamper with holy books was sacrilege'.[9] **10** is an example of this practice, and others are cited below (p. 38), as well as by Professor Wormald (1957, pp. 106–7). As he points out, however, there is a major difference between such examples and the Sherborne cartulary, for whereas the former were copied into existing books, in the latter the charters and other documents and the liturgical matter were written at the same time, and the liturgical part is almost presented as subordinate, for it appears only after thirty-seven folios of secular documents. If Professor Wormald's reconstruction is correct – and the evidence and arguments he assembled are

---

[7] For this affair see Wormald 1957, pp. 108–9; and arts 26, 33 and 35–9 in Add. 46487 (Wormald's numbering). Art. 26 is printed in Hearne, *Collections*, iii. 418; arts 33 and 35–9 appear in Holtzmann, *Papsturkunden*, nos 46–51.

[8] Wormald 1957, pp. 104–6 and 109–11. The binding may be contemporary with the manuscript or slightly later, since Wormald feels that the surviving enamel plaque belongs probably to *c.* 1200.

[9] Ibid. p. 107; and see also the discussion on the subject in pp. 61–6 of D. Jenkins and M. E. Owen, 'The Welsh Marginalia in the Lichfield Gospel, Part I', *Cambridge Medieval Celtic Studies* v (1983), pp. 37–66.

overwhelmingly compelling – then the book was especially composed so that the secular documents which ensured Sherborne's freedom 'were placed under the protection as it were of the book's sacred contents and its connection with the altar' (1957, p. 109).

The manuscript originally opened with **11**, the foundation charter of 998, and the related text **12** (arts 2 and 3). After these come the individual Sherborne estate charters: starting with the two Corscombe grants, they occur in the order **15**, **16**, **3**, **7**, **10**, **9**, **8** and **2** (arts 4–12). The sequence of pre-Conquest charters is interrupted at this point by three texts recording grants to Sherborne made by Roger, bishop of Salisbury, in the early twelfth century (arts 13–15), but it resumes with **14** (art. 16), and the three charters of liberties, **1**, **5** and **6** (arts 17–19), in chronological order. Then follows an extract from Domesday Book concerning the lands held by the bishop of Salisbury on behalf of the monks of Sherborne (art. 20: see below, pp. xxxii–xxxv), and a grant from Bishop Joscelin to Henry, abbot of Sherborne (art. 21). This is followed by a space of twenty lines (on fo. 23r). A note in a seventeenth-century hand states that a deed has been erased here, but the writer must have been misled by ink shadows from the verso, as there is no evidence (even under ultra-violet light) of writing or erasure on the lines in question. The gap is followed by the final pre-Conquest Sherborne text, **17** (art. 22). The inclusion of **17**, judging by its position, may have been an afterthought, as it would have been associated more logically with **14**, which deals with the same estate. It comes as the final text in quire 3 in the original hand. The remaining blank leaves were used shortly afterwards to record a quitclaim by Bishop Joscelin and its confirmation by Theobald of Canterbury (arts 23–4), both in a hand of s. xii^2, and later still a Middle English version of the Horton boundary, with additional boundary marks, was added (**20A**: art. 25) in a hand of s. xiii^{med}. Wormald suggested that art. 25 was written by the same hand as arts 23 and 24 (1957, p. 114), but this does not seem possible, judging both by the palaeographical dissimilarities and by the language used in **20A**.

The Horton texts proper are entered in quire 4 in the original hand, beginning with the charter of Henry I that combined Horton with Sherborne (art. 26), followed by the grant of Horton to Bovi (**20**: art. 27), and charters **19**, **21**, **18** and **22** (arts 28–31), the last being the incomplete vernacular charter of liberties of Edward the Confessor. As can be seen, there is a certain order to the arrangements: both Sherborne and Horton documents begin with foundation texts, then record individual grants, and end with grants of liberties.

The secular texts conclude with the documents concerning the dispute between the abbey and Bishop Joscelin (arts 32–3 and 35–40).[10]

(b) *The Sherborne Pontifical*

This is MS lat. 943 in the Bibliothèque Nationale in Paris. The main body of the text is written in a hand of s. x², probably at Christ Church, Canterbury, and additions of Sherborne interest have been made in the early eleventh century, including on the verso of the last folio a writ of Bishop Æthelric, printed here as **13**.[11]

(c) *BL Cotton Otho A. xviii, art. 8*

Otho A. xviii is a miscellany, presumably assembled by Cotton, ranging from eleventh-century material to poems by Chaucer.[12] Some of the manuscript was lost in the Cottonian fire, and all the surviving leaves are seriously damaged. A fragment of two leaves, formerly fos 157–8 and now fos 132–3, is described in the 1696 catalogue as arts 8–11. Art. 8 is a copy of the Sherborne foundation charter **11**, written in a hand of the first quarter of the twelfth century, and filling fo. 132r. On the verso is a copy of a Bury text, in a hand of the second quarter of the twelfth century.[13] This text is a well-known diploma of William I, dated 1081, recording a dispute between Abbot Baldwin of Bury and Bishop Arfast, who wanted to transfer his see to Bury. The text mentions that Cnut ejected priests from Bury and installed monks in their place. The diploma itself is a forgery,[14] but the replacement of priests by monks seems to be the connection between this and the Sherborne text. The next item, art. 10, is also a Bury document, a letter of Pope Alexander II to Abbot Baldwin, but the last item, art. 11, in a slightly later hand, is a short letter of thanks from King Alexander I of Scotland (d. 1124) to the prior and convent

---

[10] Wormald's arts 1, 34 and 41 are additions of various dates, s. xii²–xiv, occurring on a leaf at the beginning of the manuscript (fo. 2), on two leaves at its end (fos 87–8) and in a blank space at the end of quire 5 (fo. 38).

[11] Professor Brooks, *Church of Canterbury*, p. 244, has argued convincingly that the Pontifical was written at Canterbury for an archbishop's use, probably for Dunstan himself. That it reached Sherborne within half a century of its composition may well be another indication of the relationship between Dunstan and Wulfsige III of Sherborne (see commentary on **11**, pp. 41–2). For the date of the Sherborne additions to the Pontifical, see Ker, *Catalogue*, no. 364.

[12] The manuscript was described by T. Smith, *Catalogus Librorum Manuscriptorum Bibliothecae Cottonianae* (London, 1696), p. 69. Repr. ed. C. G. C. Tite (Woodbridge, 1985).

[13] I am gratefully indebted to Mr T. A. M. Bishop for the dating of these hands.

[14] H. W. C. Davis, *Regesta Regum Anglo-Normannorum 1066–1100* (Oxford, 1913), no. 137.

of Worcester. Whereas the first two texts were of more than local interest, the letter of thanks would seem to have been of importance to Worcester only, and is an indication that the two-leaf fragment itself came from there. How and why the Bury texts reached Worcester is not known, but the Sherborne charter could have made its way there as a result of the relationship between Bishop Wulfsige, whose reform of the Sherborne foundation is embodied in the charter, and Wulfstan, who was bishop of London from 996 until his translation to York and Worcester in 1002.[15]

Their association probably began in London, for Wulfsige was abbot of Westminster for several years before his appointment to Sherborne, and the *Vita Wlsini* (Ch. iv) claims that he retained the abbacy after his election as bishop. He may well have continued the connection with Westminster after a new abbot was appointed (by 997, when Wulfsige signs S 891 in company with Ælfwig, abbot of Westminster[16]), for Westminster possessed a copy of the Sherborne charter of 998, as is shown by S 894, a spurious Westminster text that borrowed its opening clauses from the Sherborne document (see below, p. 42), and Wulfsige is the person most likely to have supplied his old house with a copy. There is clear evidence of at least literary contact between the two men in a penitential letter issued by Wulfsige as bishop (between 993 × 995 and 1002), which was reissued by Wulfstan as archbishop, and in another text, a pastoral letter written for Wulfsige by Ælfric the Homilist, from which Wulfstan borrowed.[17] Wulfsige might well have given Wulfstan a copy of his charter, knowing that the latter would be interested in the establishment of Benedictine monasticism at Sherborne,[18] and Wulfstan could have taken the Sherborne text with him to Worcester, just as he probably took with him a copy of the penitential letter.

Only a handful of words and phrases are still legible on fo. 132r of the Otho manuscript, but the Sherborne text was copied by Henry Wharton before the Cottonian fire, and printed by him in

---

[15] Whitelock, *Sermo Lupi*, p. 10.

[16] S 876, an original dated 993, is sometimes cited as evidence that Ælfwig was appointed earlier. A gap was left for the name of the bishop of Sherborne, which implies that Æthelsige was either dead or dying when the list was drawn up. Wulfsige is named as abbot of Westminster. A different hand then filled in Wulfsige's name as bishop of Sherborne, and 'Ælfwig westm̄ abb' was added to the list of witnesses, though not necessarily in the same hand or at the same time; see *Councils & Synods with other documents relating to the English Church, I: A.D. 871–1204*, ed. D. Whitelock, M. Brett and C. N. L. Brooke, pt I: 871–1066 (Oxford, 1981), no. 39.

[17] Whitelock, *Bishops of London*, pp. 26–7.

[18] Although himself more interested in the conduct of secular clergy, Wulfstan was a supporter of the Benedictine reform party: see Whitelock, *Sermo Lupi*, p. 9.

Anglia Sacra (i. 170–1).[19] Unfortunately, he does not seem to have been an accurate copyist, for where the Otho text is still decipherable, Wharton's readings often appear to be incorrect; for instance Wharton read '... archiepiscopus se praebeat ...', where '... reser ...' is clearly visible in the Otho text, showing that it once read '... archiepiscopus reseruetur ...', as does the cartulary text. Other examples are noted below, p. 41. It is therefore difficult to accept Wharton's variations. The spelling of certain names that are still visible in the Otho manuscript suggests that the Otho scribe might have been copying from an earlier or more accurate text than that available to the cartulary scribe: Otho reads 'Wlfsinus', 'Ealdulf' and 'Ælfh ...', and conserved the ð in 'Æðelward', where Add. 46487 has 'Wlsinus', 'Eadlf, 'Ælpheagus' and 'Æthelward'. Other than these orthographical details, there is no indication in the Otho manuscript that the text being copied differed from that preserved in the cartulary.

(d) *BL Cotton Faustina A. ii.*

This is a collection of Sherborne material in hands of the fourteenth and fifteenth centuries, comprising various items, including computistical material, a church calendar, some descriptions of Sherborne estates and some devotional pieces. Arts 5 and 6, written in a hand of s. xiv², are a list of the bishops of Sherborne from Aldhelm to Hermann, with historical notes (24r–25r), occasionally inaccurate, followed by a list of pre-Conquest kings who were benefactors of the church of Sherborne, the name of each donor being followed by the name and often the hidage of the estates donated (25rv). This second list, although preserved in a late and corrupt text, is important evidence about the estates held by Sherborne, especially for the period before *c.* 909, that is, before the diocese was divided into smaller units. The list was printed fairly accurately in the 1817–30 edition of *Monasticon Anglicanum* (i. 337) and in the 1846 reissue (same page), but was omitted from other editions, so for the sake of convenience and completeness, I have included it after the charter texts as Appendix 1.

---

[19] In his Preface (i, p. xxv) Wharton gave the source of his text as 'Bibliotheca Cottoniana Otho A 17'.

INTRODUCTION xxi

(e) *The Sherborne Missal*

This is a magnificent illuminated manuscript, made for the monastery of Sherborne some time between the years 1396 and 1407, under the patronage of Robert Mitford, bishop of Salisbury, and Robert Bruynyng, abbot of Sherborne, portraits of whom appear throughout the manuscript. It has been in the possession of the dukes of Northumberland since 1800, and is now on long loan to the British Library. The Missal contains many local features: beside the numerous appearances of its sponsors, there are feasts dedicated to St Wulsin, the translation of his relics, and St Juthwara, a Cornish saint whose relics lay at Sherborne; a set of busts of the bishops of Sherborne from Aldhelm to Hermann (pp. 363–74); and various other references to Sherborne. Of particular interest here is a set of medallions decorating pp. 363–93, each of which contains a small bust of a king, bishop or monk, and a short text beneath the figure. The medallions on pp. 381–93 contain records of grants to the foundation: the first group (pp. 381–8) refers mainly to estates covered by the documents preserved in the Sherborne cartulary, and a second group (pp. 386–7 and 390–3) contains information about grants made to the foundation which must have come from a list very similar to, if not identical with, that preserved in Faustina A. ii.

4. THE DIPLOMATIC OF THE CHARTERS

(a) *Authenticity and internal connections*

As a collection, the Sherborne and Horton charters are fairly representative of Anglo-Saxon diplomatic, ranging from the most reputable (**2**) to the barely disguised forgery (**4**), and containing charters purporting to be from all five centuries of the period.

Five of the texts are quite unacceptable: **1, 4, 5, 9** and **12**. **1** is a grant of liberties, and may well show Sherborne in rivalry with Malmesbury or Glastonbury at some time after the Conquest (see below, p. 3). The text shows borrowing and influence from other charters in the cartulary, notably **5, 12** and perhaps **10**. **5** is another grant of freedom from all taxes except the three main public burdens, and is a version of the notorious '844 decimation' of Æthelwulf.[20] It also indicates almost certain contact with Malmesbury, since that is the only other house to preserve a text

---

[20] Unlike the 854 decimation, whose existence is supported by *ASC*, the 844 decimation is evidenced only by the Malmesbury and Sherborne texts, and is almost universally condemned as spurious, although Finberg (*ECW*, pp. 187–206) has argued otherwise.

of the 844 grant. **4** and **9** are grants of estates at *Osanstok* and Thornford respectively. **4** is a very poor forgery, being a mixture of seventh- and ninth-century formulas and witnesses, with some indication that it was composed after the move to Salisbury, and that the forger drew on the texts of **6** or **10** (see commentary). *Osanstok* has not been identified, but it is named in the charter of 998 as one of the monastery's possessions, and may have been part of the *Stoches* referred to later. **9** is a somewhat more professional production, with a witness-list suitable for Eadred's reign, although the date has been miscopied, and several of the formulas belong to a later century. Like the author of **4**, the composer of **9** may have borrowed material from **10**, and again Thornford is named in the charter of 998 as a Sherborne possession, and was certainly owned by the monastery by 1066. **12** is a late text connected with **11**, with very little diplomatic pretence, and a pronounced post-Conquest flavour.

Four more documents have to be regarded with suspicion, although they should not be labelled as outright forgeries. **8** is almost identical in text, date and witness-list with **7**, and it refers to the *castrum* of Sherborne, which, if taken literally, must be the castle built in the twelfth century.[21] However, other variations on the text and list are perfectly compatible with the date 933, and the estate was definitely a Sherborne possession. **15** and **16** must be treated with caution partly because of their association with **20**, a Horton charter (see commentaries). Moreover, **15** shows some confusion over its date, and **16** shares a large part of its text with an earlier Athelney charter (S 979). On the other hand, doubt must be cast on **22**, a vernacular Horton charter of liberties, because of its word-for-word accord with **6**, a charter of liberties to Sherborne which antedates **22** by some two hundred years. **22** cannot be too easily dismissed, however, because although the two houses were not amalgamated until 1122, **22** is written throughout in very good late Old English, which would fit its 1061 date admirably.

The other thirteen charters are acceptable diplomatically, and in the case of the five vernacular texts, linguistically. **11**, the foundation charter of Sherborne as a Benedictine monastery, is perhaps on the line between acceptable and suspect, and it is thus my own partiality that places it in the former group (see below, pp. 41–3). **3** appears to have a genuine text, which has suffered minor interpolations, and some tampering with its witness-lists. A witness-list has been added to **10**, although its text appears to have been untouched.

[21] See below, pp. 32–3, for discussion of this point.

INTRODUCTION   xxiii

As far as one can tell, with the exception of **20** and **22**, there is little evidence of scribes making use of earlier Sherborne documents in the composition of the genuine charters. Where an internal connection exists, as between **6** and **10**, it appears to be the result of later editing, probably the work of a copyist who supplied **10** with a witness-list borrowed from **6**, obviously feeling that even for a vernacular memorandum a witness-list was *de rigueur*.

Dr Keynes has brought to my attention what may be a significant difference between the Sherborne and Horton groups. The five Horton texts (**18–22**) are introduced by vernacular rubrics, each of which is in the conventional form and language of an endorsement, suggesting that the cartulary scribe was copying them from endorsements on single-sheet charters. The form of the first four rubrics is almost identical (**18**, **19**, **21** and the first part of **20**); **22** is rather different, being a grant of liberties rather than a land grant. This might suggest that the charters were endorsed at one and the same time, perhaps when they were bestowed on the new Horton foundation. However, there is considerable variation in the orthography (e.g. *kyning* **18**, *cingc* **19**, *cining* **20**, *kyng* **21**; *his gerefan* **19**, *hys huskarle* **20**, *his þegne* **21**; *gebocode* **18**, *gebocod* **19**, *gebocode* **20**, *let gebocygeun* **21**), and it seems safe to accept the rubrics as evidence of contemporary endorsements. The second part of the rubric to **20** is a note about the beneficiary securing the estate with a payment of money, the whole shire being witness, a matter of contemporary interest only.[22]

In contrast, twelve of the sixteen Sherborne charters in the cartulary are introduced by brief Latin rubrics: the rubrics for the land grants are in the form *Carta ~ hid' apud ~* (**2**, **3**, **4**, **7**, **8**, **9**, **10** and **15**), and the rubrics for grants of liberties are in the form *Libertas quam ~ rex concessit Scireburnensi ecclesie* (**1**, **5** and **6**); the only rubric to depart from the pattern is that introducing **16** (*Alia carta de Choriscumba*). The four remaining texts, **11**, **12**, **14** and **17**, have no rubrics at all. The treatment of the Horton texts suggests that any endorsements on the Sherborne charters would have been used by the cartulary scribe as rubrics; so the different treatment accorded to the Sherborne charters may indicate that the scribe was partly dependent on copies of the charters, and that if he had any single-sheet documents, they were not endorsed.[23] It

[22] See below, pp. 71–2, for a full translation.
[23] Professor Brooks has suggested (pers. comm.) that the cartularist might have preferred to use Latin endorsements for the rubrics when these were available (as in the case of the Sherborne texts), but used the Old English endorsements when they alone were available. However the Latin rubrics have a very different and much more consistent pattern than their Old English counterparts and moreover Professor Brown has recently suggested that they were not written by the main scribe (unlike the Horton rubrics), but by a separate rubricator.

could be that most of the original Sherborne charters, authentic and spurious alike, accompanied the bishopric to Salisbury in 1078, since according to Domesday Book it was the bishop of Salisbury who actually held most of the estates concerned, in trust for the Sherborne community. This would have been an obvious time for copies of the charters to have been made before the originals were removed, and they might well have been entered in some form of earlier cartulary. The compiler of Add. 46487 would have had access to these copies, rather than to the originals. **14** and **17** were already obsolete, as the Holcombe estate had been lost by the time of the move (see below, p. 60), and would not have been of interest to Salisbury. **14**, already entered in a gospel book, would not have had an endorsement or rubric, and there is no telling where or how **17**, the official record of a dispute settled in the shire court, was preserved. Other documents of this nature seldom have endorsements (see examples in Robertson, *Charters*). **11**, the foundation charter, probably had a different history from the other texts by virtue of its historical importance, and perhaps had been recopied several times, for it is the only formal charter in which the witness-list is not arranged in vertical columns (although **1** is a partial exception). The copy of **11** imperfectly preserved in Otho A. xviii has the same linear arrangement of the witnesses. **12** appears to have been treated as an appendix to **11**.

Dr Keynes has drawn another distinction between the Sherborne and Horton charters in his discussion of how the process of endowment reflected by the charters in a monastic cartulary can help to establish the credibility of the archive in question.[24] He has suggested that we should generally expect the late-eleventh-century possessions of a religious house (as recorded in Domesday Book) to have been accumulated in the 150 years before the Conquest, and that many of the estates would have been given to the house by local landowners, and would thus have been represented in the archive by charters granted to lay individuals rather than to the house which ultimately held the lands. A claim, represented by a cartulary, that a foundation had received a large proportion of its endowment directly from royal benefactors, would run counter to the expected pattern, and the charters which formed the basis of such a claim would thus be open to suspicion. Such suspicion would be intensified where a house produced a number of pre-Alfredian royal charters granting lands directly to

---

[24] See Keynes, *Diplomas*, pp. 6–10, and a much fuller discussion of this argument in Keynes 1976, pt I.

the foundation, where the lands were in the foundation's possession at the time of the Domesday survey.[25]

The four charters covering the Horton estates are grants to lay recipients, with no mention of an eventual ecclesiastical beneficiary, and belong to the century before the Conquest, thus fitting the general pattern of endowment outlined by Dr Keynes.[26] The Sherborne charters, however, display a very different pattern, for all but one (**3**) of the land grants are made by a king directly to the bishop or the foundation, which has led Dr Keynes to question their reliability as a group, and to associate them in this respect with the notorious charters of Malmesbury Abbey.[27] On one count the Sherborne charters can be acquitted, for whereas half the Malmesbury charters bear a pre-Alfredian date, for lands which the abbey had apparently managed to retain until the Conquest,[28] Sherborne preserved only three early land grants (excluding the grants of liberties as irrelevant to the endowment pattern). Of these, the earliest (**2**) is clearly authentic; the second (**3**) has an authentic base, although it has been tampered with, and is granted to a deacon, with no mention of Sherborne; and the third (**4**), an obvious forgery, concerns an estate that is not mentioned in Domesday Book or any subsequent list.

However, this does not meet the more weighty point that the bishop or foundation is almost invariably presented as the direct beneficiary. Nor does it address another consideration raised by Dr Keynes, that of the relationship between the charters in a particular cartulary and the estates owned by the house concerned at the time of the compilation of Domesday Book,[29] or alternatively the estates as they stood when the cartulary was compiled.[30]

In the case of the Sherborne charters, the picture is complicated by the fact that Sherborne was an episcopal see until a few years before the compilation of Domesday Book in 1086. One would expect a considerable difference in the patterns of endowment between episcopal foundations and non-episcopal monastic houses. In the Anglo-Saxon period the bishoprics were instruments of secular as well as of ecclesiastical government; they were

[25] Ibid. pp. 9–10.

[26] Although **8** may well provide a minor example of the type of alteration envisaged by Keynes: see below, p. xxvii.

[27] Ibid. p. 9: 'Certain cartularies, however, seem to convey an improbable impression of the process of endowment, and their overall authority seems thus to be suspect. Particularly blatant examples are the Malmesbury and Sherborne cartularies.'

[28] Ibid. p. 10.

[29] Ibid. p. 6 and n. 5: Keynes points out that the Sherborne cartulary is one of several that include the relevant extracts from Domesday Book.

[30] Keynes 1976, p. 219: 'The Sherborne cartulary affords a clear example of a collection of pre-Conquest texts whose selection seems to have been closely determined by the endowment of the subject house at the time of compilation.'

founded under royal patronage, and all received direct royal support in the form of land grants. It is therefore reasonable to suppose that many bishoprics would have received a greater proportion of their endowment directly from royal benefactors, and that the grants would have been distributed more widely over the pre-Conquest period.[31] At Sherborne, although the cartulary represents the estates owned by the monastery as distinct from those owned by the bishop, there may well have been some previous interchange of lands. When Wulfsige III reorganized the foundation, he formally named the estates which were to belong specifically to the monastery (see **11** and commentary). All the estates involved lie close to Sherborne, which suggests that they were deliberately chosen by the bishop, probably influenced by his determination to make Sherborne a true Benedictine monastery, and to discourage the monks from going far afield.[32] There is no way of knowing whether these lands had previously belonged to the bishop or to the monastery, or indeed whether there had been any separation of the two before Wulfsige's disposition. Certainly several of the estates covered in the cartulary are named in the list of Sherborne estates contained in Faustina A. ii, which was probably originally compiled before c. 909 (see below, pp. xxxvi–li, and Fig. 3); these estates were either episcopal or held jointly by the bishop and his *familia*.

It is worth examining the precise wording of the Sherborne charters with this consideration in mind, since it also bears on the question mentioned earlier: the extent to which the contents of the cartulary were influenced by the conditions in which it was assembled, in this instance the bitter dispute between the monastery and the bishop of Salisbury.[33] Dr Keynes has suggested that there was a tendency for some cartularists to alter the name of a charter's original grantee, if a layman, to that of the eventual ecclesiastical owner, in order to make explicit the foundation's claim to the estate.[34] Proof of such a practice would be hard to come by, as in most cases the alteration of only a few words would be necessary, but the suggestion has many implications for the study of monastic endowments. In the case of Sherborne, had the

---

[31] The question of episcopal endowments is only beginning to receive attention, but the Canterbury evidence certainly supports this: see Brooks, *Church of Canterbury*, pp. 106–7. As Keynes mentions (*Diplomas*, p. 7), there were some sees which suffered considerable dislocation, and they may display a pattern closer to that of the purely monastic foundation.

[32] See below, p. xxxiii–xxxv and Fig. 2. Lyme, the exception, was probably included to ensure the monastery's salt supply.

[33] The dispute was not, however, primarily concerned with estates, but with the autonomy of the monastery.

[34] See Keynes 1976, pt I, esp. p. 30.

cartularist felt such a tendency, one might expect to find in the charters some emphasis on the monastery – as distinct from the bishopric – being the beneficiary.

Unfortunately the charters are only occasionally helpful. **1** and **5**, both spurious charters of liberties, are granted *sedi pontificali* and *ecclesie Scireburnensis sedi episcopali*. Clearly the authors were not concerned with specifically monastic rights, but with some other circumstance connected with the bishopric (for possible reasons for the concoction of **1**, see below, p. 3). **2**, an authentic text, is a charter granted at the prompting of the bishop to the church of Sherborne, so that it could have a constant supply of salt for the preparation of food and for religious purposes, and **4**, a blatant forgery, is made *ad locum Scireburnensis ecclesie*; so neither is decisive either way. **6**, a genuine ninth-century vernacular grant of liberties, is also made to the *halgan stope æt Scireburnan*, and the confirmation mentions the charter being laid on the high altar *æt ham* at Sherborne, translated by Robertson as 'monastery', (*Charters*, p. 21) but which has a much less specific meaning; again there is nothing here to indicate awareness of any conflict of interest between bishop and monastery. **3** is granted to an individual, with no reference to Sherborne.

7 and **8** do, however, show signs of possible tampering. **7** is granted *fideli Scireburnensis monasterii familie*, and this could well be viewed as a clause inserted in the monastery's interest, although the charter goes on to call the inmates *clericorum grex*, an unlikely phrase for anyone to use of the community after 998. **8** is granted *humili Scireburnensis castri ecclesie*. Here and elsewhere (see below, p. 29) **8** shows signs of tampering or miscopying, but it is to neither party's advantage. As suggested in the commentary, the inclusion of Beorhtwulf *comes* as a recipient of prayers together with the king in **8**, may indicate that he was the original lay grantee of this estate, in which case **8** would be a good example of the kind of alteration postulated by Dr Keynes.

9 grants an estate at Thornford to Bishop Wulfsige I, with reversion *ad refectionem familie Scireburnensis ecclesie* after his death. As Thornford was a monastic possession from at least 998, there is no doubt that the text of **9**, which is spurious, was produced in order to strengthen the monastery's claim to the estate, though at what date cannot be determined. There may well have been a record of the gift as having been made to Bishop Wulfsige, which prompted the forger to name him as the immediate beneficiary, since this would be an unnecessary complication to concoct. **10**, a vernacular record originally entered in a gospel book, which has been given some approximation to charter form by the later addition of a witness-list, is made 'to God and St

xxviii INTRODUCTION

Mary', another ambiguous statement which betrays no later tampering.

Of the charters that belong to the period after Wulfsige III's reorganization, only **15** and **16** are relevant. **11**, the foundation charter, is granted to Wulfsige: it confirms the monastic estates, but confers no new endowments. **12** is a post-Conquest forgery ostensibly issued by Wulfsige to the monks, confirming that they should inherit all the possessions of the clerks whom they replaced. No estates are named, although tithes in Sherborne are mentioned. **14** is not a land grant, and **13** is not included in the cartulary.

15 and **16** both deal with an estate in Corscombe. According to Faustina A. ii, the estate was given to Sherborne in the eighth century, and unlike all the other major estates named in the charters, it was not assigned to the monastery in 998. If the history of the estate given in **15** is correct, this may have been because it had been leased out by Wulfsige's predecessor, and did not return to the monastery until the time of his successor, at which point the monastery was forced to sell it outright. Wulfgar, a *famulus* of the monastery, was able to buy back the estate and present it to the house, of which gift **15** is effectively a confirmation rather than a true grant from King Æthelred. However, it is equally possible that Wulfsige III's charter omitted Corscombe because it was being retained among the episcopal estates, and that the monastery gained possession of it only by Wulfgar's gift. Fifty years later (DB, i. 77r) it was securely held by the monastery. The wording of **15** makes clear that it was to be a monastic property: the grant is made *ad cenobiale monasterium*, and the charter lies open to a charge of later alteration, although one might wonder why no effort was made to clarify or even suppress the ambiguity of the estate's earlier history. **16**, in which Cnut regrants the same estate (with three extra hides), contains the most insistent ascription: *famosissime familiarie uenerabilium fratrum in illo sancto ac celeberrimo loco Scireburnensis ecclesie*, with a further stipulation that the grant is *ad mensam cenobialis uite fratribus Deo seruientibus*, and an anathema directed against *aliquis hominum siue episcopus – siue laicus* ... This emphasis raises the possibility of some dispute over the estate between the bishop and the monastery, which may have led to textual emendations (see below, pp. 57–8, for further commentary on the text).

From the evidence examined so far, it would appear that there was no overall attempt to 'correct' the Sherborne charters so that they favoured the monastery, although this may have been done in some cases (**8**, **9**, **15** and **16**).

With regard to the other question raised by Dr Keynes, that of the relationship between the cartulary contents and the monastic holdings, both as recorded in Domesday Book and at the time of the cartulary's compilation, the Sherborne evidence is again inconclusive. Certainly there is a correlation between the cartulary and the monastery's post-Conquest estates, but it is not a one-for-one correspondence. The question is dicussed below (pp. xxxii–xxxiii), and see also Fig. 1, a concordance between the estates named in the charters and the various lists of estates that exist for the monastery between 998 and 1146.

Dr Keynes has also drawn attention to the interest for critical purposes of the forms of pictorial invocation used in Anglo-Saxon charters.[35] In the Horton group, charters **18–21** have initial chrismons, as do **1**, **3**, **5**, **15**, and **16** among the Sherborne texts.[36] **22** (Horton), **6** and **9** (both Sherborne) are preceded by small undecorated crosses. The remainder of the texts, including the Domesday Book extracts and the post-Conquest documents, only have decorated initials.[37] **17** alone has a plain initial, strengthening the impression that it was included as an afterthought (see above, p. xvii). The cartulary scribe has normally decorated the chrismons in both the Horton and the Sherborne texts with the same flourishes as he used on the initials, and furthermore he has included in each a horizontal bar extending across the vertical stroke of the rho into its eye, possibly to suggest a cross combined with the chi-rho; this addition must have been made on the scribe's own initiative,[38] as the feature does not appear in contemporary Anglo-Saxon texts. The Horton charters are all of a date which would make a chrismon appropriate, but there is no way of telling what the original designs were like. **18**, dated 956, and **21**, dated 1042, have relatively plain forms of chrismon, but **19**, dated 1005, and **20**, dated 1033, have more elaborately decorated forms. In the Sherborne set, **15** and **16** both date from the eleventh century, so chrismons would be appropriate; but **1**, **3** and **5** (617, 841 and 844) should, if genuine, have been introduced by nothing more than a plain cross. **1** and **5** are obvious forgeries, and **3**, although basically an acceptable ninth-century text, has been altered, and a chrismon could have been added then or later. The fact that chrismons were incorporated in these three texts might be taken to suggest that the process of forgery or alteration took place before or shortly after the Conquest, rather than in the twelfth century.

[35] Ibid., Appendix A, pp. 261–72.
[36] See Pl. I for a typical example.
[37] As in Pls I and II.
[38] Keynes 1976, p. 25. **20** has a variation in which the horizontal bar does not extend through to the left side of the upright.

The plain cross preceding **6** is in keeping with its ninth-century date, and the Horton text derived from it, **22**, has retained the same motif, despite its eleventh-century date. **9**, which is unacceptable in its present form, may have derived its cross from a genuine mid-tenth-century base. Of the remaining charters, only **11** might be expected to have had some form of cross or chrismon, but this text was perhaps derived by the cartulary scribe from an earlier copy in which the form of pictorial invocation was not recorded.[39] In conclusion, it would seem that the cartulary scribe tended to accept what his exemplars offered, but was happy in some cases to add decorative details.

(b) *Connections with other archives*

As can be seen from the discussion above, and from the commentaries on the relevant texts, there are textual links (**6** and **22**; **15** and **20**, and possibly **16** and **20**) between the Sherborne and Horton charters, and at least one (**6** and **22**) seems to be pre-Conquest in nature. Horton was not refounded until some time between 1033 and 1061, and all the charters relating to its endowments preserved in the cartulary were originally issued to lay people. It is possible that **20** and **22** were drafted at Sherborne: it would be a natural place for the royal court to visit if it was travelling through the area.

As already mentioned, **1** and **5** suggest a late connection with Malmesbury texts, and we know that the two houses were in contact after the Conquest, for William of Malmesbury states that he incorporated material he found at Sherborne into his *Gesta Pontificum* (ch. 81). The archives at Malmesbury had a copy of the '854 decimation' text (S 305), and this may have supplied the first witness-list for **3** (**3A**, which belongs to 852 × 855); the lists are not, however, quite identical, and their similarity may be an innocent coincidence. **3** also shares a large part of its text with S 288, a grant to a layman issued earlier in the same year (840) and subsequently preserved at Glastonbury. The close relationship between these two charters is a strong argument for the authenticity of both, and throws valuable light on the production of charters in ninth-century Wessex (see below, p. 9): there is no suggestion here of later collusion.

16 (dated 1035) has a large part of its text in common with S 979, a charter of Cnut in favour of Athelney issued some time

---

[39] It is quite likely that many of the Sherborne charters were copied by the cartularist from an intermediate copy, but **11** appears to have had a different history from the other texts; see above, pp. xxiii–xxiv.

between 1023 and 1032. This coincidence is hard to explain, for the two cannot belong to the same date. If both are genuine then one might conclude that they had been composed by the same royal scribe, or at least been taken from the same exemplar. There is no other indication of a connection between charters preserved at Sherborne and Athelney.

18, the earliest Horton charter, is even more closely linked with S 600, a grant of an estate in Hampshire to the same lady Æthelhild, with an identical text, date and witness-list, preserved in the cartulary of the Old Minster, Winchester. The charters were evidently drawn up at the same time, and both are universally accepted as genuine.[40]

There is a possible link between Sherborne texts **7**, **8** and **5**, and S 421, a Crediton charter of liberties dated 933. Its proem, royal style and anathema are very close to those found in **7** and **8** (see below, p. 30). This in itself would not be remarkable, as all the formulas are well attested for Athelstan's charters of these years, but there is a further coincidence between the immunity and reservation clauses of S 421 and the 844 decimation text, of which versions have survived at Malmesbury and Sherborne (**5**: see below, p. 16). There must have been close connections between Sherborne and Crediton in the first decades of the tenth century, as a result of the division of the diocese *c*. 909, and it is possible that the Crediton charter was based on Sherborne material, either in 933 or later in the century.

Other than this, and the textual similarities discussed above, there is firm evidence of deliberate copying for the purpose of forgery only between Sherborne and Malmesbury. It seems rather a far-flung association, but William of Malmesbury is not the only known link between the two. As bishop of Ramsbury, Hermann had tried to shift his episcopal seat to Malmesbury because of Ramsbury's poverty, but this had been strongly repudiated by the monks of Malmesbury.[41] Later, in or after 1059, Hermann was given Sherborne to hold in plurality with Ramsbury.[42] Hermann might have had the opportunity to copy some Malmesbury documents before his intentions became clear, although after that he must have been *persona non grata*. However, Hermann also raised the question of moving his bishopric when he became bishop of Sherborne,[43] and it is noteworthy that both the linked charters, **1** and **5**, stress that their grants are made

---

[40] See commentary on **18** below, and Keynes, *Diplomas*, p. 64.
[41] *Fl. Wig.*, i. 214.
[42] His predecessor Ælfwold last signs in 1059 (S 1027).
[43] *GP*, pp. 182–3. It was Hermann who began the process of moving the seat of the bishopric from Sherborne to Salisbury.

to the *sedis episcopalis* of Sherborne. Perhaps it was the monks of Sherborne rather than its bishop who took advantage of the contact with Malmesbury to borrow some useful material against the threatened upheaval.

5. SHERBORNE LANDS: MONASTIC AND EPISCOPAL

(a) *Monastic estates*

The cartulary includes four lists of estates that belonged to or were claimed by the monastery at various times. These are: the list contained in **11**, the 998 foundation charter, which names all the estates that Wulfsige III had confirmed to the monastery; an extract from Domesday Book listing the bishop of Salisbury's holdings in Sherborne, and the nine estates he held *de victu monachorum* (Wormald 1957, art. 20); the privilege of Pope Honorius II to Abbot Thurstin of Sherborne, confirming him and his successors in their possessions, dated 30 January 1126 (1957, art. 32); and a privilege of Pope Eugenius III to the monks of Sherborne, confirming them in their possessions, dated 5 February 1146 (1957, art. 37).

As can be seen from the accompanying table (Fig. 1), no two of the lists are exactly alike in content, and none exactly matches the estates covered by the individual charters. If we consider the correlation between the estates covered by the charters and the Sherborne possessions as recorded in Domesday Book (one of the queries raised by Keynes: see above, p. xxv), it is clear from Fig. 1 that the individual charters (excluding **11**) do not correspond to the Domesday estates. The charters include texts for Holcombe and *Osanstoc*, lost by the Conquest, and omit Stalbridge, Compton, Stoke Abbott and an estate in Sherborne itself.[44] **11** is a special case, for it is both a statement of lands possessed by or assigned to Sherborne in 998, and a title to those lands, since Æthelred confirms them to the monastery and grants them the customary immunities in the charter. Dr Keynes has noted that 'only one Domesday possession of the monks [Corscombe] is not mentioned in King Æthelred's charter, giving little scope for eleventh-century additions to the endowment' (Keynes 1976, p. 222), and it is true that the two lists have very similar contents. Nevertheless, it does not appear that the list in **11** was revised to accord with the Domesday list. Had this been done, the omission of Corscombe, a sizeable estate, is hard to explain. Moreover several of the place-names in **11** are in forms earlier than those

---

[44] Halstock is omitted from Domesday Book, both in the original and in the Sherborne extract, probably purely by mistake.

11 (998)	Charters	Domesday Book	Privilege of Honorius (1126)
In Sherborne: 'centum agelli in ... Stocland ... et predium monasterii'		In Sherborne, 43 hides[1] 9½ carucates[2]	
Holancumb 9 hides	Holancumbe 9 hides (**13, 14, 17**)		
Halganstoke 15 hides	Halgan stoc 15 hides (**3**)		Halgestoc
Þorford 7 hides	Ðornford 8 hides (**9**)	Torneford[2] 7 hides	Torneford
Bradanford 10 hides	Bradan forda 10 hides (**7**)	Bradeford[2] 10 hides	Bradford et Wica
Þonburna 5 hides	Þomburnan 5 hides (**10**)	Wocburne[2] 5 hides	Woborna
Þestun 8 hides	Þest tune 5 or 8 hides (**8**)	Westone[2] 8 hides	Westona
Stapulbreicge 20 hides		Staplebrige[2] 20 hides	Staplebruge
Þulfheardigstoke 10 hides			
Cumbtun 8 hides		Contone[2] 6 hides	Comtona alia Comtona
Osanstoke 2 hides	Osanstoc 2 hides (**4**)		
Lim 1 hide	Lim 1 hide (**2**)	Lym[3] 1 carucate	Lim
	Corigescumb 13 or 16 hides (**15, 16**)	Coriscumbe[2] 10 hides less 1 virgate	Choriscumb
		Stoche[2] 6½ hides	Stocas

1. Held by the bishop of Salisbury
2. Held by the bishop on behalf of the monks of Sherborne
3. Held by the bishop, but fishermen there pay dues to the monks

Figure 1. The estates assigned to the monastery of Sherborne in various sources

found in Domesday Book: *Bradanford* (DB *Bradeford*), *Ðor[n]-ford* (DB *Torneford*), *Þonburna* (DB *Wogburne*), *Cumbtun* (DB *Contone*) and *Stapulbreicge* (DB *Stapelbrige*). If the *Stoce* of Domesday Book (Stoke Abbott) is identified with the *Þulfheardigstoke* in **11**, the latter would appear to be an earlier, more elaborate form of the name. Finally, if one accepts the hypothesis that Wulfstan took a copy of **11** with him to Worcester (see above, pp. xviii–xix), it follows that the list of estates in **11** was in this form in the early eleventh century, since the version of the list in the Worcester text of the charter (preserved in Otho A. xvii) is identical.

Fig. 2 shows the distribution of estates owned or claimed by the

xxxiv   INTRODUCTION

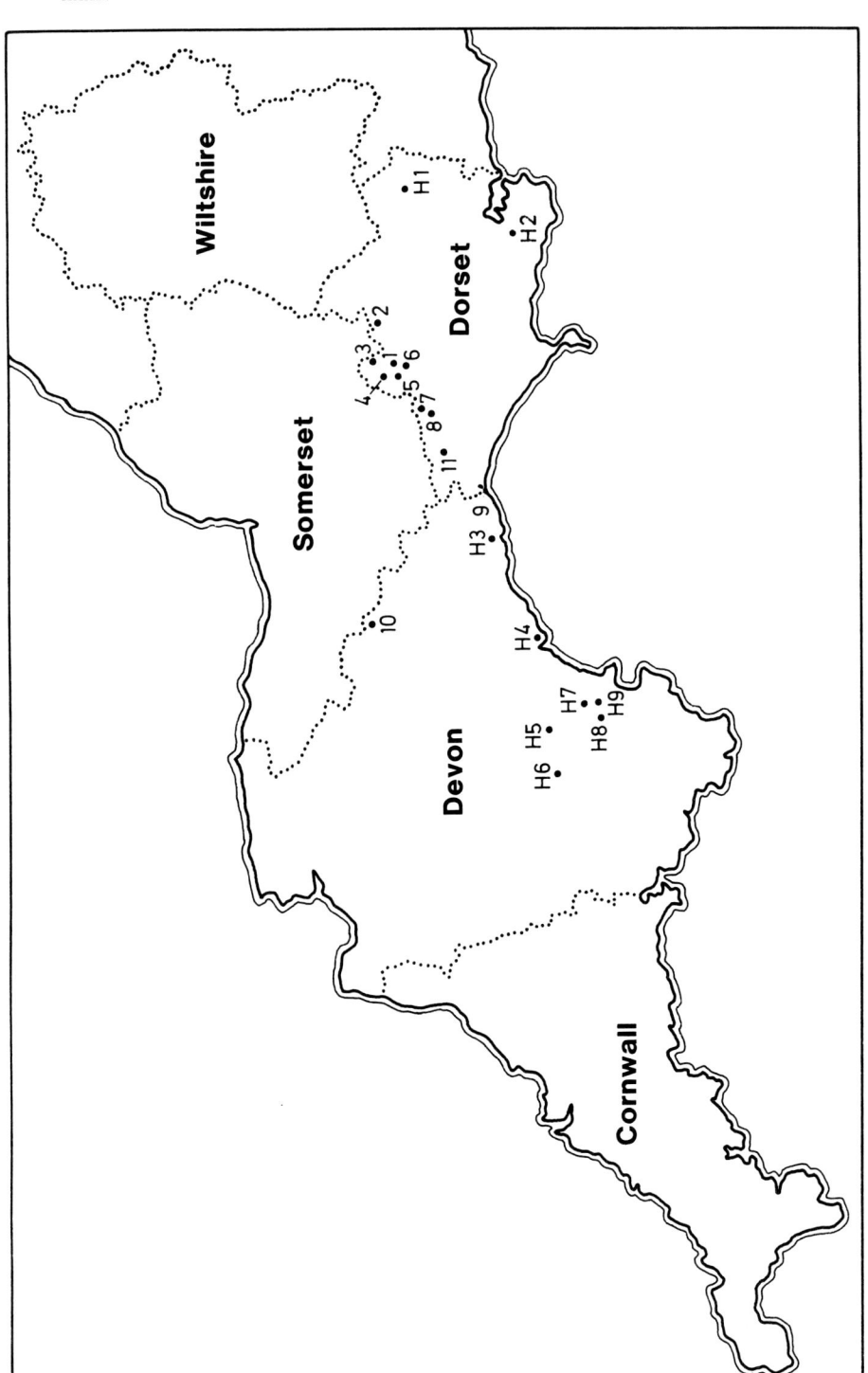

Figure 2. Map of Sherborne and Horton monastic estates c. 1060

monastery at the time of the bishopric's removal to Salisbury. With the exception of Holcombe, and to a lesser degree Lyme, all are within close reach of Sherborne, and this appears to have been the result of Wulfsige III's allotment of lands, part of his reformation of the monastic life at Sherborne (see above, p. xxvi).

The question still remains why so few grants were made to the monastery between 998 and the Domesday compilation of 1086. Part of the answer may be that Sherborne was reformed rather late in the course of the monastic revival, after the period of lavish lay endowments to new houses. Sherborne in any case was not a new house; what importance it had lay in the person of Wulfsige, and when he died – probably in 1002 – both bishopric and monastery returned to insignificance.[45] What evidence there is suggests that during the eleventh century Sherborne – both bishopric and monastery – lost land rather than acquired it: Holcombe was lost (**14** and **17**); Corscombe had been alienated before being restored in 1014 (**15**), and its loss may well have been threatened again (**16**). Even between 1035 and 1086 part of the Corscombe estate was lost, as was an episcopal estate at South Perrott.[46] Sherborne appears to have been under economic pressure during this period, perhaps *ob malorum infestationes direptionesque Danorum*, as **15** puts it.

In the next fifty years, this trend was halted but not really reversed, for the privilege of 1126 lists no new possessions for Sherborne except a small estate in Wales (granted in 1107 × 1115; Wormald 1957, art. 13), which fits well with Henry I's condem-

---

Key to Figure 2

Sherborne
1. Sherborne
2. Stalbridge
3. Oborne
4. Nether Compton
5. Bradford Abbas
6. Thornford
7. Halstock
8. Corscombe
9. Lyme
10. Stoke Abbott
11. Holcombe Rogus

Horton
H 1. Horton
H 2. Seaton (Fleote)
H 3. Littleham
H 4. Bovey Tracy (Bromleage)
H 5. Widdecombe (Bitelanwyrth)
H 6. Abbots Kerswell
H 7. Ipplepen
H 8. Dainton
H 9. Wimborne ⎫
H 10. Wareham ⎬ Town properties
H 11. Dorchester ⎭ (DB, i. 78c)

[45] Sherborne is conspicuous by its absence from most of the maps in D. Hill, *An Atlas of Anglo-Saxon England* (Oxford, 1981): it was not a burh (p. 59), a target of attack (pp. 42–3 and 65–71), or visited by any king after Æthelberht (pp. 87–94); it never acquired a mint (pp. 131–2), is not listed as a town (p. 135), and is even absent from the map of Benedictine houses c. 1060 (p. 153, the author's aberration here reflecting the Anglo-Saxon bias).

[46] DB (i. 79v) relates that Alnod held TRE five hides at *Pedret* and one hide at *Catesclive* (Catsley in Corscombe), bought for his lifetime from Bishop Ælfwold, but the lands were not restored to Sherborne.

xxxvi   INTRODUCTION

nation of Sherborne when he amalgamated it with Horton only a few years earlier (see below, pp. lxi–lxii). After this, the combined houses appear to have prospered, for the 1146 privilege names several estates not mentioned before, including Loscombe (Dorset), *Laurestocam*, *Nitherstocam* and *Curndunam* (both probably near Halstock in Dorset), Kingston (Dorset) and several town properties. This latest privilege, in which Sherborne and Horton possessions are not distinguished, includes a variety of ecclesiastical rights of which only a few are documented in the cartulary.[47] No attempt has been made to manufacture pre-Conquest claims to any of these lands or benefits, with the possible exception of **12** (see below, p. 46). Otherwise, the forgeries that are included in the cartulary do not appear to have been composed specifically for the occasion: **1** and **5** do not involve land; while **4** lays claim to an estate lost at least a century before the cartulary was drawn up and has been miscopied so that the beneficiary is in doubt. The Corscombe charters (**15** and **16**) may have been tampered with in order to emphasize that the estate belonged to the monastery rather than to the bishopric (see above, p. xxviii), but this is likely to have taken place rather earlier, and certainly neither charter could be totally a twelfth-century production. Of them all, only **9** might have been written especially for inclusion in the cartulary, and even in this case there was probably some prior note or text on which it was based (see above, p. xxviii).

This finding strengthens Wormald's theory that the secular portion of the cartulary manuscript was assembled primarily to assert and safeguard Sherborne's right to be free of interference from the bishop of Salisbury, rather than to claim specific possessions. The Anglo-Saxon charters were regarded as valuable and prestigious documents, but by the mid twelfth century their legal validity must have been waning. It is interesting to speculate why such estates as Stalbridge (by far the largest of all the monastery's holdings), Compton and Stoke Abbott had no surviving individual charters. It may be significant that all three are named in the Faustina A. ii list as early benefactions to the foundation, which suggests that a possible explanation might be that they were originally episcopal estates, and may have been assigned to the see at an early period by some other means. A similar phenomenon has been observed at certain other English sees.[48]

---

[47] Wormald 1957, arts 14, 15, 21 and 23.
[48] Canterbury, Rochester and Winchester: see Keynes 1976, pp. 132, 208 n. 2 and 249, and Brooks 1968, pp. 246–51, and *Church of Canterbury*, pp. 104–7.

INTRODUCTION xxxvii

(b) *Episcopal estates*

i) *Two fourteenth-century lists*

There is a certain amount of evidence about the estates held by Sherborne as a bishopric. For the period before *c.* 909, when the see extended over the whole south-west, two related lists, preserved in manuscripts produced at Sherborne under Abbot Robert Bruynyng (1385–1415), offer valuable, if sometimes obscure, information. One is contained in Faustina A. ii, a manuscript drawn up in the tenth year of Abbot Bruynyng [1395].[49] The list is headed *Incipiunt nomina regum eiusdem ecclesie fundatorum*; in it the name of each royal donor is followed by the names and in most instances the hidage of the estates he gave. It is printed here in Appendix 1 (below, pp. 81–2). The benefactors range from Cenwalh (king of Wessex from 643 to 672) to Cnut, but the bulk of the names fall between Cenwalh and Æthelred I, with Edgar, Æthelred II and Cnut appearing to lie outside the main sequence. Some of the place-names are obscure and some are difficult to read, but the lands that can be identified lie all over the south-west, in Dorset, Somerset, Devon, Cornwall and even in one case in Wiltshire.

The other list is preserved in a series of medallions that decorate part of the Sherborne Missal, an elaborate manuscript executed between the years 1396 and 1407, chiefly under the patronage of Abbot Bruynyng. Each medallion contains a picture bust of a king or ecclesiastic above the inscription of a record of his gifts to Sherborne. The texts within the medallions have been printed in the introduction to the Roxburghe Club edition of the Missal.[50] The first eleven medallions (pp. 381–6) contain information derived ultimately from the pre-Conquest charters preserved in the cartulary. The charters used are referred to in chronological order (**1, 2, 6, 3, 8, 9, 18, 10, 15, 19** and **20**), with the Horton texts included as if they were grants to Sherborne (e.g. no. 7: 'Rex Edwynus ratificauit donum maneri[i] de Carswylle ecclesie de Schirbor' quod idem rex antea dedit cuidam mulieri nominate Ethelhylde cum suis pertinentiis a.D. dccccº.lviº'). In some instances the texts in the medallions have altered, expanded or condensed the charter information. So no. 3 states that Æthelberht gave liberty to the Sherborne estates (**6**), and also *Abbatistocam*, *Stapilbrigg* and *Contonam*, and the date given is 788. No. 4 has Æthelwulf as the donor of Halstock (**3**), and of Bradford (as in Faustina A. ii). No. 9 states that Æthelred gave

[49] Herbert, *Sherborne Missal*, p. 12.
[50] Ibid. pp. 24–5. The twenty-six medallions concerned are on pp. 381–93; I refer to them by number for the sake of convenience only.

xxxviii   INTRODUCTION

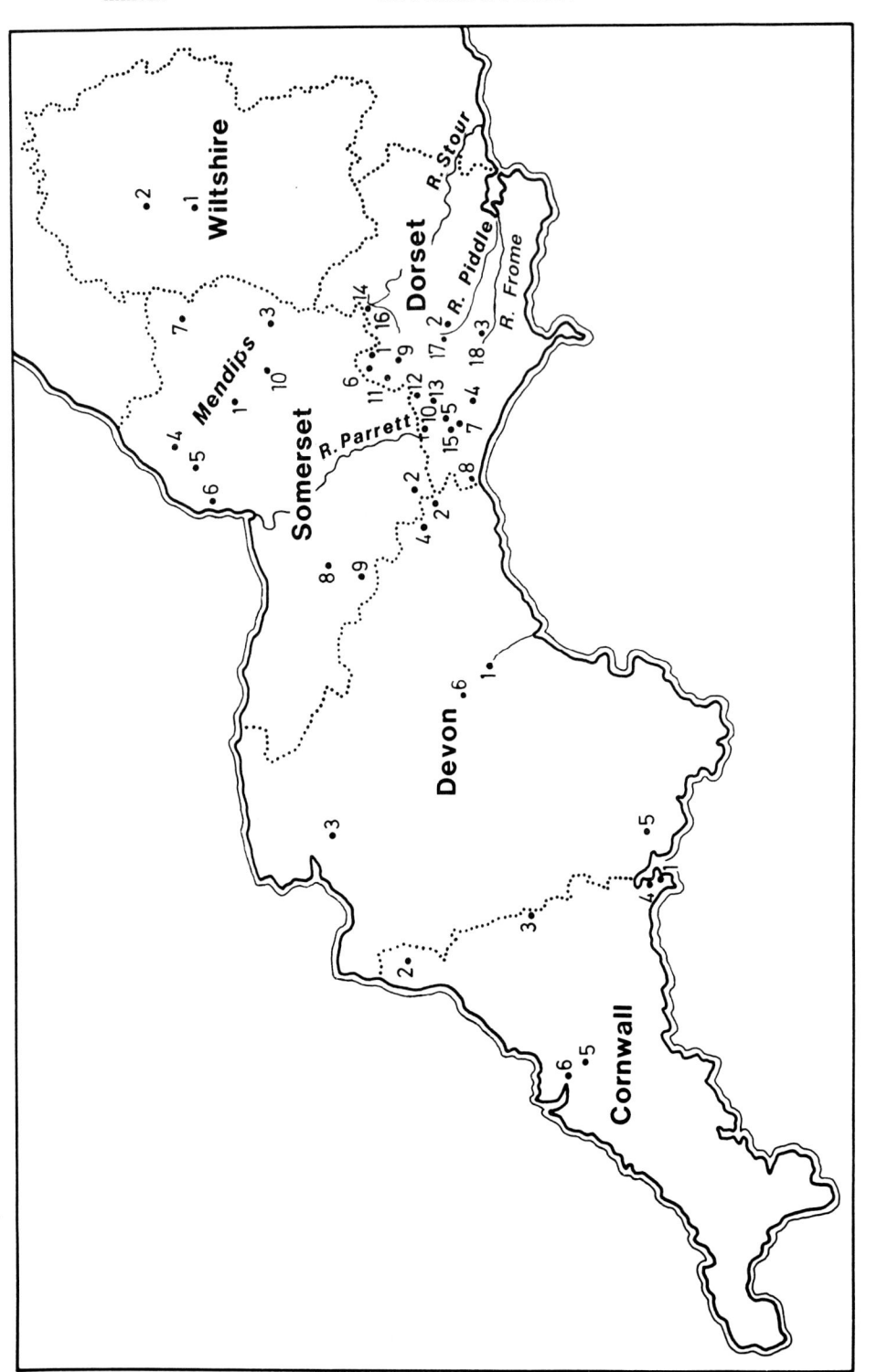

Figure 3. Map of Sherborne episcopal estates c. 900

INTRODUCTION

Sherborne the manor of Corscombe in 998 (**15**, with the date of **11**). Nos 15, 18 and 26 refer to post-Conquest documents preserved in the cartulary (Wormald 1957, arts 13 and 26). No. 17 mentions a grant by William, bishop of Exeter, giving Sherborne the churches of Abbotskerswell and Seaton.[51] No. 16 records a gift of vestments from Bishop Sigehelm on his return from India.[52]

Medallions nos 12–14 and 19–25 contain records of royal gifts, the contents of which are almost identical with those recorded in the Faustina A. ii list. Each king has a separate medallion, although Cynewulf has two (nos 20 and 21), either because he made too many donations to be fitted into one medallion, or, more

Key to Figure 3

Dorset
1. Sherborne
2. Alton Pancras
3. Charminster
4. Powerstock
5. (Beaminster)
6. Nether Compton
7. Netherbury
8. Lyme
9. Yetminster
10. South Perrot
11. Bradford Abbas
12. Halstock
13. Corscombe
14. Stalbridge and Stalbridge Weston
15. Stoke Abbott
16. R. Lidden
16. Up Cerne
18. R. Hooke (once R. Toller)

Somerset
1. Priddy
2. Chard
3. Chesterblade
4. Congresbury
5. Banwell
6. Bleadney
7. Wellow
8. (Bishop's Lydeard)
9. (Wellington and West Buckland)
10. (Wells)

Devon
1. Exeter
2. Chardstock
3. Tawstock
4. Culmstock
5. Plympton
6. Crediton

Cornwall
1. Maker
2. Kilkhampton
3. Lawhitton
4. Roseland
5. Pawton
6. Egloshayle

Wiltshire
1. Potterne
2. Calne

.... County boundaries
Chard Identification uncertain
( ) Possession by Sherborne c. 900 uncertain

[51] It is not clear whether this is William Warelwast (1107–37) or William Briwere (1224–44). Baldwin, archbishop of Canterbury, is named in the medallion, but his dates (1184–90) do not coincide with either. Perhaps William Briwere is intended, as no such grant is recorded in the cartulary (*c.* 1146).

[52] Thus perpetuating William of Malmesbury's confusion of Bishop Sigehelm of Sherborne (*c.* 909 or 918 × 925–932 × 934: see O'Donovan 1972, p. 29) with the Bishop Sigehelm who carried King Alfred's alms to India (*ASC* MS D, E and F, s.a. 883).

likely, because the original list from which these records are taken had two entries for Cynewulf, as does the list in Faustina A. ii. The entries are in no discernible order, neither in chronological order, nor in the sequence found in the Faustina A. ii list, but within each medallion the information given is identical with that in the Faustina A. ii list (except for two entries, discussed below). Each royal donor is associated with the same estates in the same order. In cases where the spelling varies, the medallion readings are preferable.

The Sherborne Missal material could have been drawn directly from Faustina A. ii, which just antedates it. The difference in arrangement could be due to the Missal scribe, since he was clearly prepared to rearrange his material (as he did with the charter entries). The difference in spelling might also be due to the scribe improving on the Faustina A. ii text wherever he recognized a name. A more likely alternative is that both manuscripts could have drawn on a third text, now lost. It may be relevant here that the Missal includes one royal donor not included in Faustina A. ii. Medallion no. 14 reads 'Rex Athelbald dedit ecclesie b. Marie de Schireborn Bedeslean .iii. hidas et G'ncric .xl. hidas et Willam .c. hidas'. Whatever the history behind the two lists, it is their contents that are of interest here. In the following discussion I shall use Faustina A. ii as the primary source, with cross-references to the Missal medallion texts where they differ from the former.

Several of the entries in the Faustina A. ii list correspond to the information given by the charters in the cartulary. The hide at Lyme is named as the gift of Cynewulf (**2**). Halstock is given as the gift of Æthelwulf (**3**), although no hidage is mentioned, and it is recorded as a gift to Sherborne rather than to the deacon Eadberht. These two grants are placed among the charter extracts in the Missal (nos 2 and 4). Faustina A. ii lists the gift of five hides at Oborne from Edgar (**10**); the Missal also lists it, but among the charter entries. The estate at Corscombe is entered twice, once as the gift of Cuthred (740–56), and again: 'Ethelredus dedit et restituit Corescumbam in oblatum et postea Cunitus eum restituit', a clear reference to the Corscombe charters **15** and **16**. The Missal also lists Corscombe as the gift of Æthelred among the charter entries (no. 9), although with the date 998, and again among Cuthred's donations. Bradford is named as the gift of Æthelwulf instead of Athelstan as in **7**. The Missal also assigns Bradford to Æthelwulf, but places it in one of the charter medallions (no. 4), and associates it with the grant of Halstock (**3**). Estates at Stalbridge and Compton, that belonged to the monastery in 998 according to **11**, but for which no charters have survived, are listed as the gift of Æthelberht. The Missal includes them among the charter texts and adds them to the grant of liberties and a grant of *Abbatistocam* which does not appear in Faustina A. ii, although the estate belonged to the monastery TRE, and is usually associated with *Wulfheardigstoke* (**11**).

Other monastic estates for which charters have survived, *Osanstok* (**4** and **11**), *Wulfheardigstoke* (**11**), Weston (**8**), Thornford (**9**) and Holcombe (**14** and **17**) are not mentioned in the Faustina A. ii list. It would appear that at one stage in the compilation of this list the author had seen or heard of the two Corscombe charters, and probably also the Oborne grant, but if he was aware of the other charters he did not allow that knowledge to influence the make-up of his own list. Nor did the Faustina list, or the list from which it was derived, have any discernible effect on the contents of the cartulary, although some form of the list must have been preserved at the monastery until it was reproduced in the two fourteenth-century lists. Nor would it have been a suitable source for the cartulary compilation, as it has a very different bias.

Below, arranged chronologically by donor, are the benefactors and their gifts, abstracted from the two lists. A name thus: *Lanprobi*[A], indicates that the estate is found in Faustina A. ii. *Wycam*[B] indicates that the name only occurs in the Sherborne Missal. *Iuxta Prediau*[AB] means that the name is found in both manuscripts. Where the Missal extracts have a significant spelling variation, this is included. Square brackets indicate an ambiguity in the manuscript.

Cenwalh (643–72)	*Lanprobi*[A]	(? in or near Sherborne, Dorset)	100 hides[A]
	Wycam[B]	(Sherborne Wyke, Dorset)	
Ine (689–726)	*iuxta Predia[u]*[A]	(beside r. Priddy, Somerset)	7 hides[AB]
	iuxta Pedrian[B]		
	Conbusburie[A]	(Congresbury, Somerset)	20 hides[AB]
	Cungresbury[B]		
Geraint of Cornwall (c. 710)	*Macuir ... iuxta Thamar*[A]	(Maker, Cornwall)	5 hides[AB]
	[ ] *... iuxta Tamer*[B]		
Cuthred (740–56)	*in Lydene*[AB]	(? valley of r. Lidden, Dorset)	12 hides[AB]
	Cor[u]scumbe[AB]	(Corscombe, Dorset)	10 hides[AB]
	aput Menedip[AB]	(by the Mendips, Somerset)	25 hides[A]
Sigeberht (756–7)	*Boselingtone*[AB]		5 hides[A]
			6 hides[B]

	in est Canne^A	7 hides^{AB}
	in Iscan[or *Ascan*]^B	
Cynewulf (757–86)	*Pidel*^{AB} (Piddle, Dorset)	5 hides^A
		15 hides^B
	Lym^{AB} (Lyme, Dorset)	1 hide^{AB}
	Snarstok^A	6 hides^{AB}
	Snarstokis Treov^B	
	Talre^A (Toller, Dorset)	8 hides^{AB}
	in Tolra^B	
	Wegentesfunte^{AB}	30 hides^{AB}
	Aueltune^A (Alton, Dorset)	
	Aulton^B	
	[*C*]*r*[*u*]*teco*[*un*]*e*^A	36 hides^A
	Cridiaton^B (Crediton, Devon)	35 hides^B
	Wytecumbe^A	
	Wlueue^B (? Wellow, Somerset)	
Offa of Mercia (757–96)	*Poterne cum pertinentiis*	
	suis^{AB} (Potterne, Wilts.)	
Egbert (802–39)	*iuxta Cernel*^{AB} (beside r. Cerne, Dorset)	10 hides^{AB}
	Power . . . iuxta flumen . . . Woch^A	7 hides^A
	(Powerstock, Dorset)	
	Ponner . . . iuxta flumen . . . Woth^B	8 hides^B
	iuxta Pedridun^{AB} (beside r. Parret,	10 hides^{AB}
	Somerset and Dorset)	
	A[*l*]*ba*[*m*]*bruth*^A	[7] hides^A
	Abbamburh^B	4 hides^B
	in Hena[*n*]*gre*^A (? Henegar in	12 hides^A
	Culmstock, Devon)	
	Kelk^A (Kilkhampton, Cornwall)	12 hides^A
	Ros^A (? Rame peninsula, Cornwall)	
	Macor^A (Maker, Cornwall)	18 hides^A
	in Chesterbled^A (Chesterblade,	10 hides^A
	Somerset)	
	Wi[*nu*]*rod*^A	15 hides^A
Æthelwulf (839–58)	*Bradford'*^{AB} (Bradford Abbas, Dorset)	
	Cerdel^A (Chard, Somerset, or	
	Chardstock, Devon)	
	Algerstoke^{AB} (Halstock, Dorset)	
	Getemynst'^A (Yetminster, Dorset)	5 hides^A
	Nutherburie^A (Netherbury, Dorset)	36 hides^{A(*)}
	Ethelbaldingham^A	
Æthelbald^{B only} (858–60)	*Bedeslean*^B	3 hides^B
	G'ncric^B	40 hides^B
	Willam^B	100 hides^B
Æthelberht (860–5)	liberty of 140 hides^A	
	liberty^B	
	Cernel^A	12 hides^A
	Tauistoke^A (Tavistock or Tawstock,	8 hides^A
	Devon)	
	Stapulbrige^{AB} (Stalbridge, Dorset)	20 hides^A
	Cuncton'^A (Compton, Dorset)	8 hides^A
	Contonam^B	
	Abbatistocam^B (Stoke Abbott, Dorset)	

INTRODUCTION   xliii

Æthelred I[A] (865–71)	Atforde[A]	[A attributes the grant of both these estates to Æthelred; B names Alfred as the donor of the same estates]	
Alfred[B] (871–99)	Acford[B]		
	Cletha[n]gre[A]		
	Cleihangra[B]		
Edgar (959–75)	Woburnam[AB]	(Oborne, Dorset)	5 hides[A]
Æthelred II (978–1016)	Corescumbam[AB]	(Corscombe, Dorset)	
Cnut (1016–35)	Corescumbam[A]	(Corscombe, Dorset)	

*See below, Appendix 1, p. 81. It is not clear from the manuscript whether the '36 hides' refer to *Cerdel et Algerstoke*, possibly including the five hides at *Getemynst'*, or to *Nutherburie* et *Ethelbaldingham*.

Of the identifiable estates in Dorset, several became the property of the monastery at Sherborne: Sherborne Wyke, Corscombe, Bradford Abbas, Halstock, Stalbridge, Compton, Stoke Abbott and Oborne. Lyme seems to have been in dispute between the monastery and the bishopric, but ended up in the former's possession. The subsequent history of the remaining estates – albeit not fully investigated – reveals a distinct pattern.

The record in Faustina A. ii of a gift of 100 hides at *Lanprobi*, made by Cenwalh, could have had its origin in a genuine tradition of the foundation of Sherborne as an Anglo-Saxon religious house. The bishopric was established in 705, but most probably there was already a church or monastery there, since it was customary to set bishops in already existing foundations.[53] The first element of *Lanprobi* is a Brittonic word for an enclosed cemetery or church, generally the latter where it occurs in place-names,[54] and it has been suggested that *Lanprobi* was the name of a British monastic site on which Sherborne was later founded.[55] There is support for some form of church associated both with Sherborne and with the name *Probi* in the appearance of a *Propeschirche* in the 1146 papal privilege, and a *capella sancti Probi* in a papal bull of 1163,[56] although its whereabouts is unclear. The etymology of the word *Lanprobi* is also puzzling, and since both this and the possible siting of Sherborne in a British monastery are questions of some intricacy, they are discussed in more detail in Appendix 2 (see below, pp. 83–8). In Domesday Book the bishop of Salisbury held forty-three hides and sixteen

[53] See Keen 1984, pp. 208–9, with ref. to Sherborne.
[54] *DEPN*, s.v. 'lann'; and see O. J. Padel, 'Cornish Names of Parish Churches', *Cornish Studies*, iv/v (1976–7), pp. 15–27, esp. 26.
[55] Finberg, *Lucerna*, p. 98.
[56] *Mon. Angl.*, i. 339.

carucates in Sherborne, which had presumably been inherited from the bishopric of Sherborne, as well as nine and a half carucates held on behalf of the monks of Sherborne. This could be the remains of Cenwalh's grant.[57] The Sherborne Missal, interestingly, makes no mention of *Lanprobi*. The first medallion of the series derived from the charters records that Cenwalh gave privileges and liberty to Sherborne, as well as *Wycam cum omnibus suis pertinenciis*. There is no way of determining whether the scribe of the Missal omitted the reference to *Lanprobi* by mistake (as he apparently omitted several of Æthelwulf's gifts listed in Faustina A. ii while combining estates from that list with the charter information), or on purpose, or whether his source did not contain the reference. Another possibility is that he equated *Lanprobi* with *Wycam*, which would add yet another complication to the question of where to place *Lanprobi*, since *Wycam* must lie to the west of Sherborne, whereas indications are that *Lanprobi* (if it is to be located near Sherborne) lay to the east of the town (see below, pp. 85-7).

Other estates that can be securely assigned to Dorset are Piddle, Alton, Powerstock, Yetminster, Netherbury, *iuxta Cernel* and perhaps *iuxta Pedridun* (the river Parret forms part of the boundary between Somerset and Dorset). Almost all have connections with the bishopric of Salisbury. An estate at Piddle was held by the bishop of Salisbury in 1086 for four hides (DB, i. 77r).[58] Alton was held by the same bishop in 1086 for six hides (DB, i. 75v), and is also named as one of the original endowments of the bishopric in the *Registrum Osmundi* in 1091 (i. 198). *Iuxta Cernel*, an estate of ten hides, is probably to be identified with the ten hides at Charminster held by the bishop of Salisbury in 1086 (DB, i. 75v), and similarly named in the *Registrum Osmundi* as an original endowment.[59] The estate *iuxta Pedridun* could be in either North Perrott in Somerset or South Perrott in Dorset. Domesday Book records that Alnod held an estate of five hides at *Pedret* TRE, which he had bought from Bishop Alwold (Ælfwold of Sherborne) for his lifetime only, on condition that after his death it should be restored to the church, although this apparently never happened. An estate of fifteen hides was held by the bishop of Salisbury at Yetminster (DB, i. 75v), which is also named as one of the original endowments in *Registrum Osmundi*. An estate at Netherbury is likewise listed as one of the Salisbury possessions in the same two sources. Æthelberht's grant of twelve hides at

---

[57] Although it is equally possible that the attribution to Cenwalh is a late assumption based on **1**, since a hundred hides would be a most unusually large gift to a monastery.

[58] Although the bishop held this in part exchange for the manor of Shipley.

[59] Ibid. i. 198. Charminster means 'minster on the Cerne'.

Cernel may be a regrant of the earlier *iuxta Cernel*, although in 1086 the bishop of Salisbury also held a small estate of two and a half hides at Up Cerne. *Power ... iuxta ... Woch* was identified by Finberg (*ECW*, p. 157) as Powerstock on the river Mangerton, whose old name was Woth or Woch. It was held TRE by a layman for six hides, and is not listed among Salisbury's original estates, but it is worth noting that the bishopric had an interest in the church of *Porstoke* in the mid-twelfth century,[60] and that it was finally given to Salisbury by the abbey of Montebourg in 1213.[61] *Talre* or *in Tolra* must refer to the river Toller in Dorset (now called the Hooke), and probably to some estate in the river valley now unknown: it seems unlikely that the higher land around Toller Whelme, which Sherborne possessed in the eleventh century (**16**), was the intended reference.

So of the identifiable place-names in Dorset listed by Faustina A. ii and the Sherborne Missal, Piddle, Alton, Charminster, Yetminster, Netherbury and possibly Up Cerne coincide with estates held by the bishopric of Salisbury in 1086, four of them also being listed as part of the original endowment of the bishopric, which must mean that they were inherited from the bishopric of Sherborne. The bishopric of Salisbury also held a large estate in Sherborne itself, which must also have been part of the Sherborne endowment. An estate at South Perrott had been held and lost by the bishop of Sherborne, and the bishopric of Salisbury was interested in Powerstock in the twelfth century.

Only one estate, at Potterne, can be assigned to Wiltshire. Potterne is included among the original endowments of Salisbury,[62] and although the majority of these estates in Wiltshire must have been inherited from the bishopric of Ramsbury, it is possible that Potterne had originally been granted to Sherborne by Offa. The gift could have been made after Cynewulf's death in 786, since charter evidence shows that he was in control of north Wiltshire (S 264). The period between Beorhtric's accession to Wessex in 786 and Offa's death in 796 would be the most likely time for such a gift. It is also remotely possible that the grant was actually from Beorhtric, with confirmation by Offa, but this seems unlikely, for there is no Mercian confirmation in any of the three surviving charters issued by Beorhtric (S 267, dated 794; S 268, dated 801; and S 269, issued between 786 and 793).[63]

---

[60] *Charters and Documents*, pp. 26–9.

[61] *Registrum Osmundi*, i. 224–5.

[62] Ibid. i. 198–9. All the estates in this part of the *Registrum* are listed by county rather than by bishopric of origin.

[63] I am assuming that Wiltshire was part of the diocese of Winchester until the division of the West Saxon sees *c*. 909 (for which see Stenton, *Anglo-Saxon England*, pp. 349–40),

With regard to the lands in Somerset the picture is far less clear. *Iuxta Prediau* and *apud Menedip* indicate lands a few miles to the north-west of Wells, and suggest that in the early eighth century the area was only in the process of being settled by the English. Wells held many estates round the Mendips, such as Easton, Wookey, Binegar and others,[64] but there is no way of distinguishing possible Faustina A. ii estates.

Ine is said to have made a grant of twenty hides at Congresbury. This estate has an involved history. Other than the mention in Faustina A. ii and the Missal, it first appears as a Christmas gift from King Alfred to Asser, along with Banwell (*Vita Alfredi*, ch. 81). Later Asser was given Exeter, and its *parochia* in Saxon lands and in Cornwall, where he was most probably intended to act as a suffragan bishop for the western part of the Sherborne diocese,[65] and later still he became bishop of Sherborne. When the diocese of Sherborne was divided at his death into three sees, it would have been appropriate that the lands owned by Sherborne in Somerset should be allotted to the new bishopric of Wells, and a similar arrangement made for the bishopric of Crediton.[66] Wells certainly claimed both Congresbury and Banwell, although its later ownership of the estates was precarious, and is not relevant here.[67] The link made between Congresbury and Ine in the two fourteenth-century lists raises the question of whether the estate had been given to Sherborne before it was granted to Asser. The lists do not appear to have been influenced by the longstanding link between Congresbury and Banwell, which appears in Asser and in Cnut's gift of both estates to Dudoc.[68] It is possible that Alfred transferred Congresbury from Sherborne to Asser in preparation for giving him further authority in the south-west. There is also the strange legend recounted in the *Historiola de primordiis episcopatus Somersetensis* to be considered; it states that the see of Somerset was placed at Congresbury until the reign of Ine, when it was transferred to

---

despite William of Malmesbury's statement that it was originally part of Sherborne (*GP*, p. 175). Nothing seems to be known about the ownership of Potterne until the post-Conquest period, when it is named as one of the original endowments of Salisbury. If it was a Sherborne estate (as Faustina A. ii claims), it might well have been transferred to Ramsbury *c.* 909, since geographically this would have made sense, and it would have been necessary to endow the new bishopric with suitable estates in Wiltshire.

[64] See Robinson, *Wells*, pp. 52–3, and S 1042.

[65] Whitelock, *Genuine Asser*, p. 14. See also Keynes and Lapidge, *Alfred the Great*, pp. 264–5 n. 193.

[66] Robinson, *Wells*, pp. 18–24 and 52–5.

[67] See Keynes and Lapidge, *Alfred the Great*, p. 264 n. 192, for the later history of the two estates.

[68] Hunter, *Ecclesiastical Documents*, p. 15.

Wells.[69] A date in the late twelfth century has been suggested for the composition of the *Historiola*, although it has only survived in an early-fourteenth-century copy.[70] This story would be another possible source for the Congresbury–Ine link found in the lists, if it does not have a basis in fact.[71]

Of the other Somerset estates mentioned in the lists, Finberg suggests (*ECW* 394 and 395) that the *Wlueue* given by Cynewulf may be the same as the eleven *manentes* at *Wluue* (r. Wellow) given by him to St Andrew at Wells (S 262: Whitelock, *EHD*, no. 70, dated 766 for ?774), since Wells lay within the diocese of Sherborne at the time. The spelling of the river name is almost identical, but a grant to Wells would not have counted as a grant to Sherborne, and Cynewulf might well have made two grants along the Wellow. Egbert is said to have made a grant of ten hides at Chesterblade, and Wells later claimed an estate there (S 1042, dated 1065). It was not held by Wells in 1086, but the church had lost several estates in the preceding half-century.

Æthelwulf is recorded as granting an estate at *Cerdel*. This could be either Chard in Somerset, held in 1086 by the bishop of Wells, or Chardstock, a rather bigger estate in Devon held in 1086 by the bishop of Salisbury. The two places are very close, and Chardstock was probably a part of Chard.[72] Chardstock in particular lies very close to the borders of Somerset and Dorset, and could have been retained by Sherborne when Chard was passed on to Wells.

There are very few estates that can be identified even tentatively with places in Devon. The twelve-hide grant *in Henangre* has been identified by Finberg (*ECDC*, p. 8) as Henegar in Culmstock, since *heanhangre* appears among the boundary marks in S 386, in which five hides at Culmstock are granted by Athelstan to Exeter. The charter is dated 670, but is written in a mid-eleventh-century hand, and was probably forged then, perhaps in connection with Bishop Leofric's campaign to regain lost estates for his church.[73] But it seems unlikely that the Culmstock estate was ever known as *in Henangre*, so the identification is questionable.

The Sherborne Missal (medallion no. 20) lists as one of Cynewulf's gifts thirty-five hides at *Cridiaton*, which in Faustina

---

[69] Ibid. pp. 10–14.
[70] Ibid. pp. 5–6.
[71] Professor Whitelock has suggested (pers. comm.) that events might have been reversed, and that a charter or note recording the gift of Congresbury by Ine, passing with the estates from Sherborne to Wells, might have been the original source of the legend.
[72] See *DEPN*, s.v.: 'The name means *stoc* belonging to Chard.'
[73] Chaplais 1966, pp. 4–5.

A. ii is rendered as thirty-six hides at *Erutecoune* (or *Crute-*; capital *C* and *E* are sometimes indistinguishable in the manuscript). If one accepts the reading of the Missal, which can only be intended for Crediton, an interesting possibility emerges. The monastery at Crediton was founded by Forthhere, bishop of Sherborne, in or shortly after 739, with an endowment from King Æthelheard of twenty hides (S 255; see below, p. liv). However, the late-tenth-century bounds for Crediton (printed as *Crawford Charters* II) outline an area of land which Finberg estimated at about 50,000 acres,[74] vastly more than twenty hides, however calculated.[75] It is very tempting to conclude that Sherborne received more land around Crediton which was transferred to the new bishopric *c*. 909. The equivalent name in Faustina A. ii, *Erute-* or *Crutecoune*, could be a mangled form of Yarcombe, Devon,[76] but no trace remains there of an estate of thirty-six hides, and Crediton remains the more attractive version.

Not even a tenuous link can be established for the other Devonshire estates. *Tauistoke* (eight hides) could be either Tawstock just south of Barnstaple, or Tavistock. Finberg favours Tawstock, as the north was more settled by the English (*Lucerna*, p. 108). Moreover, Sherborne already possessed an estate near Tavistock, at Plympton (see below, p. liv), and it makes sense to assume that estates given to a bishopric were intended as suitable centres for episcopal visitations as well as sources of income, at least in the early centuries. Tawstock is recorded as having been held TRE by Earl Harold for five hides (DB, Exon. i. 94v), which is inconclusive, since the earl held vast lands, and was known as a despoiler of churches, but it is interesting to note that the nearby Bishop's Tawton, with which Tawstock has at least an etymological link, belonged to the bishopric of Exeter (DB, Exon. i. 117v).

For Cornwall, the lists record a grant of five hides at Maker from Geraint. Finberg interprets this as an attempt to buy off the English enemy,[77] but it is equally possible that the grant took place perforce after some campaign of Ine's. The estate was either confirmed or enlarged in a grant by Egbert, which included lands at *Kelk* and *Ros* (only mentioned in Faustina A. ii). The latter has been identified as Roseland,[78] which was held by the bishop of

---

[74] *WCHS*, pp. 44–52.

[75] In DB (Exon. i. 117r) the bishop of Exeter held fifteen hides at Crediton, but the assessment must have been very biased in favour of the Church, for the land could support 185 ploughs.

[76] I am grateful to Dr Mills for this suggestion; in S 391 the name appears as *Ercecombe*, and in DB (i. 194v) as *Erticoma*.

[77] Finberg, *Lucerna*, p. 100.

[78] Ibid. p. 106.

Exeter in 1086.[79] However, Mr Padel (pers. comm.) has recently suggested an alternative to Roseland: the Rame peninsula, in which Maker lies. His reasons are firstly that Faustina A. ii reads *Et Ros et Macor de xviii hidis*, which suggests adjacent estates, and secondly that Roseland is too far south and west for such an early grant.[80] *Ros* simply means 'peninsula' or 'promontory', and could well have been applied to the Rame peninsula before it received a later, probably Anglo-Saxon name (*DEPN*, s.v.). In a rather dubious text of 981 (S 838), Rame is granted or confirmed to Tavistock Abbey. By 1066 Maker belonged to the king, whilst *Kelk* (Kilkhampton) was in the hands of Earl Harold. Another interesting variation found in the Sherborne Missal is a grant made by Cynewulf of six hides at *Snarstokis Treov*, where Faustina A. ii reads simply *Snarstok*. *Treov* looks like the Cornish prefix *trev-* (homestead, village), but this does not help much with the identification of *Snarstok*, except to suggest that it might lie in Cornwall.

Several places remain completely unidentified. *In Lydene* probably refers to the valley of the river Lidden, Dorset. Finberg suggests Lydlinch (*ECW*, p. 156), but there is no evidence to support this against some other place in the valley. *Boselingtone* is unidentifiable, as is *Wegentesfunte*, although its association with Alton in both lists suggests that it was situated in Dorset. *Ethelbaldingham* is untraceable, although its absence from the Sherborne Missal, and the appearance in the latter (but not in Faustina A. ii) of King Æthelbald as a donor, suggests that there may have been some confusion in the original source. The Missal omits other gifts of Æthelwulf (*Cerdel*, *Getemynst*' and *Nutherburie*), but includes as gifts of Æthelbald three hides at *Bedeslean*, forty hides at *G'ncric* and 100 hides at *Willam*, none of which are clearly identifiable. There are various place-names in Dorset derived from the OE *welle*, *wiella*, but none which could be associated with such a large estate. It seems more likely that Wells in Somerset was intended, although the grant seems very large for a period when the area had been settled by the English for a considerable time. In Domesday Book (i. 89r) the bishop of Wells held fifty hides at Wells, some of which presumably had belonged to the minster of St Andrew's, and some of which could well have been transferred from Sherborne.

The two lists also differ in their readings of Sigeberht's gift of seven hides *in est Canne* (Faustina A. ii) or *in Iscan* (altered to or

[79] If Henderson's identification of Trigel with Tregear is correct; cf. *VCH Cornwall*, viii. 65, 68 and 103.

[80] Pawton, which may have been granted to Sherborne in the same period (see below) was much closer to English territory.

from *Ascan*: Missal, no. 23). The element '*in*' suggests that the estate was located in a river valley (as *in Lydene, in Tolra*; though not in the case of *in Chesterbled*). *In Ascan* could well refer to the valley of the river Axe, but there are rivers of that name in Dorset, Somerset and Devon. S 1042, the spurious Wells charter, lists an estate at *Æsce* claimed by the bishop (identified by Finberg, *ECW* 542, as Ash Priors, Somerset), and it is tempting but unwise to associate the two names. The Faustina A. ii reading also has possibilities: *in est Canne* could refer to Cann in Dorset or in Devon. Alternatively it might refer to Calne in Wiltshire, listed as one of the bishopric of Salisbury's original possessions in the *Registrum Osmundi* (in Domesday Book the name is given as *Cauna*, and the Faustina entry could be read as *Canne* or *Caune* with equal justification).

Other unidentifiable names are *Snarstok*, whether in Cornwall or nor, and *A[l]bambruth* (Faustina A. ii) or *Abbamburh* (Missal).[81] *Wytecumbe* is probably one of the several Whit[e]combes in Dorset, none of which has retained any link with Sherborne or Salisbury. *Wi[nu]rod* might be a form of *Winfrod (from a British stream name), which lies behind the place-names Winford, Somerset, and Winfrith Newburgh and Wynford Eagle, both in Dorset. None of these has any early episcopal connection. *Acford* (to be preferred to the *Atford* of Faustina A. ii; Dr Mills, pers. comm.) could be Oakford, Devon, or one of several Okefords in Dorset; and *Cleihangre* (a better reading than the Faustina A. ii *Clet*-) must be the modern Clinger or Clayhanger, of which there are four in Dorset and one in Devon: none of these has any helpful associations.

The place-name evidence offered in the two fourteenth-century manuscripts and examined above strongly suggests that their exemplar embodied a record of royal grants made to Sherborne before the bishopric was divided *c.* 909. A large number of the Dorset estates are found in the possession of the bishopric of Salisbury by 1086, as is one, or possibly two, of the Wiltshire estates. Several of the Somerset estates were claimed by the bishopric of Wells in S 1042, giving support to Robinson's hypothesis that the bishopric of Wells was endowed with many of the estates that the bishop of Sherborne had originally held in Somerset.[82] There are no secure links between the estates in Devon and Cornwall listed in the fourteenth century and the later endowments of the bishopric of Crediton and its successor Exeter

---

[81] Finberg, *ECW* 402, read this in Faustina A. ii as *Awam-*, and identified it as Wambrook in Somerset, but the manuscript lacks any trace of the distinctive downstrokes displayed in other *w*s, and the reading in the Missal is clearly *Abbam-*.

[82] Robinson, *Wells*, pp. 52–3; and see also S 380, discussed below, p. liv.

(except perhaps for an estate at Crediton itself), but this may well reflect the irregular history of that see. Both the Plegmund narrative and the Dunstan letter, which concern three estates in Cornwall (see below, pp. lv–lvi), assume that episcopal estates should belong to the diocese administering the area in which they are situated.

The origin of the list that lay behind the fourteenth-century versions is unknown. The donor's names, together with a note of their gifts, might have been entered in some form of calendar or obituary list, as people for whom prayers would regularly be said, like those in some of the lists in the *Liber Vitae* of the New Minster, Winchester.[83] However, judging by the few obits that are available, the Faustina A. ii list is not organized in such a way. The Sherborne Missal extracts afford even less evidence, since three of the kings for whom obits are available (Æthelwulf, Edgar and Æthelred II) are only included in the charter groups of medallions. The Missal names Alfred (instead of Æthelred I, Faustina A. ii) and places him shortly after Offa, so their obits (26 or 29 July; 26 October) are in chronological order but Egbert, who probably died in the second half of 839 (802 + 37 years and 7 months; *ASC*, preface) is near the head of the list, and would be out of sequence. There is no other discernible organizing principle in either list.

Whatever its purpose, the list was apparently abandoned after the division of the bishopric of Sherborne, perhaps because it was seen as invalid, even as a prayer record, after so many of the estates concerned had been dispersed. Being no longer relevant, it might have remained with the monastic records rather than among the episcopal muniments that were transferred to Salisbury late in the eleventh century. At some later date a few more names were added (as least to the exemplar of Faustina A. ii), perhaps with the intention of converting it into a list of benefactors of the monastery, although the project, if it was such, did not get far.

No charters survive for those estates listed in Faustina A. ii and the Missal which might have passed to the other bishoprics of the south-west. It has already been suggested (see above, p. xxxvi) that some early episcopal endowments may not have been accompanied by charters. It is possible that, in the south-west, it was accepted that a bishopric might possess an old-established nucleus of estates without benefit of charter, for neither Salisbury nor Wells appears to have preserved or later produced any specific documents to support their ownership of episcopal lands.

---

[83] There is another good example in Cambridge, Trinity College O. 2. 1, from Ely.

For St Osmund of Salisbury it was enough to list in his foundation charter for the new cathedral church the various estates which should belong to the bishopric: there is no mention of earlier documents, nor were any preserved among the Salisbury muniments. Wells likewise preserved no early titles to its episcopal estates: S 1042, a dubious document dated 1065, but most probably a post-Conquest production, is the earliest surviving text to name the estates claimed by the bishopric. No charters have survived at Crediton for estates which passed to the bishopric from Sherborne, although a copy of the foundation charter of the original monastery has been preserved (S 255, dated 739, with some later alterations; see below, p. liv). This would be in accordance with the normal practice of 'booking' land for the purpose of monastic endowment. The next Crediton documents to have survived are S 405 (930), in which Athelstan granted the bishop and his *familia* three hides at Sandford, and S 421 (933), a grant of privileges to the bishopric by the same king, neither of which is wholly acceptable.[84] It is worth considering whether during the early period in the south-west, until about the mid ninth century, many episcopal lands were held not as bookland but by some other tenure closer to the conditions under which estates were held by royal officials, for in many ways the bishops were just that.[85] The difference between such episcopal estates and other church lands lay perhaps more in the degree of control exercised by the king over the bishopric, and the secular duties performed by the bishop, than in the various immunities from secular burdens enjoyed by church lands.[86]

However, by the second half of the ninth century both the immunities and the reservation of military obligations were becoming more standardized, and it may have become necessary to clarify the status of lands held without charter. One of Sherborne's most impressive texts is the charter of immunities granted by Æthelberht in 864 (**6**), which frees the foundation from all secular obligations except those of army-service and bridge-work. Moreover both Crediton and St Germans were apparently granted similar charters quite soon after being made sees and receiving estates from the parent diocese (i.e. Sherborne in the case of Crediton, and Crediton in the case of St Germans).

---

[84] See Chaplais 1966, pp. 10–12.

[85] This is better established for the later period: see Stenton, *Anglo-Saxon England*, p. 546, and F. Barlow, *The English Church 1000–1066*, 2nd edn (London, 1979), pp. 96–8; but from the earliest evidence available it can be seen that bishops took a prominent place in the *witan* and in the judicial system.

[86] Although evidence is scanty for this period, see W. H. Stevenson, 'Trinoda Necessitas', *English Historical Review* xxix (1914), pp. 689–703, esp. pp. 700–1, and Brooks 1971, pp. 75–7.

INTRODUCTION

The Crediton text, S 421 (933), frees the episcopal church of Crediton from all secular obligations except those of army-service and fortress-work. It exists as a single-sheet manuscript in a hand of s. x^2, or perhaps s. x/xi.[87] The date 933 is consistent with the inclusion of Bishop Eadulf in the text,[88] but the witness-list must have been added later, since it is based on one which must date from the period between 937 and September 939.[89] The formulas have close links with three Sherborne charters: the proem, royal style and anathema show only minor variations in vocabulary from those used in **7** and **8**, while the immunity and reservation clauses are almost identical with that found in **5**, also a grant of liberties to the bishopric, although not an acceptable one.[90] The St Germans text, which has only recently been published, survives only in a very late and abbreviated copy.[91] It records that Athelstan restored the lands of the bishopric of St Germans: 'partim abstracto jugo servitutis addicti ab omni censu Regalis fisci, exceptis hijs rebus, scilicet expeditione contra hostes et vigilijs marinis liberum restituo ...' The extract is dated 838 (*recte* 936).[92] It is too brief to allow any decision on the original charter's authenticity, although, as its editor points out, the phrase *in diocesi* (for *diocesim*) *perpetuam* would accord with a tenth-century Cornish provenance,[93] and the substitution of *vigilijs marinis* for the usual fortress- and bridge-work would make excellent sense in view of Cornwall's position and circumstances.[94] *Cum titulo sanctae crucis*, used in Athelstan's attestation, is a phrase first found in Eadwig's charters (e.g. S 628, dated 956), but it is only a minor variant on the common *cum sigillo sanctae crucis*, and could well have occurred earlier. Whether the Crediton and St Germans texts are accepted as genuine or not, they indicate that both bishoprics found it necessary to clarify not the extent of their episcopal estates but their fiscal position.[95]

---

[87] See refs *sub* S 421. Mr T. A. M. Bishop suggested s. x^2; in Chaplais 1966, p. 11, it is 'tentatively ascribed to the end of the tenth or the beginning of the eleventh century'.

[88] O'Donovan 1972, pp. 36–7. He died between June 934 and 937.

[89] Chaplais 1966, p. 11.

[90] For **5**, see below, pp. 15–18. If, as I suspect, the original of S 421 was composed at Sherborne, or with the aid of Sherborne documents, this casts an interesting light on the date at which **5** was composed. The omission of bridge-work in the reservation clause of S 421 could well be due to a scribal error.

[91] Padel 1978, pp. 26–7. The extract comes from a s. xvii copy of the Register of Plympton Priory, now lost.

[92] This is the date given by Leland for Conan's establishment at St Germans: see for comment Padel 1978, pp. 26–7, and O'Donovan 1972, pp. 35–6.

[93] Padel 1978, p. 27.

[94] This is the earliest occurrence of this phrase. The same phrase is found in a somewhat later charter dealing with estates in Cornwall (S 932, dated 977), although here it only replaces bridge-work (see Whitelock, *EHD*, no. 115, and Chaplais 1966, p. 16).

[95] This is yet another topic that needs a much fuller treatment than can be afforded here.

INTRODUCTION

ii) *Early charter evidence*

The fourteenth-century lists are not the only sources of information about the holdings of the see of Sherborne before 900. There is a Glastonbury charter dated 712 (but with an indiction for 718) which records a grant made to Glastonbury by Forthhere, bishop of Sherborne (S 1253). The grant was of one hide at Bleadney, Somerset, and a small island, and at St Martin's Church. Sherborne must have owned land at Bleadney from which such a grant could have been made, and an estate at Bleadney was claimed by Wells in S 1042.

Another charter, S 255 (739), records a grant to Bishop Forthhere of land at *Cridie* (Crediton) for the foundation of a monastery. The charter has survived in an eleventh-century copy, and appears to have an authentic text and witness-list, although the bounds are of later date.[96] The amount of the grant is given as twenty hides, although, as Dr Chaplais has observed, both in the text and in the endorsement the number 'xx' is written over the erasure of a number which originally occupied a smaller space.[97]

A third charter, S 380, preserved at Wells in a late cartulary copy, records an exchange of lands between Edward the Elder and Asser, bishop of Sherborne, in which Asser gave the king the monastery at Plympton in exchange for *tres villas*: six hides at Wellington, five hides at Buckland and twelve hides at Bishop's Lydeard. The charter is undated, but the transaction must belong to the period between 899 and 909 (the years of Edward's accession and Asser's death respectively). The text itself is not above suspicion, although its authenticity is hard to determine because there are so few genuine charters of Edward the Elder available for comparison. The use of *villa* to refer to the estates involved is most unusual in tenth-century diplomatic, and is reminiscent of the *tres villas* in the Plegmund narrative (discussed below). The three estates acquired by Sherborne lay in Somerset, and belonged to Wells at the time of the Conquest.[98] There is no mention of Plympton in the fourteenth-century lists, and it may have been acquired only shortly before the exchange: Robinson suggested that it was one of King Alfred's gifts to Asser.[99]

S 255 and 380 are only calendared in this volume, although both record grants to Sherborne, as both lands and charters passed to other foundations before the Conquest. They will be fully edited in later volumes of this series.

---

[96] See Whitelock, *EHD*, no. 69; Chaplais 1966, pp. 10–11; Finberg, *WCHS*, pp. 61–4; and Brooks 1971, pp. 75–6 and 80.

[97] Finberg, *WCHS*, pp. 62–3, suggests that the number was corrected to make the grant correspond to the Domesday hundred assessment.

[98] DB, i. 156. Buckland was part of the Wellington estate: see Robinson, *Wells*, pp. 53–4.

[99] Ibid. p. 53.

INTRODUCTION   lv

iii) *The Dunstan letter and the Plegmund narrative*

Further evidence of Sherborne episcopal estates is afforded in a vernacular text known as the Dunstan letter.[100] It is a letter from the archbishop (who must be Dunstan by internal evidence)[101] to King Æthelred, written in a hand alternatively assigned to s. x^{ex} and s. x/xi.[102] It gives the history of three Cornish estates, *Polltun, Cællwic* and *Landwiþan*, from their gift to Sherborne by King Egbert to their final assignation to the bishopric of Cornwall, which the author urges the king to reconfirm for the new bishop. In the middle of this account is a shortened version of the Plegmund narrative, itself concerned with the same three estates, although from a different angle. The narrative, an inaccurate account of the division of the West Saxon sees, survives in several manuscripts, the earliest being of mid or late s. x.[103] It names the five bishops consecrated for Wessex, and mentions that to Ealdulf of Crediton were assigned *tres villas* in Cornwall, namely *Polltun, Cællincg* and *Landuuithan*, so that he could visit the Cornish people yearly to 'wring out' (*exprimendos*) their errors, since they had in the past resisted the truth and not obeyed apostolic decrees.[104]

The Dunstan letter gives a different reason for the gift of the estates to Crediton: to punish the Cornish people for disobeying the West Saxons. It goes on to relate that when a separate see was created for Cornwall, the estates were transferred to that bishopric, and to urge that this disposition should be continued under the new bishop of Cornwall. Clearly both documents were intended to support a claim to the Cornish estates: the Plegmund narrative supported their possession by Crediton, and would have been composed some time in the mid-tenth century before the estates passed to Cornwall;[105] whilst the Dunstan letter supported

---

[100] *Crawford Charters*, no. VII; S 1296.
[101] Ibid. p. 103.
[102] The hand itself cannot be dated precisely: the differences in dating reflect various scholarly assessments of how the document came to be written. Chaplais 1966, pp. 16–19, accepted it as the original text written at Dunstan's instigation for Ealdred, bishop of Cornwall, between the years 980 and 988. The editors of the *Crawford Charters*, pp. 102–3, regarded their text as a copy of a letter actually sent to the king between 980 and 988, and dated it s. x/xi (but see n. 106 below). Robinson, *Wells*, p. 27, accepted the latter date, although he questioned Dunstan's authorship, pointing out that the bishopric of Cornwall would have been interested in protecting the three estates involved against a claim made by the bishopric of Crediton (as set forth in the Plegmund narrative). The whole issue is not strictly relevant here, but for Chaplais' general point see the commentary on **13**.
[103] A strip of parchment, BL Add. 7138: see Robinson, *Wells*, pp. 18–27. For a recent discussion of the two documents and the division of the West Saxon sees, see Brooks, *Church of Canterbury*, pp. 210–13.
[104] Presumably a reference to the variant practices of the British Church.
[105] Robinson, *Wells*, p. 20, suggests a date within the episcopacy of Æthelgar of Crediton.

their ownership by St Germans, having been written shortly after Wulfsige of Cornwall's death.[106] What is of concern here is the reliability of the opening statement of the letter: that the three estates were originally given to Sherborne by Egbert. Neither fourteenth-century list mentions the three Cornish estates in question, although they list several gifts from Egbert, including, in Faustina A. ii, three other estates in Cornwall. It is possible that the author of the letter had some reason for pushing back the known history of the three estates (for in the Plegmund narrative this only goes back to the early tenth century), perhaps to emphasize that the estates had always been intended to form part of an episcopal endowment, for the support of whichever bishopric was charged with the cure of Cornwall. There is no external evidence to support the additional statement that Egbert gave a part of the land [Cornwall] to God, and Robinson (*Wells*, p. 27) suggested that this was derived from the account of Æthelwulf's decimation in the *Anglo-Saxon Chronicle* (s.a. 855). It is conceivable that the author of the Dunstan letter, who must have had some knowledge of the bishopric of Cornwall, knew that Egbert had given estates in Cornwall to Sherborne, which had eventually passed to the see of Cornwall, and connected Egbert's name with the three disputed estates.[107]

The three estates have been identified as Pawton, a large manor comprising six or seven parishes, and Lawhitton, which included Launceston and four other parishes; the third, *Cællwic* or *Cællincg*, is probably Kelly in Egloshayle.[108] Pawton and Lawhitton were held by the bishop of Exeter in 1086 (by then Devon and Cornwall again formed one diocese), although the parish of Launceston had been lost to Earl Harold. Kelly is not mentioned in Domesday Book, but the bishops of Exeter held much of the parish as part of their manor of *Berner(h)*.[109] All three have been included in Fig. 3 as probable possessions of Sherborne, *c.* 900.

iv) *The writ of Bishop Æthelric* (**13**)

For the period after *c.* 909, when the diocese of Sherborne was confined to Dorset, there is a possible source of information about the episcopal estates in **13**, a writ issued by Bishop Æthelric which lists a number of places from which the bishop expected to

---

[106] Wulfsige's last appearance was in 981 (S 838, a suspect text, but its witness-list is acceptable for the date: see Keynes, *Diplomas*, pp. 157 n. 9 and 239).

[107] See Robinson, *Wells*, p. 27, for other sources of information for the letter. Robinson was sceptical of the reliability of its early information.

[108] See *Crawford Charters*, p. 107; Henderson, *Cornish Church Guide*, pp. 26, 57 and 113-16; and W. M. M. Picken, '143: Callington and Kelliwic', *D&CN&Q* xxvii (1956-8), p. 225.

[109] Henderson, *Cornish Church Guide*, p. 57.

collect shipscot, but was no longer able to do so.[110] The wording of the writ does not imply that the bishop owned either the lands named or the 300 hides from which he had to collect the tax, although it might well have eased the administrative burden of collection to include some or all of the episcopal estates in the 300 hides allotted to the bishop. One might assume that the bishop would experience difficulty in dealing with those estates which were not part of the episcopal endowment, but the picture is obscured by the mention of Holcombe (Holcombe Rogus, Devon: see below, p. 148), of which Sherborne did claim possession. The other places named seem to be mostly situated within the hundreds of Sherborne, Yetminster and Beaminster, but only occasionally do they coincide with estates known to be in possession of Sherborne or Salisbury. *Apultune* is Alton Pancras, which was an episcopal possession (see above, p. xliv). According to the writ, the bishop lost two hides here. According to Faustina A. ii, Alton together with another estate was worth thirty hides, while in Domesday Book it was assessed at six hides. At *Upcerle*, probably Up Cerne, seven hides were missing: in 1086 the bishop held two and a half hides there (DB, i. 75v). None of the other places has a demonstrable link with either Sherborne or Salisbury (see Harmer, *Writs*, pp. 484–5).

There is no way of telling whether Æthelric's appeal was successful, or whether the bishopric lost the authority to collect shipscot from the estates named. Holcombe was technically in Sherborne's possession for the next few decades, but none the less when mentioned it always appears to be in lay hands (**14, 17** and DB; see commentaries), so Æthelric's fears were well founded.

v) *Other sources*

The *Vita Wlsini*, ch. vi, records that Wulfsige's death took place in his *mansionem* called *Bega monasterium*. This can only be Beaminster in Dorset, and its pre-Conquest ownership by the bishopric of Sherborne is consistent with its possession by the bishop of Salisbury in 1086 (DB, i. 77r),[111] and it is listed as one of the original endowments of the see in the *Registrum Osmundi* (i. 198).

There is a tenth-century charter, S 445 (dated 939), which records a grant made by King Athelstan of land at *Archet* (West

---

[110] I am following Harmer's interpretation of the writ, as well as her discussion of the place-name identifications: *Writs*, pp. 266–70 and 482–6.

[111] There is no evidence that it was a monastic possession, *pace* K. Barker, 'Early Ecclesiastical Settlement in Dorset: a Note on the Topography of Sherborne, Beaminster and Wimborne Minster', *Proceedings of the Dorset Natural History and Archaeological Society* cii (1982 for 1980), pp. 107–12, at 107.

Orchard, Dorset), to a bishop Alfric or Alfrid, who immediately regranted it to Beorhtwyn, the daughter of Wulfhelm. The bishop is most probably Alfred, bishop of Sherborne, although there was another contemporary Bishop Alfred, probably a Mercian.[112] Beorhtwyn is also called *uxor fratris illius Beorhtere*, which must in the context refer to the bishop's brother, making Beorhtwyn Alfred's sister-in-law, an interesting (if irrelevant) piece of biographical detail. The text has no outstanding anachronisms and may well be authentic. It is preserved in the Shaftesbury cartulary, BL Harley 61, and will be published in the volume of Shaftesbury charters; it is only calendared in the present volume.

The original endowments of the bishopric of Salisbury, as recorded in the *Registrum Osmundi*, include estates in Dorset, Somerset, Wiltshire and Berkshire. The lands named in Dorset are Yetminster, Alton Pancras, Charminster, Beaminster and Netherbury, and all have been shown above to have been possessions of Sherborne before they passed to Salisbury. Writhlington in Somerset might also have come from Sherborne, but it has no known history before its appearance in Domesday Book. The estates in Wiltshire and Berkshire listed in the *Registrum Osmundi* must have been inherited largely from the bishopric of Ramsbury, although possibly Potterne and Calne were once owned by Sherborne (see above, pp. xlv and xlix–l). The *Registrum Osmundi* does not give any indications of the provenance of these lands; they are listed by county.

6. THE EARLY HISTORY OF HORTON ABBEY

The early history of Horton is obscure, and only the barest outline is distinguishable. Horton was originally founded as a house of nuns, at some unknown date. The earliest evidence for its existence is to be found in the *Liber Vitae* of New Minster, Winchester, which contains the entry *Wulfhild abbatissa Hortun coenobia* in a list of *Feminarum Illustrium*.[113] The entry is in the main hand of the manuscript, dated s. xi^1; internal evidence suggests that it may have been compiled *c.* 1020.

The only other reference to Horton as a nunnery is to be found in a life of St Wulfhild written by Goscelin of St Bertin, which must have composed between 1086 and 1098 × 1099.[114] In this dramatic tale Wulfhild, a nun of Wilton, was abducted by King Edgar, but before either could give way to temptation the king

---
[112] O'Donovan 1973, pp. 105–6.
[113] *Liber Vitae*, p. 57.
[114] M. Esposito, 'La Vie de Sainte Vulfhilde', *Analecta Bollandiana* xxxii (1913), pp. 10–26.

had a change of heart. He released Wulfhild, and gave her the abbey of Barking. Later, in ch. viii, Goscelin relates how Wulfhild was ejected from Barking, largely due to the machinations of Queen Ælfthryth, and how she retired to Horton: *ad hereditarium monasterium suum Hortunam recessit*, where she stayed for twenty years until the queen repented, and Wulfhild could return to Barking for the last seven years of her life. She died in 996,[115] which would imply that Horton was in existence by *c*. 970. Horton is also mentioned, implicitly as a nunnery, in ch. iv, where Goscelin describes it as at the centre (*quasi umbilicus tetrapolis*) of four other houses, all equally spaced at twenty miles distant from each other. The four are named as Wilton, Shaftesbury, Wareham and Hampton. The last house Esposito tentatively identified as Hampton in Gloucestershire; but it is more likely that Southampton was intended, for Horton lies equidistant from and in the centre of the circle formed by these four places. No nunnery is recorded for Southampton (or any other Hampton) in Knowles' *HRH*, but a short-lived foundation could well have left no trace. Horton is also named in ch. xi, in which a woman of Horton (presumably a member of the community) was healed at Barking, a miracle performed after Wulfhild's death.

It is likely that the Wulfhild of Barking was the same person as the abbess of Horton recorded in the *Liber Vitae*, although there is no evidence other than the coincidence of names, and a possible later connection with Barking (see below, p. lxi n. 126). There is also no way of knowing how accurate Goscelin's information, most of which must have come from Barking, may be. At least it is clear that he knew of Horton's earlier existence as a nunnery.

Dr Ker refers to Horton as a nunnery dedicated to St Wolfrida.[116] This information comes from *VCH Dorset*,[117] which gives no indication of its source. St Wolfrida (Wulfthryth) was abbess at Wilton, and died in 1000.[118] This would seem too late to have inspired the original dedication of Horton, although a suitable one for the nunnery. It could have been added later. It would however have been an unusual choice for the new monastic foundation, and moreover **22**, the charter of liberties granted to the refounded house in 1061, mentions a dedication to St Mary. Sherborne was also dedicated to St Mary, but this is not mentioned in **6**, the exemplar for **22**, so that the reference in **22** was independently added to the text (see below, p. 79). St Mary is also named in the rubric to **22**, most probably copied from the charter's endorsement. Possibly the idea of a dedication to St

[115] Ibid. pp. 21–2.
[116] *Medieval Libraries*, p. 103.
[117] ii. 71.
[118] Knowles, *HRH*, p. 222.

Wolfrida was due to a confusion with St Wulfhild of Barking and Horton.

What happened to the first foundation is not known: it had ceased to exist by 1033, when Bovi received the grant of seven hides at Horton (**20**). Around the turn of the century Viking armies had ravaged the area several times (*ASC*, s.a. 998, 1001 and 1003), and in 1015 Cnut ravaged Dorset, Wiltshire, and Somerset. Horton was not necessarily destroyed by direct action; there could well have been economic causes for its failure, perhaps resulting from the Danish depredations and general disruption.

A similar veil covers the second foundation at Horton, this time as a monastery. It must have taken place between 1033, when Bovi received the land (**20**), and 1061, when it is first referred to as a foundation (**22**). It has been suggested that this foundation was connected with, and perhaps founded by, a member of the powerful Wessex family brought into prominence by Ordgar, father-in-law to King Edgar through his daughter Ælfthryth, the villain of Goscelin's story. Ordgar's son Ordulf founded the monastery of Tavistock, and a second Ordgar, prominent in charters in the 1030s and 1040s, was the original grantee of **21**, which relates to an estate at Littleham in Devon. A garbled account of the family and of the founding of Tavistock was related by William of Malmesbury,[119] and has been discussed by Finberg.[120] In William's version the foundation of Tavistock is attributed to Ordgar, the father of Ælfthryth, and both he and his son Ordulf are said to have been buried there. Ordulf was a giant and very strong, having on one occasion torn down the gate and part of the city wall of Exeter with his own hands, when he and his kinsman King Edward were kept waiting without. Ordulf died at Horton, which was one of the houses to have benefited from his generosity (*ejus liberalitate inter abbatias numerabatur*), and he wished to be buried there, but the abbot of Tavistock, Sihtric, took both the body and the legacies for his own church.[121] Finberg suggests that William confused the first Ordgar, the ealdorman and father-in-law of Edgar, who died in 971, with the second Ordgar, who was most likely a relative and perhaps a grandson; and that he also confused the first Ordulf, the real founder of Tavistock, with a later man of the same name, who attested charters between 1044 and 1050, and who appears in Domesday Book as one of the great landowners in Devon at the time of the Conquest.[122] Although the king named as a relative could be

---

[119] *GP*, i. 202–4.
[120] Finberg 1943, pp. 190–201.
[121] *GP*, i. 203–4.
[122] Finberg 1943, p. 197.

either Edward the Martyr or Edward the Confessor, the mention of Sihtric implies the second Ordulf. Finberg suggests that Littleham (**21**) came to Horton from Ordgar,[123] but it is equally possible that Ordulf was the benefactor, having inherited the land at Ordgar's death *c*. 1050. With regard to William's story about Sihtric's actions, Finberg points out that in Domesday Book one of the Tavistock estates in Cornwall, half a hide at Antony, was claimed by Horton, so that there was obviously some dispute between the two houses, and William's tale may well have had some basis in fact. This increases the likelihood that Horton was intimately connected with the family of Ordgar, and may indeed have been refounded by Ordgar II or Ordulf II.[124] There is, however, no easy way of dating the foundation more closely within the period between 1033 and 1061. Horton may or may not have been in existence when Ordgar was granted Littleham in 1042. The only indication – a tenuous one – is that Sherborne supplied the exemplar of the charter of 1061 (**22**), which suggests that Horton might not have been organized long enough to be able to supply its own draft.

Horton's later history is equally obscure. The abbey appears in Domesday Book as a landowner on a small scale in Dorset and Devon, holding some of the estates mentioned in the charters, and in addition some town properties in Wareham, Wimborne and Dorchester. Only the Wareham property is named in the papal privileges of 1126 and 1146. The name of only one abbot is known (*Osirich*, who appears in 1075),[125] and only one manuscript from the Horton library has survived (a Boethius, which was given to Horton in the middle of the eleventh century).[126] The second foundation survived independently not much longer than the first, for early in the twelfth century it was merged with Sherborne, then still a priory. The charter of Henry I which recorded this was included in the Sherborne cartulary as the introduction to the group of Horton charters (fo. 26). In the text, the reason for the combination is given as Horton's poor location and inadequate endowment (*pro loci importunitate et terrarum eidem adiacentium paucitate*), but clearly Sherborne was not too highly rated either, since the charter continues *ut de duabus exiguis et debilibus*

---

[123] Ibid. p. 195.
[124] Davidson 1883, pp. 144–62, suggested that Horton was founded by Ordgar I, destroyed, and then refounded by Ordulf, which is chronologically possible, but leaves Bovi's interim possession of the Horton estate unaccounted for.
[125] Knowles, *HRH*, pp. 23 and 53, and Wilkins, *Concilia*, i. 364.
[126] Ker, *Catalogue*, no. 115. An Old English inscription records that the book was given to Horton by Ælfgyth. There was an abbess of Barking at about this time called Ælfgyth or Ælfgyva, and it is possible that she is the Ælfgyth in question, since there may well have been an earlier connection between the two houses (see above, p. lix).

una sit in substantiis maior. The charter is undated, but the appearance of Ralph as archbishop of Canterbury limits it to the years 1114 × (20 October)1122. There is nothing in the charter about altering the status of either foundation, but in the Faustina A. ii manuscript the date of both the amalgamation and the reversal of status is given as 1122 (fos 25 and 26), at which time Thurstin was elevated from prior to abbot of Sherborne. There is an alternative tradition that places the amalgamation in 1122, and the shift in Horton's status from abbey to priory in 1139.[127] Certainly Sherborne had been upgraded by 1126, since Thurstin is addressed as abbot of Sherborne in the papal privilege of that year, but it is possible that Horton was not demoted immediately.

Henry I's charge about the scanty nature of Horton's endowment was well justified. The estates covered by the four charters (**18**, **19**, **20** and **22**) add up to twenty-four hides, but by 1066 (according to Domesday Book) Horton only held ten hides. It is possible that the lands included in **18**, which lists estates at five places in Devon (Abbotskerswell, Ipplepen, Dainton, Brimley and Bittleford), totalling fifteen and a half hides, were not all given to Horton. Abbotskerswell is listed in Domesday Book, for one and a half hides, and the papal privileges mention only Abbotskerswell and Brimley. Perhaps the grant embodied in the charter was divided before Horton received a portion. This would explain how the foundation apparently lost fourteen hides so quickly. In the cartulary the scribe preceded his copy of **18** with a vernacular rubric which records the booking to Æthelhild of *Iplanpenne* 7 ... *Doddingtune* 7 ... *Cærspylle*, but if this is a copy of the orginal endorsement, it is not necessarily proof that all three estates were transferred to Horton. The distribution of Horton estates is illustrated in Fig. 2.

---

[127] Sherborne Missal, p. 388, and Knowles, *HRH*, p. 70.

ABBREVIATIONS

Bibl. Nat.	Paris, Bibliothèque Nationale
BL	London, British Library
OS	Ordnance Survey
s.	*saeculo*
s.a.	*sub anno*
TRE	Tempore regis Eadwardi

BIBLIOGRAPHICAL ABBREVIATIONS

Anglia Sacra	H. Wharton, *Anglia Sacra*, 2 vols (London, 1691)
ASC	*Anglo-Saxon Chronicle*
Asser	*Asser's Life of King Alfred*, ed. W. H. Stevenson (Oxford, 1904)
BAR	British Archaeological Reports
Barker 1980	K. Barker, 'The Early Christian Topography of Sherborne', *Antiquity* liv (1980), pp. 229–31
Barker 1982	K. Barker, 'The Early History of Sherborne', *The Early Church in Western Britain and Ireland*, ed. S. M. Pearce, BAR British Series cii (1982), pp. 77–116
Bede, *HE*	Bede, *Historia Ecclesiastica*
Birch	W. de G. Birch, *Cartularium Saxonicum*, 3 vols and index (London, 1885–99)
Brooks, *Church of Canterbury*	N. Brooks, *The Early History of the Church of Canterbury: Christ Church from 597 to 1066* (Leicester, 1984)
Brooks 1968	N. Brooks, 'The Pre-Conquest Charters of Christ Church, Canterbury', unpubl. D.Phil. thesis, Oxford University (1968)
Brooks 1971	N. Brooks, 'The Development of Military Obligations in Eighth- and Ninth-Century England', *England before the Conquest: Studies in Primary Sources presented to Dorothy Whitelock*, ed. P. Clemoes and K. Hughes (Cambridge, 1971), pp. 69–84
Brotanek, *Texte*	E. Brotanek, *Texte und Untersuchungen zur altenglischen Literatur und Kirchengeschichte* (Halle, 1913)
Chaplais 1966	P. Chaplais, 'The Authenticity of the Royal Anglo-Saxon Diplomas of Exeter', *Bulletin*

	of the Institute of Historical Research xxxix (1966), pp. 1–34 (repr. in *Essays in Medieval Diplomacy and Administration* (London, 1981), pp. xv 1–34 and Addendum)
Charters and Documents	*Charters and Documents Illustrating the History of the Cathedral, City and Diocese of Salisbury in the Twelfth and Thirteenth Centuries*, ed. W. H. R. Jones and W. D. Macray, RS (London, 1891)
Crawford Charters	*The Crawford Collection of Early Charters and Documents now in the Bodleian Library*, ed. A. S. Napier and W. H. Stevenson (Oxford, 1895)
Davidson 1883	J. B. Davidson, 'On the Ancient History of Exmouth', *Transactions of the Devonshire Association* xv (1883), pp. 144–62
Davis, *Cartularies*	G. R. C. Davis, *Medieval Cartularies of Great Britain: a Short Catalogue* (London, 1958)
DB	Domesday Book
DB, Exon.	Exon. Domesday
D&CN&Q	*Devon and Cornwall Notes and Queries*
DEPN	E. Ekwall, *The Concise Oxford Dictionary of English Place-Names*, 4th edn (Oxford, 1960)
EETS	Early English Text Society
EPNS	English Place-Name Society
Fägersten, *Place-Names of Dorset*	A. Fägersten, 'The Place-Names of Dorset', *Uppsala Universitets Årsskrift, Filosofi, Språkvetenskap och Historiska Vetenskaper* 4 (1933), pp. 1–335
Finberg, *ECDC*	H. P. R. Finberg, *The Early Charters of Devon and Cornwall*, 2nd edn, Department of English Local History, Occasional Papers ii, (Leicester, 1963)
Finberg, *ECW*	H. P. R. Finberg, *The Early Charters of Wessex* (Leicester, 1964)
Finberg, *Lucerna*	H. P. R. Finberg, *Lucerna* (London, 1964)
Finberg, *WCHS*	H. P. R. Finberg, *West-Country Historical Studies* (Newton Abbot, 1969)
Finberg 1943	H. P. R. Finberg, 'The House of Ordgar and the Foundation of Tavistock Abbey', *English Historical Review* lviii (1943), pp. 190–201
Fl. Wig.	*Florentii Wigorniensis Monachi Chronicon ex Chronicis*, 2 vols, ed. B. Thorpe, English Historical Society (London, 1848–9)
Förster, *Themse*	M. Förster, 'Der Flussname Themse und seine Sippe', Sitzungsberichte der

	Bayerischen Akademie der Wissenschaften, Philosophisch-historische Abteilung i (1941)
Förster, *Zur Geschichte*	M. Förster, 'Zur Geschichte des Reliquienkultus in Altengland', *Sitzungsberichte der Bayerischen Akademie der Wissenschaften*, Philosophisch-historische Abteilung viii (1943)
Gelling, *ECTV*	M. Gelling, *The Early Charters of the Thames Valley* (Leicester, 1979)
GP	*Willelmi Malmesbiriensis Monachi De Gestis Pontificum Anglorum Libri Quinque* ed. N. E. S. A. Hamilton, RS (London, 1870)
Grundy 1933, 1934, 1935, 1936, 1937, 1938, 1939	G. B. Grundy, 'Dorset Charters', *Proceedings of the Dorset Natural History and Archaeological Society* lv (1933), pp. 239–68; lvi (1934), pp. 110–30; lvii (1935), pp. 114–39; lviii (1936), pp. 103–36; lix (1937), pp. 95–118; lx (1938), pp. 75–89; and lxi (1939), pp. 60–78
HAA, HAB	*Historia Abbatum auctore anonymo, Historia Abbatum auctore Beda*, in *Venerabilis Baedae Opera Historica*, ed. C. Plummer, 2 vols (Oxford, 1896)
Harmer, *Writs*	F. E. Harmer, *Anglo-Saxon Writs* (Manchester, 1952)
Harrison, *Framework*	K. Harrison, *The Framework of Anglo-Saxon History to A.D. 900* (Cambridge, 1976)
Harrison 1973	K. Harrison, 'The Beginning of the Year in England, c. 500–900', *Anglo-Saxon England* ii (1973), pp. 51–70
Hart 1965	C. Hart, 'Some Dorset Charter Boundaries', *Proceedings of the Dorset Natural History and Archaeological Society* lxxxvi (1965 for 1964), pp. 158–63
Hearne, *Collections*	*Remarks and Collections of Thomas Hearne*, ed. C. E. Doble (D. W. Rannie, H. E. Salter), 11 vols, Oxford Historical Society (Oxford, 1885–1921)
Hearne, *Leland's Itinerary*	*Leland's Itinerary*, ed. T. Hearne (Oxford, 1712)
Henderson, *Cornish Church Guide*	C. Henderson, *The Cornish Church Guide and Parochial History of Cornwall* (Truro, 1925)
Herbert, *Sherborne Missal*	*The Sherborne Missal: Reproductions of Full Pages and Details of Ornament from the Missal executed between the years 1396 and 1407 for Sherborne Abbey Church and now preserved in the Library of the Duke of*

	Northumberland at Alnwick Castle, with an Introduction by J. A. Herbert, The Roxburghe Club (Oxford, 1920)
Holtzmann, *Papsturkunden*	W. Holtzmann, *Papsturkunden in England* iii (Berlin, 1952)
Hunter, *Ecclesiastical Documents*	J. Hunter, *Ecclesiastical Documents*, Camden Society (London, 1840)
Keen 1984	L. Keen, 'The Towns of Dorset', in *Anglo-Saxon Towns in Southern England*, ed. J. Haslam (Chichester, 1984), pp. 203–47
Kemble	J. M. Kemble, *Codex Diplomaticus Aevi Saxonici*, 6 vols (London, 1839–48)
Ker, *Catalogue*	N. R. Ker, *Catalogue of Manuscripts containing Anglo-Saxon* (Oxford, 1957)
Ker, *Medieval Libraries*	*Medieval Libraries of Great Britain: a List of Surviving Books*, ed. N. R. Ker, 2nd edn, Royal Historical Society Guides and Handbooks iii (London, 1964)
Keynes, *Diplomas*	S. Keynes, *The Diplomas of King Æthelred 'the Unready' 978–1016: a Study in their Use as Historical Evidence* (Cambridge, 1980)
Keynes 1976	S. D. Keynes, 'Studies on Anglo-Saxon Royal Diplomas', 2 vols, unpubl. Fellowship thesis, Trinity College, Cambridge (1976)
Keynes and Lapidge, *Alfred the Great*	S. Keynes and M. Lapidge, *Alfred the Great: Asser's* Life of King Alfred *and other Contemporary Sources* (Harmondsworth, 1983)
Knowles, *HRH*	*The Heads of Religious Houses: England and Wales 940–1216*, ed. D. Knowles, C. N. L. Brooke and V. C. M. London (Cambridge, 1972)
Latham, *DML*	R. E. Latham, *Dictionary of Medieval Latin from British Sources*, fasc. ii (London, 1981)
Liber Vitae	*Liber Vitae: Register and Martyrology of New Minster and Hyde Abbey, Winchester*, ed. W. de G. Birch, Hampshire Record Society (London and Winchester, 1892)
Mon. Angl.	W. Dugdale, *Monasticon Anglicanum*, ed. J. Caley, H. Ellis and B. Bandinel, 6 vols (London, 1846)
O'Donovan 1972, 1973	M. A. O'Donovan, 'An Interim Revision of Episcopal Dates for the Province of Canterbury, 850–950: Part I', *Anglo-Saxon England* i (1972), pp. 23–44; '... Part II', *Anglo-Saxon England* ii (1973), pp. 91–113
Padel 1978	O. J. Padel, 'Two New Pre-Conquest Charters for Cornwall', *Cornish Studies* vi (1978), pp. 20–7

Pierquin, *Recueil*	H. Pierquin, *Recueil général des chartes anglo-saxonnes: les Saxons en Angleterre, 604–1061* (Paris, 1912)
PN Devon	J. E. B. Gover, A. Mawer and F. M. Stenton, *The Place-Names of Devon*, 2 vols, EPNS x–xi (Cambridge, 1931–2)
Registrum Osmundi	*Vetus Registrum Sarisberiense alias dictum Registrum S. Osmundi Episcopi*, ed. W. H. Rich Jones, 2 vols, RS (London, 1883–4)
RMLWL	R. E. Latham, *Revised Medieval Latin Word-List from British and Irish Sources* (London, 1965)
Robertson, *Charters*	*Anglo-Saxon Charters*, ed. A. J. Robertson, 2nd edn (Cambridge, 1956)
Robinson, *Somerset*	J. Armitage Robinson, *Somerset Historical Essays* (London, 1921)
Robinson, *Wells*	J. Armitage Robinson, *The Saxon Bishops of Wells: a Historical Study in the Tenth Century*, British Academy Supplemental Papers iv (London, 1918)
RS	Rolls Series
S	For 'Sawyer' in citations of charters
Sawyer	P. H. Sawyer, *Anglo-Saxon Charters: an Annotated List and Bibliography*, Royal Historical Society Guides and Handbooks viii (London, 1968)
Sawyer, *Burton*	*Charters of Burton Abbey*, ed. P. H. Sawyer, Anglo-Saxon Charters ii (London, 1979)
Stenton, *Anglo-Saxon England*	F. M. Stenton, *Anglo-Saxon England*, 3rd edn (Oxford, 1971)
Stenton, *Latin Charters*	F. M. Stenton, *The Latin Charters of the Anglo-Saxon Period* (Oxford, 1955)
Stenton 1918	F. M. Stenton, 'The Supremacy of the Mercian Kings', *English Historical Review* xxxiii (1918), pp. 433–52 (repr. in *Preparatory to Anglo-Saxon England, being the Collected Papers of Frank Merry Stenton*, ed. D. M. Stenton (Oxford, 1970), pp. 44–66)
Thorpe, *Diplomatarium*	B. Thorpe, *Diplomatarium Anglicum Ævi Saxonici* (London, 1865)
VCH Cornwall	*A History of Cornwall*, ed. W. Page, ii, pt 8, Victoria History of the Counties of England (repr. Folkestone, 1975)
VCH Dorset	*A History of Dorset*, ed. R. B. Pugh, iii, Victoria History of the Counties of England (London, 1968)
Vita Wlsini	'The Life of Saint Wulsin of Sherborne by Goscelin', ed. C. H. Talbot, *Revue Bénédictine* lxix (1959), pp. 68–85

Whitelock, *Bishops of London*	D. Whitelock, *Some Anglo-Saxon Bishops of London*, Chambers Memorial Lecture 1974 (London, 1975)
Whitelock, *EHD*	*English Historical Documents c. 500–1042*, ed. D. Whitelock, 2nd edn, English Historical Documents i (London, 1979)
Whitelock, *Genuine Asser*	*The Genuine Asser*, Stenton Lecture 1967 (Reading, 1968)
Whitelock, *Sermo Lupi*	*Sermo Lupi ad Anglos*, ed. D. Whitelock, 3rd edn (London, 1963; rev. repr. Exeter, 1976)
Whitelock 1979	D. Whitelock, 'Some Charters in the Name of King Alfred', *Saints, Scholars and Heroes: Studies in Medieval Culture in Honour of Charles W. Jones*, ed. M. H. King and W. M. Stevens, 2 vols (Collegeville, Minn., 1979) i. 77–98
Wilkins, *Concilia*	*Concilia Magnae Britanniae et Hiberniae*, ed. D. Wilkins, 4 vols (London, 1737)
Wormald 1957	F. Wormald, 'The Sherborne "Chartulary"', *Fritz Saxl: a Volume of Memorial Essays*, ed. D. J. Gordon (London, 1957)

LIST OF CHARTERS

CHARTERS OF SHERBORNE ABBEY

1. King Cenwalh grants liberties to the church and bishopric of Sherborne. A.D. 671

2. King Cynewulf grants one hide at Lyme, Dorset, to the church of Sherborne. A.D. 774

3. King Æthelwulf grants, and later confirms, fifteen hides at Halstock, Dorset, to the deacon Eadberht. A.D. 841 [for 840]

4. King Æthelwulf grants two hides at *Osanstoc* to the place of the holy church of Sherborne. A.D. 844

5. King Æthelwulf grants liberties to the church of Sherborne. A.D. 844

6. King Æthelberht grants liberties to the holy foundation at Sherborne. A.D. 864

7. King Athelstan grants ten hides at Bradford Abbas, Dorset, to the *familia* of the monastery of Sherborne. A.D. 933

8. King Athelstan grants five (or eight) hides at Stalbridge Weston, Dorset, to the church of Sherborne 'castle'. A.D. 933

9. King Eadred grants eight hides at Thornford, Dorset, to Wulfsige, bishop of Sherborne. A.D. 903 [for ?953]

10. King Edgar grants five hides at Oborne, Dorset, to God and St Mary. [A.D. 959 × 975]

11. King Æthelred grants Bishop Wulfsige permission to convert Sherborne into a Benedictine monastery, and confirms possession to the monastery of its lands (listed). A.D. 998

12. Bishop Wulfsige grants all the possessions of the former clerks of Sherborne to the monks of the monastery, as well as making other concessions. [A.D. 998]

13. A writ of Bishop Æthelric to Æthelmær concerning various lands (listed) which should have contributed to the *shipscot* to be collected by the bishop, and mentioning a threat to the community's ownership of the estate of Holcombe Rogus, Devon. [A.D. 1002 × 1014]

14. The community at Sherborne leases the estate at Holcombe Rogus, Devon, to Edmund Ætheling for his lifetime, in return for twenty pounds. [A.D. 1007 × 1014]

15. King Æthelred grants thirteen (or sixteen) hides at Corscombe, Dorset, to the monastic community at Sherborne. A.D. 1014

16. King Cnut grants sixteen hides at Corscombe, Dorset, to the monastic community at Sherborne. A.D. 1035

17. Agreement between Bishop Ælfwold and the community at Sherborne, and Care, Toki's son, regarding the estate at Holcombe Rogus, Devon. [A.D. 1045 × 1046]

CHARTERS OF HORTON ABBEY

18. King Eadwig grants fifteen and a half hides at Ipplepen, Dainton and Abbotskerswell, Devon, to Æthelhild, *nobilis femina*. A.D. 956

19. King Æthelred grants one hide at Seaton, Devon, to Eadsige, *minister*. A.D. 1005

20. King Cnut grants seven hides at Horton, Dorset, to Bovi, *minister*. A.D. 1033

20A. A Middle English version of the bounds of the estate at Horton, Dorset, conveyed to Bovi in **20**

21. King Edward grants half a hide at Littleham, Devon, to Ordgar, *minister*. A.D. 1042

22. King Edward grants liberties to the holy foundation at Horton, Dorset. A.D. 1061

Grants to bishops of Sherborne not included in this volume

I. King Æthelheard grants twenty hides at Crediton, Devon, to Bishop Forthhere, for the foundation of a monastery. A.D. 739 (S 255)

II. King Edward grants six hides at Wellington, five hides at West Buckland and twelve hides at Bishop's Lydeard, Somerset, to Asser, bishop of Sherborne, and his *familia*, in exchange for the minster of Plympton, Devon. [A.D. 899 × 909] (S 380)

III. King Athelstan grants five hides at West Orchard, Dorset, to Bishop Alfred (Alfric), who then grants the land to Beorhtwyn. A.D. 939 (S 445)

CONCORDANCE OF THIS EDITION
WITH SAWYER'S LIST AND THE EDITIONS
OF BIRCH, KEMBLE, ROBERTSON AND OTHERS

	Sawyer	*Birch*	*Kemble*	*Robertson*	*Others*
1	228	26			
2	263	224			
3	290				Finberg, *ECW* 567
4	295				Finberg, *ECW* 642
5	294				Finberg, *ECW* 566
6	333	510		11	
7	422	695			
8	423	696			
9	516	894			
10	813	1308		50	
11	895		701		
12	1382		702		
13	1383		708		Harmer, *Writs* 63
14	1422		1302		
15	933		1309		
16	975		1322		
17	1474		1334	105	
18	601	952			
19	910		1301		
20	969		1318		
21	998		1332		
22	1032		1341	120	

NOTE ON THE METHOD OF EDITING

All the charters (except **13**) have been preserved in and are printed from BL Add. 46487 (given the siglum B). Only **11** exists in a second copy, in BL Cotton Otho A. xviii (siglum C), although much of the text was rendered illegible by the Cottonian fire. Wharton printed his reading of C, made before the fire, in *Anglia Sacra* (AS). **11** has been printed from B; variants from C and AS are indicated in the textual notes. **13** has only survived in Paris, Bibl. Nat., lat. 943, printed here as siglum D.

The punctuation and orthography of the manuscripts have been followed throughout, except for obvious scribal errors, which have been corrected and noted. Latin texts in B are mostly punctuated in typical twelfth-century fashion: for major pauses, point and capital; for minor pauses, either point, *punctus elevatus* (⸵), or a short, heavy 'dash'; and for words divided between lines, a light hyphen after the first part. *Punctus elevatus* is absent only from **9** and **11**. Punctuation on the Old English texts is mostly limited to point and capital, and point, for major and minor pauses respectively; but *punctus elevatus* occurs in **7** and **10** only, and the 'dash' in **7** and **22** only. Typical pre-Conquest marks occur in **17** (;· and :–), in **18** and **21** (:–), and in **22** (;). The scribe of B also used a system of accents, apparently to indicate word stresses (e.g. line 21 on Pl. I), although their use is not consistent. They have been omitted in this edition as the committee felt that they were unlikely to reflect pre-Conquest practice.

Capital letters have been normalized, as have word-divisions in both the Latin and – as far as possible – the Old English texts. The letters u and v, i and j have not been normalized; æ, ae and ę are distinguished, as are uu, w and ƿ, th, þ and ð.

Standard abbreviations have been expanded silently, except for ⁊ and ꝥ, which has been retained. *Minisƚ, miñ* and *m̄* have all been expanded as *minister*, although where the charter has only *m̄*, this has been indicated in the textual notes: *miles* could be a possible alternative expansion. Interliniations are indicated by ` ´, and glosses have been recorded in the textual notes.

In the commentaries it will be apparent that I have done very little work on the charter boundaries other than giving references to already published studies. For personal reasons I was unable to undertake any field-work, nor would I have felt competent in the attempt. I hope that someone reading this will be inspired by my default to do the job themselves.

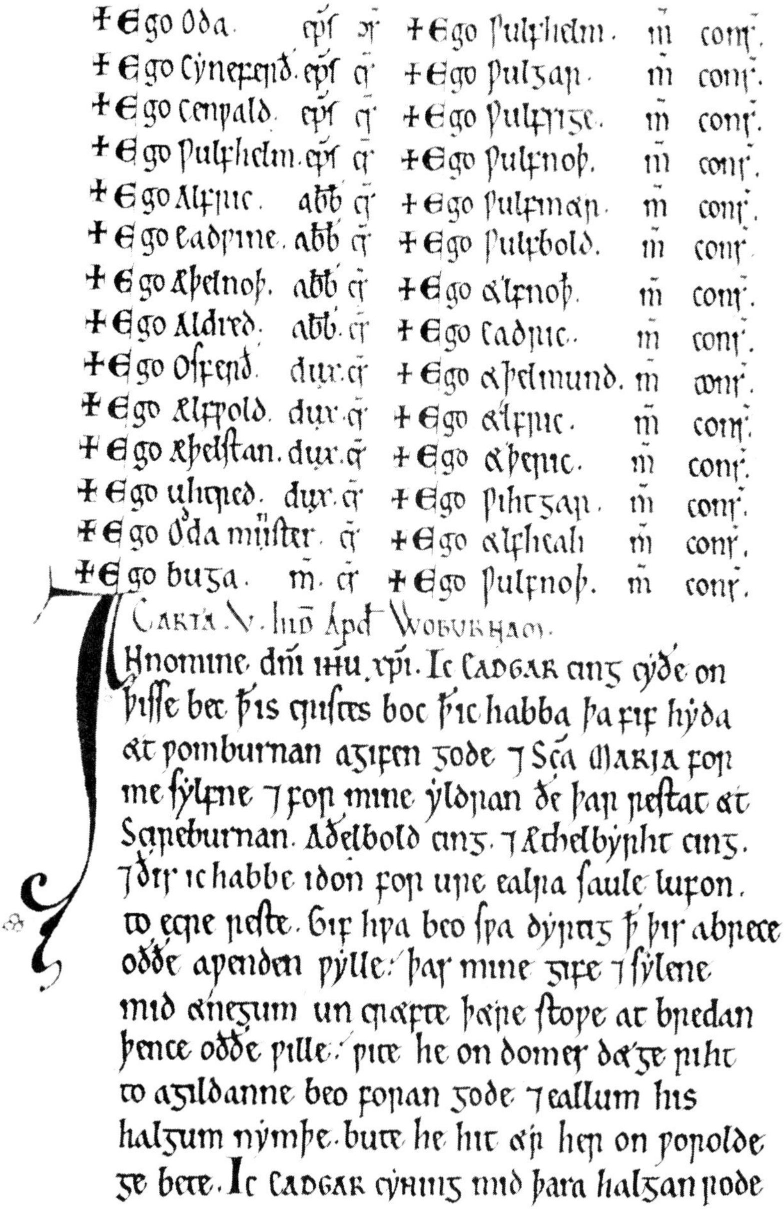

✠ Ego Oda. epſ ⁊   ✠ Ego Pulfhelm. m̄ conſ.
✠ Ego Cyneperd. epſ cō   ✠ Ego Pulȝar. m̄ conſ.
✠ Ego Cenpald. epſ cō   ✠ Ego Pulfriȝe. m̄ conſ.
✠ Ego Pulfhelm. epſ cō   ✠ Ego Pulfnoþ. m̄ conſ.
✠ Ego Alfpic. abb cō   ✠ Ego Pulfman. m̄ conſ.
✠ Ego Eadpine. abb cō   ✠ Ego Pulfbold. m̄ conſ.
✠ Ego Aþelnoþ. abb cō   ✠ Ego Alfnoþ. m̄ conſ.
✠ Ego Aldred. abb. cō   ✠ Ego Eadpic. m̄ conſ.
✠ Ego Osfred. dux. cō   ✠ Ego Aþelmund. m̄ conſ.
✠ Ego Alfpold. dux. cō   ✠ Ego Alfpic. m̄ conſ.
✠ Ego Aþelstan. dux. cō   ✠ Ego Aþepic. m̄ conſ.
✠ Ego ulfcyted. dux. cō   ✠ Ego Pihtȝar. m̄ conſ.
✠ Ego Oda miniſter. cō   ✠ Ego Alfheah. m̄ conſ.
✠ Ego buȝa. m. cō   ✠ Ego Pulfnoþ. m̄ conſ.

CARTA V. IN͞D Apd WOBURHAM.

In nomine dn̄i ih̄u. xp̄i. Ic CADGAR cyng cy̅ðe on þiſſe bec þis criſtes boc þic habba þa fif hyda æt Pomburnan aȝifen ȝode ⁊ Sc̄a Maria for me sylfne ⁊ for mine yldran ðe þar reſtað æt Sapeburnan. Aðelbold cyng. ⁊ Æðelbyrht cyng. ⁊ þiſ ic habbe idon for ure ealra ſaule lufon. to ecre reſte. Gif hpa beo ſpa dyrſtiȝ þ þis abrece odde apenden pylle: þar mine ȝife ⁊ ſylene mid ænegum uncræfte þæpe ſtope æt bredan þence odde pille: pite he on domer dæȝe riht to agildanne beo foran ȝode ⁊ eallum his halȝum nympe. butte he hit ær her on populde ȝe bete. Ic CADGAR cyning mid þara halȝan rode

PLATE I. BL Add. 46487, 10v, illustrating the twelfth-century scribe's version of Anglo-Saxon minuscule (reduced from *c.* 192 × 115 mm)

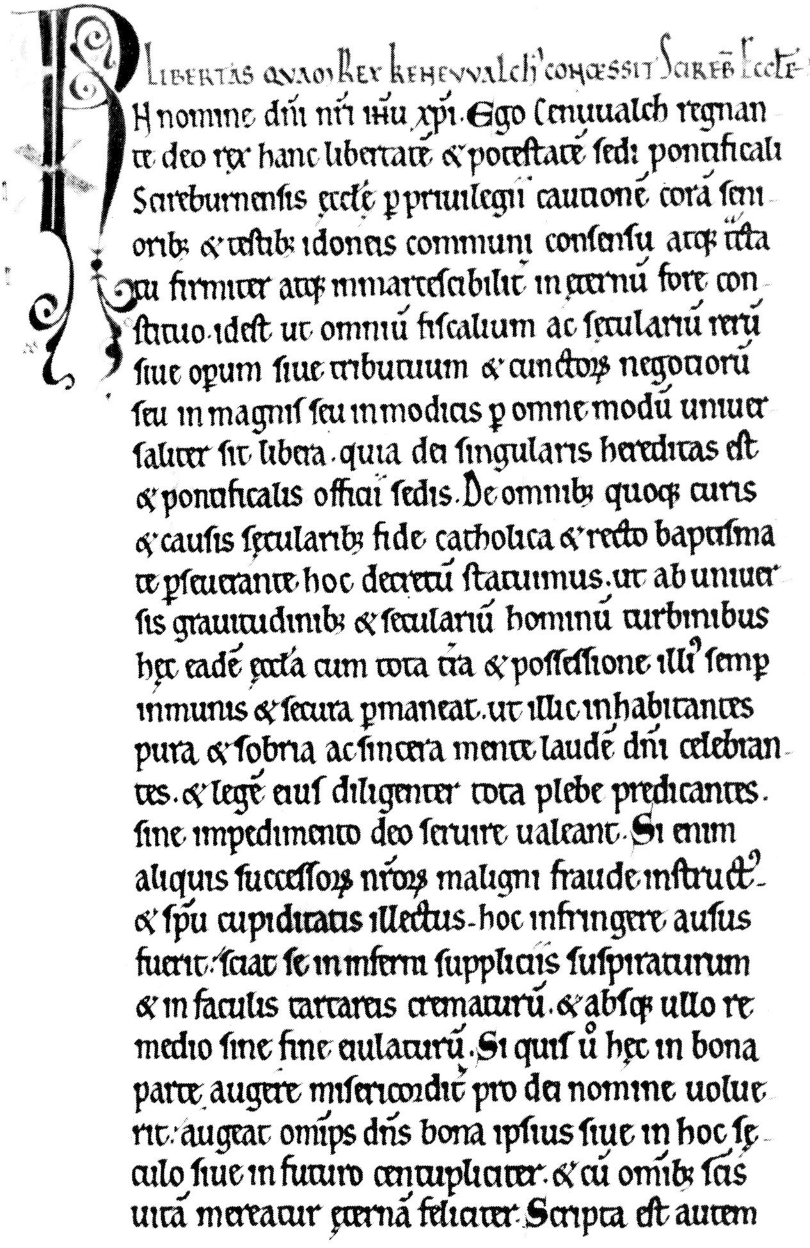

LIBERTAS QVAM REX KENEVVALCH' CONCESSIT SAREB ECCLE

IN nomine dñi nri ihu xpi. Ego Cenuualch regnante deo rex hanc libertate & potestate sedi pontificali Sareburnensis eccle p priuilegii cautione cora senioribz & testibz idoneis communi consensu atq̃ tota seu firmiter atq̃ inmartescabilit in eternu fore constituo. idest ut omniu fiscalium ac seculariu reru siue opum siue tributuum & cunctor negotioru seu in magnis seu in modicis p omne modu uniuersaliter sit libera. quia dei singularis hereditas est & pontificalis officii sedis. De omnibz quoq̃ curis & causis secularibz fide catholica & recto baptismate pseuerante hoc decretu statuimus. ut ab uniuersis grauitudinibz & seculariu hominu turbinibus hec eade parta cum tota tra & possessione illi' semp immunis & secura pmaneat. ut illic inhabitantes pura & sobria ac sincera mente laude dñi celebrantes. & lege eius diligenter tota plebe predicantes. sine impedimento deo seruire ualeant. Si enim aliquis successor nror maligni fraude instructus & spu cupiditatis illectus. hoc infringere ausus fuerit. sciat se in inferni supplicis suspiraturum & in faculis tartareis crematuru. & absq̃ ullo remedio sine fine eulaturu. Si quis u hec in bona parte augere misericordit pro dei nomine uoluerit. augeat omips dñs bona ipsius siue in hoc seculo siue in futuro centupliciter. & cu omnibz scis uita mereatur eterna feliciter. Scripta est autem

PLATE II. BL Add. 46487, 17r, illustrating the protogothic *litera textualis* used throughout the Latin texts (reduced from c. 192 × 115 mm)

CHARTERS OF SHERBORNE ABBEY

1

King Cenwalh grants liberties to the church and bishopric of Sherborne. A.D. 671

B. BL Add. 46487, 17rv: copy, s. xii^{med}

Ed.: a. Hearne, *Collections*, iii. 450 (incomplete)
    b. Thorpe, *Diplomatarium*, pp. 6–7 (incomplete)
    c. Birch 26, from Thorpe (incomplete)

Listed: Sawyer 228; Finberg, *ECW* 550

LIBERTAS QVAM REX KENEVVALCHUS
CONCESSIT SCIREBURNENSI ECCLESIE .[a]

☧ In nomine domini nostri Iesu Christi . Ego Cenuualch regnante Deo rex hanc libertatem et potestatem sedi pontificali Scireburnensis ęcclesię per priuilegii cautionem coram senioribus et testibus idoneis communi consensu atque tractatu firmiter atque inmarcescibiliter in ęternum fore constituo . id est ut omnium fiscalium ac sęcularium rerum siue operum siue tributuum et cunctorum negotiorum seu in magnis seu in modicis per omne modum uniuersaliter sit libera . quia Dei singularis hereditas est et pontificalis officii sedis . De omnibus quoque curis et causis sęcularibus fide catholica et recto baptismate perseuerante hoc decretum statuimus . ut ab uniuersis grauitudinibus et secularium hominum turbinibus hęc eadem ęcclesia cum tota terra et possessione illius semper inmunis et secura permaneat . ut illic inhabitantes pura et sobria ac sincera mente laudem domini celebrantes . et legem eius diligenter tota plebe[b] predicantes . sine impedimento Deo seruire ualeant . Si enim aliquis successorum nostrorum maligni fraude instructus – et spiritu cupiditatis illectus – hoc infringere ausus fuerit ; sciat se in inferni suppliciis suspiraturum et in faculis tartareis crematurum . et absque ullo remedio sine fine eiulaturum . Si quis uero hęc in bona parte augere misericorditer pro Dei nomine uoluerit ; augeat omnipotens dominus bona ipsius siue in hoc sęculo siue in futuro centupliciter . et cum omnibus sanctis uitam mereatur ęternam feliciter . Scripta est autem hęc cartula huius priuilegii consentiente et confirmante Laurentio archiepiscopo . simul rege Merciorum Wlfherio . ceteris patricia potestate preditis corroboranti-

bus ac subscribentibus . anno dominicę incarnationis . dclxxi .
+ Ego Coenuualh rex hęc omnia confirmans propria manu signum Crucis subscripsi . + Ego Wlfhere rex similiter corroborans signum Crucis impressi. + Ego Laurentius archiepiscopus hęc similiter corroborando signum Crucis subscripsi .
+ Signum manus Hugg principis . + Signum manus Romani abbatis .

^aLIBERTAS ... ECCLESIE . *rubric*   ^b*For* tote plebi

This charter is a manifest forgery: amongst many other errors, the forger's most glaring mistake was to link Cenwalh and the date of 671 to the bishopric, which did not come into existence until 705. The forger has borrowed formulas from various periods, including many from other Sherborne and Horton charters: for example, the invocation appears in **18** (956), **10** (959 × 975) and **21** (1042), and the anachronistic clause *sedi pontificali Scireburnensis ęcclesię* is echoed in the *ęcclesię Scireburnensis sedi episcopali* of **5** (844, also spurious). *Constituo*, an unusual dispositive verb, also occurs in **12** (998, again unacceptable). The immunity has several clauses in common with S 255, a grant of land at Crediton to Forthhere, bishop of Sherborne (see above, pp. lii and liv). However where S 255 explicitly reserves the king's right to exact military service (see Brooks 1971, pp. 75–6), **1** conveys sweeping and unqualified immunity to the episcopal lands. Although the Crediton estate passed to the new bishopric of Crediton *c*. 909, it is quite possible that a copy of the charter was available at Sherborne even after that date. The immunity in **1** also has wording similar to that in S 245, a Malmesbury text dated 704 which may have an authentic substratum (Brooks 1971, p. 75 n. 1), and its associate S 246 from Glastonbury, although again **1** is much more verbose.

Among the witnesses, Cenwalh of Wessex and Wulfhere of Mercia are acceptable for the date, and Wulfhere might have been entitled to endorse West Saxon charters as overlord (see Stenton 1918, pp. 433–5). Laurentius was archbishop of Canterbury from 604 to 619, so his name may have been confused with that of Leutherius, bishop of Wessex from 670 to 676, in which case the rank was altered to match. 'Hugg' is an uncommon name element for the Anglo-Saxon period. If there is an early witness-list underlying that of **1**, it is possible that the name was miscopied from 'Hag-', as happened in S 235 (688 for 685 × 687), where the open *a* in 'Hagona' was misread as a *u*, giving rise to 'Hugon'. The second *g* found in the name in **1** could have resulted from a misinterpretation of an abbreviation sign thus: 'Hag''. Hagona appears as a witness in the late seventh century, being called *presbyter et abbas* in S 1171 (685 × 693). Perhaps the Sherborne forger wrongly expanded the abbreviation *pr* as *princeps*. Romanus *abbas* is unidentifiable. The only recorded person of this name was the Kentish priest mentioned by Bede as being present at the synod of Whitby (Bede, *HE*, iii. 25), and who is also referred to in connection with Lyminge in an eighth-century

Kentish Charter (S 24). However, it does seem a distinct possibility that a genuine witness-list of the late seventh century was the basis for the list in **1**.

No such original can be traced beneath the main body of the text, and the motives that prompted its forgery remain obscure. It seems a singularly pointless document. At first sight, the insistence on Sherborne's episcopal status would indicate a pre-Conquest date, but the bishopric already had a much more impressive and reputable charter in Æthelberht's grant (**6**). Nor would it have been of much use in the twelfth-century dispute with the bishop of Salisbury.

Cenwalh is mentioned as a benefactor of Sherborne in the fourteenth-century Faustina A. ii list, in which he is recorded as granting 100 hides at *Lanprobi* to the Church (see above, pp. xliii–xliv, and Appendix 2, below). The list itself must have been compiled originally at a much earlier date than the cartulary, and may have been available to the composer of **1**. In this case one might have expected him to forge a grant embodying the gift of *Lanprobi*. It is possible, however, that Cenwalh was chosen for his antiquity rather than for his beneficence, for **1** does have close parallels with the pair of charters S 245 and 246 (see above), and it is here that one might look for its *raison d'être*. There was undoubtedly rivalry between the great monastic houses, especially in the post-Conquest period, on the counts of prestige and antiquity: one has only to look at the elaborations of fantasy provoked by the rivalry between Glastonbury and Westminster (see Robinson, *Somerset*, pp. 1–25). The removal of the see from Sherborne to Salisbury must have meant a great loss of prestige for the monastery, and it is conceivable that the monks looked to the past to bolster up their foundation's sagging image. Considering the similarities between **1** and S 245 and 246, not just in wording, but in content and purported date, it is possible that the Sherborne writer was inspired by the documents of the neighbouring houses to reassert the merit and priority of his own monastery. Glastonbury and Malmesbury possessed liberties from Ine, so Sherborne was given liberties by his predecessor Cenwalh, and at the same time the fact that Sherborne was the original seat of the bishopric was strongly emphasized. This may seem a tenuous argument, for we do not know whether Sherborne did attempt to rival the larger and richer houses. But there may have been a time at Sherborne after the episcopal transfer to Salisbury when the monks were reluctant to surrender their former position of honour, and tried, however ineffectively, to preserve at least its shadow.

2

King Cynewulf grants one hide (mansio) *at Lyme, Dorset, to the church of Sherborne.* A.D. 774

B. BL Add. 46487, 13v–14r: copy, s. xii^{med}

Ed.: Birch 224

Listed: Sawyer 263; Finberg, *ECW* 550

CARTA . I . HIDAE APUD LIM .[a]

Regnanti[b] imperpetuum domino nostro Iesu Christo . et hoc sęculum iusto moderamine dispensanti[c] . cuncta tamen fugitiuę tempora uitę . et omnes prosperitates sęculi huius aduersis causis misceri cernimus . uelocissimoque cursu hęc relinquentia ad futura festinant . Quapropter ego Cynepulfus rex . uenerabilis episcopi mei exortationibus Æthelmodi – instructus saluberrimis . Scireburnensi ęcclesię unius mansionis terram ad elemosinam diurnam pro expiatione peccaminum meorum condonare dignatus sum – iuxta occidentalem ripam fluminis illius quod uulgo Lim uocatum est ∴ haut procul a loco ubi meatus sui cursum in mare mergit . quatinus illic prefatę ęcclesię sal coqueretur ad sustentationem multiforme necessitatis . siue in condimentum ciborum . siue etiam ut in diuinis officiorum usibus haberetur . et quibus cotidie christianę religionis causa multipliciter indigemus . Si quis autem hanc donationem augere et amplificare uoluerit ∴ augeat dominus locum eius in terra uiuentium . Scripta est autem hęc cartula anno incarnationis domini nostri Iesu Christi . dcc° . lxx° iiii° . consentientibus patriciis et principibus meis . quorum nomina infra tenentur asscripta .

+ Ego Cynepulf rex predictam agelli portionem subscribens sic signo Crucis Christi confirmo .
+ Ego Æthelmodus seruus seruorum Dei hanc largitionem signo Crucis roboraui .
+ Signum manus Scilling .
+ Signum manus Hemele .
+ Signum manus Cærdic .[d]
+ Signum manus . Æthelnoþ .
+ Signum manus . Æthelmund .
+ Signum manus . Þigferth .[e]
+ Signum manus Ecgbaldi episcopi hanc munificentiam consentientis .

[a]CARTA ... LIM . *rubric* [b]*For* regnante [c]*For* dispensante [d]*First column of subscriptions ends here* [e]*Second column of subscriptions ends here*

This appears to be an authentic charter. Its formulas occur in or are closely paralleled by many other acceptable documents of the same period (see e.g. S 29, 105, 262, 264 and 265). Several charters mention land grants connected with salt production, e.g. S 23 (732), S 254 (737) and S 123 (785). *Mansio* is not the word usually used to describe a unit of land, but it does occur in S 256 (745, a dubious charter), where it appears to be the equivalent of *manens*, or *cassatum*, and it is also found in S 265 (dated 808, but an acceptable charter for Cynewulf, with witnesses belonging to the years 757 × 760: see Whitelock, *EHD*, p. 498). In Domesday Book the estate at Lyme, then in the bishop of Salisbury's possession, appears assessed as land for one plough (DB, i. 75v). The charter does not contain an immunity clause, an omission which is quite usual in West Saxon charters of this period (cf. Brooks 1971, p. 81).

The witness-list is perfectly acceptable. Cynewulf ruled Wessex from 757 to 786. Æthelmod was bishop of Sherborne from 766 × 774 to 789 × 794. Ecgbald was bishop of Winchester; he signs here and in 778 (S 264), and last appears in 781 (S 1257). The lay witnesses all appear in contemporary charters, usually with the title *praefectus*. Birch suggested a possible alternative date of 778, perhaps because of the similarity between the witness-lists of 2 and S 264, but there is no other reason to reject the given date of 774.

There is no boundary clause attached to this charter: the land is simply described as lying on the west side of the river Lyme, not far from where it enters the sea (see Grundy 1936, p. 136). The outline of the estate can however be deduced from a set of bounds attached to S 442, a Glastonbury charter, describing another estate at Lyme Regis (see Barker 1982, pp. 90–1 and Fig. 7.6; on S 442 see also Finberg, *ECDC* 11, and Hart 1965, pp. 160–1). Appropriately, the bounds in S 442 include a *saltforde* at a point which would probably touch the Sherborne estate.

3

King Æthelwulf grants, and later confirms, fifteen hides (cassati) *at Halstock, Dorset, to the deacon Eadberht.*
A.D. 841 [*for* 840]

B. BL Add. 46487, 7v–9r: copy, s. xii[med]

Ed.: a. Hearne, *Collections*, iii. 447 (incomplete)
    b. Finberg, *ECW* 567

Listed: Sawyer 290; Finberg, *ECW* 567

CARTA . XV . HIDARUM APUD HALGASTOKE .[a]

✠ Regnante inperpetuum domino nostro Iesu Christo. Omnia speciosa regna huius labentis uitę regnorumque dispensatores cum uelocitate deficiunt . et cuncta quę uidentur cassabunda et morituri*b* sunt ׃ quę autem non uidentur – ęterna sunt ׃ ideo caducis et uanis rebus iugiter mansura gaudia mercanda sunt. Qua de re ego Æþelpulfus domino largiente Occidentalium Saxonum rex – pro unicę animę meę redemptione . et criminum meorum remissione – et pro stabilitate regni mei – aliquam agri partem – id est . xv . cassatos in loco qui dicitur Halgan stoc ׃ cum consilio et licentia episcoporum ac principum meorum pro Dei omnipotentis honore et sancti archangeli Michaelis amore cuius ęcclesia in eodem monasteriunculo manet . Eadberhto diacono pro eius fideli seruitio inibi in elemosinam sempiternam deuota mente liberaui . id est ut omnium*c* regalium tributum*d* et principalium rerum et *e*penalium causarum*e* furisque comprehensione . et ab omnium sęcularium seruitutum molestia . secura et inmunis ęternaliter permaneat . Et qui hoc augere et obseruare uoluerit . augeat Deus bona illius in regione uiuentium . Si autem aliquis quod absit diabolica fraude deceptus – et tyrannica potestate illectus – in magnis aut in minimis hoc infringere uel irritum facere temptauerit ׃ nouerit se ab omni ęcclesia catholica sequestratum . et in die magni examinis quando cęlum mouetur et terra . *f*Christo domino Deo et sancto Michaele pro quorum dilectione liberata est ׃*f* coram exercitu cęlesti nisi ante emendauerit rationem reddat . Scripta est autem huius libertatis cartula anno ab incarnatione Christi . dccc . xli . indictione . iiii . die qua Sancti Stephani protomartiris solennitas*g* celebratur in uilla regali quę apellatur Æscantun . his testibus consentientibus et subscribentibus quorum nomina infra prenotata cernentibus clare patescunt.

+ Ego Æðelpulf rex ad confirmandum istius libertatis testimonium sanctę Crucis imposui .

+ Ego Ælfstan	episcopus
+ Ego Spiðun	episcopus
+ Ego Æþelbald .	dux
+ Ego Eanpulf	dux
+ Ego Osric	dux
+ Ego Þulfhere	dux
+ Ego Æðelbreht	dux
+ Ego Eanuulf	dux
+ Ego Lullede	dux
+ Ego Þulflaf .	abbas
+ Ego Þærferð	abbas
+ Ego Æþelred	filius regis .
+ Ego Ælfred	filius regis .
+ Ego Esne	minister .*h*
+ Ego Cynepulf	minister

+ Ego Cyneheah	minister
+ Ego Cuðulf	minister
+ Ego Niðmund	minister
+ Ego Ecgheard	minister
+ Ego Osmund	minister
+ Ego Milred	minister
+ Ego Ecgulf	minister
+ Ego Lullric	minister
+ Ego Ulfred	minister
+ Ego Alfstan	minister
+ Ego Kyma	minister
+ Ego Aldred	minister
+ Ego Eahmund	presbiter .[i]

Þis synd þæs landes landgemære æt Halgastoke . Ærest up on þone esc . ðonne ut on preosta lege an ane dic . ðonene on þone ealdan herpað æt niþerstoce . ðonne on þonne ford on liuedic . ðonne up of liuedic oð holan broc . ðonne up an holan broc . ðonne on hlosbroc . of hlosbroce on piþighege . ðonne on horsford . ðonne up on horsford on fyres hylleford . ðonne up on hlidan . ðonne ut on huna lege . ðonne up on cric . of cric on hunda troh. ðonne on tymbercumb . þonne on æsc lege . of æsc lege on faldhege . ðonne on readan peg . þonne up on stigele . ðonne an piþbelescumb . up on æsc eft .

Pro ampliore itaque adstipulatione iterum adducta est hęc scedula coram Æðelpulfum regem et optimates eius in loco qui dicitur Ethandun ibique ab his testibus cum signo Sanctę Crucis similiter corroborata est .

+ Ego Æðelpulf rex ad confirmandum istius libertatis testimonium signum Sanctę Crucis imposui.

+ Ego Alhstan . episcopus	consensi et subscripsi .
+ Ego Helmstan . episcopus	consensi et subscripsi .
+ Ego Æðelbald . filius regis	consensi et subscripsi .
+ Signum manus[k] Ceorli .	principis .
+ Signum manus Eanpulfi .	principis .
+ Signum manus Osrici .	principis .
+ Signum manus Æðelpulfi .	principis .
+ Signum manus Æðelrici	principis .
+ Signum manus Þulflaui .	abbatis
+ Signum manus Osrici .	abbatis .
+ Signum manus Þihthelmi	abbatis .[l]
+ Signum manus Æðelheardi .	ministri .
+ Signum manus Alhstani .	ministri .
+ Signum manus Aldberhti .	ministri .

+ Signum manus Ulfredi .   ministri .
+ Signum manus Þulfhardi .   ministri .
+ Signum manus Osrædi .   ministri .
+ Signum manus Þulfhere .   ministri .
+ Signum manus Herepulfi .   ministri .[m]

Territoria huius agelli hęc sunt . Habens in oriente fossam antiquam de amne lyfdic usque ad aliam lyfdic . et in meridie bropoldesham . et in occidente cric . et in aquilonali parte æsc leage . deinde in radicem on ðone æsc . et sic iterum in antiquam fossam .

[a]CARTA ... HALGASTOKE . *rubric*   [b]*For* moritura   [c]*Should read* ut ab omnium   [d]*For* tributuum   [e–e]*Glossed* Þite rædenna ond ælces ðeof fenges   [f–f]*Probably an interpolation: see below, p. 10*   [g]*For* solemnitas   [h]*First column of subscriptions ends here.* Esne minister *is written out in full in* B; *all the following* minister *titles have been expanded from* m̄   [i]*Second column of subscriptions ends here*   [k]*Throughout abbreviated* siḡ mū   [l]*First column of subscriptions ends here*   [m]*Second column of subscriptions ends here*

The text of this charter is generally supported by contemporary diplomatic practice. The invocation occurs in S 275 (826), S 289 (841) and in variations throughout the first half of the ninth century. The sentiments expressed in the proem are common for the period (see S 275, dated 825; S 198, dated 845; and S 202, dated 852), and the superscription, dispositive and consent clauses have fairly close ninth-century parallels, as in S 298 (847), S 320 (880 for 844), S 202 (852), S 316 (855 with a miscopied indiction) and S 217 (880). The clause 'for the love of the holy archangel Michael' is rather unusual. Other charters mention the saints to which the churches concerned were dedicated, but the two contemporary examples, S 271 (823 for ?826 or 828) and S 203 (840 × 852), are both dubious. The church at Halstock is now dedicated to St Mary, but there is mention of another chapel (see Finberg, *ECW*, p. 161 n. 1), or the dedication could have been changed, as often happened during the Middle Ages. However, the emphasis on St Michael rather unfortunately recalls the appearance of his name in **5**, the Sherborne version of a spurious Malmesbury production.

The immunity clause is matched both in language and content by S 298 (847), S 328 (858) and several others. There is no clause reserving the burdens of bridge-building, fortification and military service, but this is a common omission for the period, as can be seen in S 289, 291, 296 and 301 (841, 842, 845 and 850) and many others (see Brooks 1971, pp. 73–4). The anathema is very closely paralleled in S 1862 (854) and in S 328 (858), and its sentiments are very similar to those expressed in **6**, a vernacular text dated 864. The clause 'Christo domino Deo et sancto Michaele pro quorum dilectione liberata est' has been inserted into the formula 'quando cęlum mouetur et terra coram exercitu celesti' with little regard for the sense of the passage, and must be a later interpolation, as can be seen by comparing it with the same formula found in S 328. The dating clause is echoed in S 277, dated St Stephen's Day 833, and other charters mention Christmas (S 196, dated 841) and Easter (S 1862, dated 854; S 208, dated 857). These were the great feasts at which a full court would be assembled, and thus a very suitable time for grants to be made and witnessed.

Much of the text of **3** is almost exactly mirrored by S 288, a charter of King Æthelwulf dated 840, preserved in the archives of Glastonbury. The text appears to be quite acceptable, but at some time its witness-list was abbreviated. S 288 differs from **3** only in its anathema and in the dating clause, where it has only the year, the indiction (3), and a statement that the charter was issued at *Hamptone*. **3** was issued at *Æscantun* on St Stephen's Day 841, in the fourth indiction. This in modern reckoning was probably 26 December 840, since the year and indiction would most likely have changed on Christmas Day (see Harrison, *Framework*, pp. 115-17. The evidence for this particular period in Wessex is scanty, but **6**, only twenty years later, certainly shows a change of year at Christmas: see below, pp. 23-4). The textual coincidence is striking, and suggests that at this date anyway the author of both texts was to be found within the royal entourage rather than at an ecclesiastical centre (cf. Keynes, *Diplomas*, p. 80 and n. 159). Eadberht, the deacon to whom the grant is made, may be the same man as the deacon Eadberht who witnesses the confirmation of S 1438 (838) in Æthelwulf's retinue. Two contemporary copies of S 1438 have an almost identically worded confirmation clause, written by a West Saxon scribe, probably trained at Sherborne or Winchester (see P. Chaplais, 'The Origin and Authenticity of the Royal Anglo-Saxon Diploma', *Journal of the Society of Archivists*, iii (1965), pp. 57-8, and Brooks, *Church of Canterbury*, pp. 324-5). Other ninth-century Wessex charters that include confirmations are S 281 (838), S 287 (839), **6** (864) and S 338 (867).

As Professor Finberg pointed out (*ECW*, p. 164), the two witness-lists have been transposed. The first list (**3A**), which contains the subscriptions of both Alfred (b. 848 or 849) and Swithun, bishop of Winchester (who succeeded Helmstan c. 852: see O'Donovan 1973, p. 108), cannot belong to 841, whereas the second list (**3B**), with the subscription of Helmstan, must come before the first. **3A** must belong to the period between 852 and King Æthelwulf's departure for the continent in 855; 'Ælfstan episcopus' is presumably a mistake for Ealhstan, bishop of Sherborne. In fact **3A** is virtually identical with the witness-list in the 854 version of the decimation charters (e.g. S 308), although none makes the same mistake over Ealhstan, and since all the names are acceptable for the date, it seems possible that they derive from a genuine charter produced at Easter in 854. Alternatively, one could argue that it would be possible for the same court to have met twice within a few days with almost the same personnel, since the confirmation of **3** took place at Edington, Wiltshire, and the decimation was enacted at Wilton, only twenty miles distant.

The second list (**3B**) should therefore belong to 26 December 840, and all the witnesses are possible for this year. Moreover there is an appropriate change in the atheling Æthelbald's title. In **3B**, the earlier list, he is called *filius regis*, as he is in 847 (S 298) and 850 (S 299). He has the same title in S 344, a charter with the date 873, but with lists belonging probably to *c*. 840, and in S 1196, dated 859, but again with a list apparently belonging to *c*. 840. In **3A** he signs as *dux*, a 'promotion' which happened perhaps during 850 (S 300 and 301, although neither is a reputable charter), and had certainly taken place by 854 (see S 1862, where he is referred to as 'ealdorman', and the 854 decimation texts).

Each witness-list is followed by a set of bounds, and here again there is evidence of the transposition. **3B**, the earlier list, is followed by a short set of Latin bounds in an early form, describing the boundaries of the estate to the east, south, west and north (see Chaplais 1968, p. 319). Although vernacular bounds are usual by the ninth century, there are several Kentish Latin examples from the first half of the ninth century, as in S 169 (812), S 178 (815) and S 1266 (824); S 169 also uses *signum manus* for its witnesses as does **3B**. S 270 (773 for 833) is a charter apparently issued by Egbert which uses Latin bounds in the early form, but it cannot be accepted as a reliable guide to ninth-century usage (see Stenton 1918, p. 451 n. 84). **2** has a short Latin description, so evidently this was a possible form in late-eighth-century Wessex. It is difficult to know whether to regard the bounds which follow **3B** as an unusual use of an older style, or perhaps as a reusing of part of an older charter dealing with Halstock (as may have been the case with S 270).

The vernacular bounds associated with **3A** are much fuller, but they follow the same outline as the Latin marks. They delineate the modern parishes of Halstock (Dorset) and Closworth (now in Somerset). To the south the boundary runs along part of the northern boundary of the Corscombe estate (**15** and **16**). Both sets of Halstock bounds have been discussed by Grundy (1936, pp. 112–15).

It is clear that as a whole **3** is not an untouched text. At least the second occurrence of St Michael should probably be regarded as an interpolation, perhaps made under the influence of **5**. The vernacular gloss may also have been borrowed from **5** and **6**: **5** has '... taxationibus quod nos dicimus *piteraeden*', and **6** has *ðeoffenges*. The transposition of the witness-lists must have involved more than just miscopying, since the connecting phrase 'Pro ampliore itaque ... corroborata est' has been correctly replaced between the two lists. The text is introduced by a chrismon, which would suggest a late-tenth- or early-eleventh-century date (see above, p. xxix), so the original text could have been recopied and altered then.

Halstock is mentioned in the charter of 998 (**11**) as belonging to Sherborne, and although it is not mentioned by name in Domesday Book as being one of the nine estates held by the bishop of Salisbury for the support of the monks of Sherborne, it is named as a possession of the monastery in a papal letter of 1126 (BL Add. 46487, fo. 32, printed in Holtzmann, *Papsturkunden*, no. 13). It is a further argument for the authenticity of the original text that although the estate already belonged to Sherborne by 998, the charter makes no mention of the foundation, but is issued unconditionally to Eadberht.

4

King Æthelwulf grants two hides (cassati) *at* Osanstoc *to the place of the holy church of Sherborne.* A.D. 844

B. BL Add. 46487, 14r: copy, s. xii[med]

Ed.: a. Hearne, *Collections*, iii. 449 (incomplete)
    b. Finberg, *ECW* 642

Listed: Sawyer 295; Finberg, *ECW* 642

CARTA . II . HIDARUM APUD OSANSTOKE .[a]

In nomine Dei nostri saluatoris . Omnia quę uidentur temporalia sunt – et quę non uidentur ęterna sunt. Quapropter ego Æþelþulf rex Occidentalium Saxonum dabo . ii[as] .[b] cassatos eo in loco qui Osanstoc nuncupatur . ad locum sanctę Scireburnensis ęcclesię pro redemptione animę meę et pro redemptione filiorum meorum qui ibi requiescunt . hoc est Aþelbald rex et Æþelberht rex cum omnibus bonis quę ad illum locum pertinent . Si quis uero hanc donationem meam minuere temptauerit ; sciat se coram Christo reddere rationem in die iudicii . Scripta est autem hęc syngrapha anno dominicę incarnationis . dccc⁰ . xl⁰ iiii⁰ . his testibus consentientibus .

+ Ego Æthelþulf	rex .
+ Ego Hædde .	episcopus .
+ Ego Aldhelm .	episcopus .
+ Ego Freanþulf .	dux .[c]
+ Ego Hamgyls	abbas .
+ Ego Hunfrið .	abbas .
+ Ego Osric	dux .[d]

[a]CARTA ... OSANSTOKE . *rubric*   [b]*Sic*   [c]*First column of subscriptions ends here*   [d]*Second column of subscriptions ends here*

This charter makes, as Professor Finberg says, 'hardly any pretence of authenticity' (*ECW*, p. 181). Not only are there obvious mistakes and anachronisms, but also small errors, which give it the appearance of having been written in a hurry by someone who was familiar with

Anglo-Saxon diplomatic but who was not in this instance concerned to produce a credible document.

The formulas are not directly paralleled in ninth-century texts, and the brevity of the text is more reminiscent of the seventh century. For instance, the proem occurs in S 53, S 237 and others of the late seventh century, although it is incorporated in longer proems two centuries later, as in S 275 (826) and S 190 (836). Other formulas echoing those in **4** are found in S 274 (826), S 289 (841), S 299 (850) and S 300 (850). *Syngrapha* does not come into respectable usage as a synonym for *cartula* until the tenth century, although it is often found in spurious or altered documents allegedly produced in earlier centuries. The Sherborne charters **8** and **14** both use the word, so the forger had examples close at hand.

The way the grant is made 'ad locum sanctę Scireburnensis ęcclesię' is peculiar. Grants were generally made to a person or a church. Here the intention is clear but the wording is quite untypical. I have found no parallel to it except in **6** (864), where the grant is made to the *halgan stope* at Sherborne. To make a grant for the salvation of others (especially kinsmen) as well as for the salvation of the donor was not too uncommon, but the writer of **4** did not bother to check the dates of those concerned: he assumed that Æthelwulf outlived his two sons Æthelbald and Æthelberht. He was correct, however, in placing their bodies at Sherborne (*ASC*, s.a. 860 and 865). The forger may have been inspired to add this unnecessary complication by two other Sherborne charters which made specific provision for kings buried there. **6** was granted by Æthelberht for himself, for his father Æthelwulf, and for his brother Æthelbald, who was buried at Sherborne. **10** (959 × 975) is even closer, being made by Edgar for himself and 'for mine yldran ðe þar restat æt Scireburnan. Aðelbold cing 7 Æthelbyrht cing'.

The witness-list is a mixture of ninth-century names (Æthelwulf, Hunfrith and Osric) and seventh-century names (Hædde, Aldhelm and Hamgyls), with one (*Freanwulf dux*) who appears nowhere else. Hædde, bishop of Wessex from 676 to 703 × 705, should not attest in the presence of Aldhelm, his successor 'west of the wood'.

Although this charter is quite unacceptable, the estate it was supposed to convey was in Sherborne's possession by 998, according to the foundation charter (**11**). *Osanstoke* is not mentioned in Domesday Book or in the papal letter of 1126 (Holtzmann, *Papsturkunden*, no. 13), but it may have formed part of the larger estate of Stoke Abbott, which is mentioned as Sherborne property in both these sources. The monks of Sherborne did not provide themselves in the cartulary with charters for all the estates they owned, so one might surmise that at some time their ownership of *Osanstoke* was in dispute. There is no indication as to when the charter was forged, except perhaps the stress on *ad locum*, which might suggest that it was composed after the bishopric had been moved to Salisbury, when the monks might have wished to emphasize that the grant was made to the foundation at Sherborne rather than to the episcopal seat, to counter a Salisbury claim; but this can only be conjecture.

5

King Æthelwulf grants liberties to the church of Sherborne.
A.D. 844

B. BL Add. 46487, 17v–18v: copy, s. xii^{med}

Ed.: a. Hearne, *Collections*, iii. 450–1 (incomplete)
    b. Finberg, *ECW* 566

Listed: Sawyer 294; Finberg, *ECW* 566

LIBERTAS QVAM ÆTHELVVLFVS REX CONCESSIT SCIREBURNENSI ECCLESIE .[a]

✠ Regnante domino nostro in perpetuum.
Dum in nostris temporibus bellorum incendia – et direptiones opium nostrarum . necnon et uastantium crudelissima depredatione hostium – barbarorum – paganorum – et gentium multiplici tribulatione affligentium . usque ad internitionem tempora cernimus incumbere periculosa . Quam ob rem . ego Æthelwlfus rex Occidentalium Saxonum cum consilio episcoporum ac principum meorum hanc libertatem ęcclesię Scireburnensis sedi episcopali perpetuo iure optinendam famulis et famulabus Dei – Deo seruientibus perdonare diiudicaui . ut sit tuta atque munita ab omnibus sęcularibus seruitutis fiscis . regalibus tributis . maioribus et minoribus siue taxationibus . quod nos dicimus piteraeden . sitque libera ab omnibus causis regalibus – pro remissione animarum et peccatorum nostrorum Deo soli ad seruiendum . sine expeditione . et pontis instructione . et arcis munitione . ut eo diligentius pro nobis ad Deum preces sine cessatione fundant . quo eorum seruitutem sęcularem in aliqua parte leuigamus . Placuit autem tunc postea episcopis – Alhstano Scireburnensis ęcclesię et Helmstano Wintancastrensis ęcclesie – cum suis abbatibus et seruis Dei consilium iniere[b] . ut omnes fratres et sorores nostri in una quaque ęcclesia omni ebdomada mercoris die hoc est Wodnes dæg . omnis congregatio cantet quinquaginta psalmos . et unusquisque presbiter duas missas . unam pro rege Æthelpulfo . et aliam pro ducibus eius hoc dono consentientibus . pro mercede et refrigerio delictorum suorum . Pro rege uiuente ⁏ Deus qui iustificas . Pro ducibus uiuentibus ⁏ Pretende domine . Postquam autem defuncti fuerint ⁏ pro rege defuncto singulariter . pro principibus defunctis ⁏ communiter . Et hoc sit firmiter constitutum omnibus diebus christianitatis quamdiu fides crescit in gente Anglorum . Et hoc sub testimonio satrapum nostrorum plurimorum ad confirmationem . quorum nomina subter adnexa notantur.
Scripta est autem hęc donationis cartula anno dominicę incarna-

tionis . dcccxliiii . indictione . iiii . die quoque nonas Nouembris . in ciuitate Wentaneę . in ęcclesia Sancti Petri . ante altare capitale . Et hoc fecerunt pro honore Sancti Michaelis archangeli . et Sanctę MARIĘ reginę et gloriosę Dei genitricis . simulque et beati apostolorum principis . necnon et Sancti patris nostri Gregorii papę atque omnium sanctorum . Et tunc pro ampliori firmitate rex Æthelwlfus posuit cartulam supra altare Sancti Petri . et episcopi pro fide Dei acceperunt . et postea per omnes ęcclesias transmiserunt in suis parrochiis secundum quod predictum est . Et qui hoc augere uoluerit . augeat Deus bona illius in regione uiuentium . Si autem aliquis diabolica fraude deceptus . in magnis aut in modicis hoc infringere uel minuere temptauerit ; sit anathematizatus ab omnibus fidelibus hic et in futuro sęculo . nisi ante satisfactione emendauerit.

+ Ego Æðelpulf rex
+ Ego Alhstan .   episcopus .
+ Ego Helmstan .   episcopus .
+ Ego Æþelric .   dux .
+ Ego Æþelpulf .   dux .
+ Ego Eanpulf .   dux .
+ Ego Eanulf .   dux .
+ Ego Osric .   dux .
+ Ego Ceorl .   dux .
+ Ego Þulflaf .   abbas .
+ Ego Æþelmund .   abbas .
+ Ego Beorhthelm .   abbas .
+ Ego Ecgheard .   minister .
+ Ego . Milræd .   minister .[c]
+ Ego Cyneheah .   minister .
+ Ego Dudda .   minister .
+ Ego Æþelred .   minister .
+ Ego Aella .   minister .
+ Ego Cyneheah .   minister .
+ Ego Þulfhere .   minister .
+ Ego Ceolmund .   minister .
+ Ego Æþelbald .   minister .
+ Ego Osmund .   minister .
+ Ego Ealhstan .   minister .
+ Ego Eanræd .   minister .
+ Ego Ceolmund .   minister .
+ Ego Þihtgar .   minister .
+ Ego Lulling .   minister .[d]

[a] LIBERTAS ... ECCLESIE . rubric   [b] For inire: see S 322   [c] First column of subscriptions ends here   [d] Second column of subscriptions ends here

This is one of the strangest of all the Sherborne charters. It is a version of the 'decimation' of Æthelwulf, dated 844, and adapted rather poorly to apply only to the Sherborne estates. The 844 text is found only at Malmesbury and Sherborne, and almost certainly originated at Malmesbury, where several versions were preserved (see Finberg, *ECW*, pp. 206–9; S 322). Almost all critics have condemned the text in all its versions as spurious, although Professor Finberg defends it as a concession made by Æthelwulf to all landowners in 844, which did not take effect because the Viking attacks caused such disruption (*ECW*, pp. 187–91).

The theme of the proem is unacceptable for the mid ninth century, in that it makes a direct reference to historical events: '... crudelissima depredatione hostium – barbarorum – paganorum ...' 'Historical' proems (indeed allusions to historical events anywhere in the text) are uncommon in ninth-century charters, and are generally to be regarded as a suspicious feature (Stenton, *Latin Charters*, p. 27). They become diplomatically acceptable only in texts of the late tenth century. The phrases found in the proem of **5** are not found elsewhere until the early eleventh century, when they occur almost verbatim within the longer proem of an Eynsham charter, S 911 (1005), which appears reliable (see Keynes, *Diplomas*, p. 114 n. 103). Somewhat reminiscent wording, though with a more generalized meaning, appears in S 380 (*c.* 900, from Wells), and in S 1034 (1061, from Bath), a text apparently modelled on S 380. S 380 has a strong association with Sherborne, as it records an exchange of lands between Edward the Elder and Asser, bishop of Sherborne (see above, p. liv), but there is no reason to suggest a connection with the 844 texts.

The royal style, which occurs in the same form in both Sherborne and Malmesbury texts, is unadorned, and there are other unelaborated examples from the ninth century, as in S 274 (826, dubious) and S 282 (830). The dispositive section betrays the Sherborne author's clumsy adaptation of the underlying text. The Malmesbury version reads 'ego Ethelwlfus ... consilium salubre atque uniforme remedium affirmaui . ut aliquam porcionem terrarum hereditarium antea possidentibus gradibus omnibus siue famulis et famulabus Dei Deo seruientibus . siue laicis ⁊ semper decimam mansionem ⁊ ubi minimum sit . tamen decimam partem in libertatem perpetuam perdonare dijudicaui' (from S 322), where **5** has 'hanc libertatem ęcclesię Scireburnensis sedi episcopali perpetuo iure optinendam famulis et famulabus Dei – Deo seruientibus perdonare diiudicaui'. **5** omits any mention of decimation, but presents the grant as a general charter of liberties for the Sherborne estates. The mention of *famulis et famulabus* shows how carelessly the adaptation was made, for there were no nuns at Sherborne. The grant is made to the *sedi episcopali* at Sherborne, echoing the *sedi pontificali* of **1**. It is not at all a common practice, and the only other ninth-century example occurs in S 274 (826), a very dubious text from the Old Minster, Winchester. The wording 'pro remissione animarum et peccatorum nostrorum' is odd, for such clauses refer almost invariably to a single donor, as is the case in the 854 decimation version. The occasional 'royal' plurals where the kingdom is referred to, as in S 274 ('ad remedium animae meae ... et pro omni populo in regno nostro') and S 217 ('pro ... stabilitate regni Merciorum nobis') are not really close parallels. The clause 'ut eo diligentius ... leuigamus', instituting perpetual intercession for the donor, is echoed elsewhere in three charters – S 11 (*c.* 690, Kentish), S 54 (706) and S 1035 (1062), only the first being a reliable text.

The closest parallel for the description of services remitted is found in a Crediton charter, S 421 (933), though many of the remitted dues are mentioned in ninth- and tenth-century charters in various forms, as in S 335 (862), S 331 (862) and S 539 (probably 865 × 871). Several charters of the period specify a service by its vernacular name, as in S 186 (822) and S 293 (843), both from Kent. *Witereden* is mentioned in a spurious Abingdon charter, S 278 (835), and also in a more acceptable Winchester document, S 1277 (877). The use of *sine* to introduce the reservation of the three public burdens occurs occasionally in ninth-century West Saxon diplomas, but is more commonly found in the mid tenth century. Other than in the 844 decimation it occurs over a dozen times between 944 and 968. The order of these clauses is unusual, for the *pro remissione* generally comes after the councillors' assent and before the terms of the grant.

Then follow the elaborate liturgical arrangements which are common to both the 844 and 854 versions of the decimation, unparalleled elsewhere in Anglo-Saxon diplomatic. Specific prayers on behalf of a benefactor are mentioned in a few charters, two of the earliest being a vernacular Canterbury document of the early ninth century (S 1188), and a Mercian charter (S 209, dated 862) from Gloucester, and there are a few examples from Athelstan's reign: two closely related Sherborne charters specify that the psalter and masses shall be said for the king every All Saints' Day (**7** and **8**, both dated 933; one at least is genuine: see below, p. 30), and a fairly acceptable Shaftesbury charter (S 419, dated 932) states that the land is given to the community upon the condition that a mass should be said and fifty psalms sung for the king daily. Other charters including such stipulations are S 414 (931, a dubious text), S 476 (941), S 876 (933), S 979 (?*c.* 1030) and **16** (1035). So such provisions, though not often recorded, were not unknown, certainly in the tenth and eleventh centuries. However, whereas in the examples cited above the masses and psalms are an integral part of the grant, a form of spiritual payment for the land, in the decimation charters the proposal of weekly services is made by the bishops, abbots and 'servants of God' as a response to the king's generosity. The naming of particular masses is unparalleled elsewhere in the charters. This passage is the only portion of text common to both the 844 and the 854 versions. In the 844 texts it is followed by a clause which would normally precede a witness-list. This includes the phrase 'quamdiu fides crescit in gente Anglorum', which is similar to many others found in the eighth and especially the ninth centuries (Stenton 1918, p. 445 n. 57), although the verb *crescere* only occurs once elsewhere, in **9** (903 for ?953), a dubious Sherborne charter (see below, pp. 35–6, and also the note on *peaxan* in **6**, p. 23).

Then follows an elaborate description of when and where the charter was issued. Various ninth-century charters record the exact day on which they were issued (see above, p. 9); usually these were high feast days, but there were exceptions, such as S 1194 and 296 (both dated 845). The indiction (4) is wrong for 844, and has presumably been miscopied from an original '7': the same mistake occurs in several of the Malmesbury versions (see Finberg, *ECW*, pp. 194-5). The text declares that the charter was 'written in front of the high altar in the church of St Peter in the city of Winchester'. Apart from the practical difficulties this would have entailed, such a circumstantial account arouses suspicion. A number of ninth-century charters record where they were issued, but they name only an estate or town. *Civitas* is used very occasionally to refer to an ecclesiastical seat of Roman origin (as in S 1194, dated 845, or in several episcopal professions of the ninth century, e.g. nos 8, 13 and 20, in *Canterbury Professions*, ed. M. Richter, Canterbury and York Society lxvii (Torquay, 1973)).

The dedication of a grant to the patron saint of the foundation concerned is not unknown (see above, p. 8), but only the 844 decimation names four specific saints. For greater security, the charter was then placed on the altar, an accepted if not common practice: in S 1258 (798) a turf and charters were placed on the altar of the church to which the lands were being conveyed; the confirmation of **6** (864) declares that King Æthelwulf laid the charter on the altar at Sherborne, and S 1021 (1050) contains a similar passage. **5** then continues with the provisions for promulgating the decimation throughout the dioceses, another feature unique to the 844 texts, and ends with an anathema found only here and in **9**, although all its elements occur separately in ninth-century charters.

The witness-list is acceptable for the year 844. Beorhthelm *abbas*, Aella and Eanred are unknown elsewhere, as is the second Ceolmund, and Lulling appears only here and in the 854 decimation texts.

It is obvious that **5** is the result of a clumsy attempt to concoct a charter of liberties for Sherborne from a version of the 844 decimation text, similar to those found at Malmesbury, which was meant to apply to one-tenth of all the heritable lands of Wessex. But most scholars (the present writer included) find this 'original' version as unacceptable as the Sherborne adaptation. Although the witness-list is in accord with the date, and although some of the formulas would fit a ninth-century context, there are too many inconsistencies and improbabilities. The terms of the grant are an outstanding example. They imply that every tenth hide (or tenth part of a small estate) was to be free of the secular burdens, an impossible arrangement when one considers that at this date actual services were involved. How, for instance, was the entertainment of the king's messengers to be reduced by a tenth? This sort of concept would fit far more readily into a later period when most of the services had already been commuted into a money payment, or when there was some form of land tax, such as the geld of the early eleventh century. Another strong argument against the 844 version is the fact that it survives only at Malmesbury and Sherborne, despite the arrangements for its distribution. Professor Finberg suggests (*ECW*, pp. 190–1) that the decimation never took effect, and this explanation was presumably intended to account for its poor survival rate. But according to the text the charter incorporating the grant and the liturgical details was placed on the altar, after which the two bishops sent copies to all the churches in their bishoprics. All the arrangements were therefore apparently completed before the text was drawn up as it now stands. If the scheme was then abandoned, it would have meant another round of instructions. One would have expected the Old Minster at least to have preserved some trace of the affair among its voluminous archives.

That there was a decimation made by Æthelwulf is attested by the *Anglo-Saxon Chronicle*, s.a. 855, and it must have been incorporated into various documents, as e.g. S 315, but the 'decimation texts' of 854 are not acceptable, although their composer may have had access to a genuine text of 854 (Whitelock, *EHD*, p. 525). The 844 version is most easily understood as an elaboration of the 854 text, probably produced at Malmesbury, judging by the proliferation of texts there. The reason for its production is not clear, since Malmesbury already had a copy of the 854 text, which offered wider tax concessions. We know that Sherborne and Malmesbury were in contact after the Conquest, for William of Malmesbury incorporates material he found at Sherborne in his *Gesta Pontificum*, so Sherborne could have obtained a copy and adapted it to apply to all the Sherborne estates, thus bringing it into line with the other two general grants of liberties by Cenwalh and Æthelberht, with which it is grouped in the cartulary.

6

King Æthelberht grants liberties to the holy foundation at Sherborne. A.D. 864

B. BL Add. 46487, 18v–20v: copy, s. xii[med]

Ed.: a. Thorpe, pp. 124–7 (incomplete lists), with translation
    b. Birch 510, from Thorpe (incomplete lists)
    c. Robertson, *Charters*, no. 11, with translation

Listed: Sawyer 333; Finberg, *ECW* 573

LIBERTAS QVAM ATHELBERTVS REX
CONCESSIT SCIREBURNENSI ECCLESIE .[a]

+ Regnante in perpetuum domino nostro Iesu Christo. Ricsiendum urum dryhtne hælendun Criste in ecnisse . ðæm hiehstan 7 ðæm untosprecendlican ealra þinga . 7 ealra tida

scippende . se þe on manegum ðingum his mihtum setteþ 7 ƿaldeð .
Eac sƿylce ðam ure hefenlican 7 þæm unasecgendlican rice . Þte he
ðisses lifes eadinysse 7 gesælinysse on ænigum þingum ne forlæte .
For þon ic Æþelbreht mid Godes gife Þestsaxna kyning piToðlice
ic þence 7 me on gemynde is mid þissum eorþlicum ðingum þa
ecelican gestreon to begitanne . Sicut Salomon dixit . redemptio
animę proprię diuitię . Spa spa Salomon cƿæþ . ðæt þe sceoldon
mid urum spedum urum saulum þa ecen gesælinesse begitan . For
þon ic cuþlice mid geðeahte 7 mid geðafonge 7 leafe minre biscepa
7 ældormanna . 7 nohte þon læs minra broðera . Æþelredes 7
Ælfredes . 7 ealra þara selestena piTona ures rices . Ic forgyfo for
me selfne . 7 for mine þa liofestan lifiende frynd . 7 eac sƿylce for
arƿuþnesse[b] Æþelƿulfes saule mines fæder . 7 Æþelbaldes mines
broþor . soþlice þisne freols . to þære halgan stoƿe æt Scireburnan
ðær Æþelbaldes cyninges lichama hine resteð . Þ hit sy fæstlice 7
unanƿended 7 ecelice gefreod . alra cynelicra 7 alra domlicra
þeoƿdoma . ge ðeoffenges . ge æghƿelcre ieðnesse[c] ealles ƿorldlices
broces . nymþe fyrde 7 brycge ƿeorces . Gyf hƿa þonne sye Þ he
hine for Godes lufan to þan geeaðmedan ƿille Þ he þas ure gyfe
geieacnan ƿille oððe gemonifældan ƿille . geiece him ælmihti God
eal god her on ƿorlde . 7 his dagas gesundfulle . Gyf þanne hƿilc
man to þan geþristlæce oððe mid deofles searƿum to þam besƿicen
sye Þ he þis on ænigum þingum lytlum oððe myclum þence to
gebrecanne oððe to onƿendanne . ƿite he þonne Þ he þæs riht
agieldende sie byforan Cristes ðrymsetle – þonne ealle hefonƿare 7
eorþƿare on his andƿeardnesse beoð onstyrede 7 onhrerede .
nymþe he hit ær her on ƿorlde mid ryhte gebete.
Ðis ƿæs geƿriten þæs gære þe ƿæs agan fram Cristes acennednesse
eahta hund ƿintra 7 feoƿer 7 sixtig . 7 in þam tacencircole Þ tƿelfte
gear . ðe dæg þæs septimo kalendis Ianuariis . Þis ƿæs gedon in
þam cynelican setle on þære stoƿe ðe is genæmned Dornƿara
ceaster . beforan þissum ƿitum geþafigendum þe hære namon her
benioþan geƿritene 7 geseƿene siondon . + Ic Æþelbreht cyning
mid þære halgan rode tacne þis het spiþe geornlice getrymman 7
gefæstnian.

+ Ic Alhstan .   episcopus .
+ Ic Eanƿulf .   dux .
+ Ic Ælfstan .   dux .
+ Ic Æþelred .   filius regis .
+ Ic Ælfred .   filius regis .
+ Ic Osmund .   minister .
+ Ic Þulfhere .   minister .
+ Ic Alhhard .   abbas .

+ Ic Heahmund .	presbiter .
+ Ic Hpita .	prępositus .
+ Ic Cyma	minister .[d]
+ Ic Þulfred .	minister .
+ Ic Ecgbreht .	minister .
+ Ic Monnel .	minister .
+ Ic Eadpulf .	minister .
+ Ic Þistan .	minister .
+ Ic Æþelpulf .	minister .
+ Ic Þynsige .	minister .
+ Ic Goda .	minister .
+ Ic Coenpald .	minister .
+ Ic Æþelric .	minister .
+ Ic Þulfhelm .	minister .[e]
+ Ic Beocca .	minister .
+ Ic Æþelmod .	minister .
+ Ic Beorhtnoþ .	minister .
+ Ic Denegils .	minister .[f]
+ Ic Hunred .	minister .
+ Ic Ecgulf .	minister .
+ Ic Ælfhere .	minister .[g]

Þa æfter þyssum hit gelamp þan ilcan geare þæs þe þis on midne pinter pæs gedon . Þ Æþelbreht se cining on frigedæg tpam nihtum ær estron þisne freols mid his agenre hande unnende mode ufan in þone heah altare alegde æt ham æt Scireburnan – in andpeardnesse ealre þære broþorlican gesamnunga ealdra 7 giongra . 7 eac spylce his mægan Æðelredes 7 Ælfredes . 7 his opræ pitona þe þær þa mid him pæron . for hine selfne lifigende . 7 for his tpegen broþre þe þæt þa andpearde stodon . 7 for hyra ealra fæder saule Æþelpulfes cyninges . 7 Æþelbaldes cyninges hyra broþor þe his lichama in þære stope resteð . He þisne freodom on ælmihtiges Godes namon 7 on ealra his halgra fæstlice bebead . þæt hine nan his æfterfylgendra eft ne onpende . ne on anegum dælum læssan ne on maran hine ne on cyrde . ac he spa ecelice forþ þurhpunedæ . spa lange spa God polde Þ Cristen geleafa mid Eongolcynne untosceacen peoxa . Ealra þara porldcundra hefinesse þe her beforan nemde syondon . 7 se hæbbe Godes miltse 7 his halgra . se þe þis mid Gode trymman pille 7 healdon . Gyf þonne hpa sie Þ he þis on ænegum dæle panian þence oððe brecan . þanne næbbe he naþer ne Godes miltse ne his haligra . nymþe he hit ær mid ryhte gebete . Þis pæs gedon beforan ðære gepitnesse þe hyro naman her bynyoþan gemearcode standað .

+ Ic Æþelbreht .   rex .
+ Ic Alhstan .   episcopus .
+ Ic Æþelred .   filius regis .
+ Ic Ælfred .   filius regis .
+ Ic Heahmund .   presbiter .
+ Ic Osmund .   minister .
+ Ic Beorhtmund .   minister .
+ Ic Cyma .   minister .
+ Ic Ecgbreht .   minister .
+ Ic Babba .   minister .
+ Ic Mucel .   minister .
+ Ic Cynelaf .   minister .
+ Ic Torhthelm diaconus prępositus .
+ Ic Burghelm .   presbiter .
+ Ic Heoteman .   presbiter .
+ Ic Rædnoþ .   presbiter .
+ Ic Æþelheah .   presbiter .
+ Ic Ospuulf .   presbiter .
+ Ic Þistan .   presbiter .
+ Ic Ceolmund . diaconus .
+ Ic Luhha .   minister .
+ Ic Beorhtþulf . diaconus .
+ Ic Ceolred .   minister .
+ Ic Eanþulf .   minister .[h]
+ Ic Ealhferþ .   minister .
+ Ic Ceolþulf .   minister .
+ Ic Cynemund .   minister .
+ Ic Ealhstan .   minister .
+ Ic Æþelmund .   minister .
+ Ic Ceofa .   minister .
+ Ic Duda .   minister .
+ Ic Þulfheard .   minister .
+ Ic Hereþulf .   minister .
+ Ic Æscmund .   minister .
+ Ic Ceolred .   minister .
+ Ic Burhgred .   minister .
+ Ic Þulfric .   minister .
+ Ic Cyrred .   minister .
+ Ic Æþelþulf .   minister .
+ Ic Ceolhelm .   minister .
+ Ic Eadulf .   minister .
+ Ic Ealhstan .   minister .
+ Ic Ecgstan .   minister .
+ Ic Heorhtric .   minister .[i]

+ Ic Ceolheah .   minister .
+ Ic Þulfheah .   minister .
+ Ic Eardulf .   minister .
+ Ic Cuðred .   minister .[k]

[a]LIBERTAS ... ECCLESIE . *rubric*   [b]*For* -purþ-   [c]*For* unieðnesse, *see* 22   [d]*First column of subscriptions ends here, bottom of folio*   [e]*Second column of subscriptions ends here, bottom of folio*   [f]*Third column of subscriptions ends here*   [g]*Fourth column of subscriptions ends here*   [h]*First column of subscriptions ends here*   [i]*For* Beorht-   [k]*Second column of subscriptions ends here*

This charter is one of the very few Anglo-Saxon diplomas that may well have been composed originally in the vernacular, rather than being a translation of a Latin original (Stenton, *Latin Charters*, pp. 36–7 and 46–7), although this has been questioned (e.g. by Professor Whitelock, who compared it to the free style of translation from Latin into the vernacular evidenced by the Alfredian translations; pers. comm.). Although much of the wording corresponds to contemporary diplomatic formulas, sometimes it is independent of them, and is far more freely expressed than was possible for scribes restrained by the set phrases of diplomatic Latin. There is no obvious explanation for such an important document being produced in the vernacular rather than in Latin, although Stenton linked it with a growing use of English in legal records and even for a while in land grants in Mercia (S 204), and also pointed to the decline in Latin scholarship in ninth-century England (ibid. pp. 43–6 and 47–9).

The opening of the charter is modelled on a proem found in several ninth-century texts, e.g. S 1274 (858), S 329 (860) and S 341 (869): a longer version of the proem occurs in the 854 decimation text (e.g. S 304). But where the Latin goes on to speak of God setting an end to life, and the advisability of performing good deeds here in order to win felicity hereafter, the Old English pursues a more cheerful and very unusual note: 'þ(æ)te he ðisses lifes eadinysse 7 gesælinysse on ænigum þingum ne forlæte' (in Robertson's translation: 'he [Christ] ... by no means neglects the happiness and prosperity of this life'). No Latin equivalent is found for this idea of God concerning himself with temporal happiness. Since in the next sentence the king declares that it is for this reason that he intends to win everlasting treasure by means of temporal wealth, it seems possible that the author intended to follow the standard Latin proem, which would have made better sense in the context, but was led away from it by his own thoughts.

The royal style is found also in S 342 (?870: see Stenton, *Latin Charters*, p. 47 n. 1, for the suggestion that this document may be another example of a charter composed in the vernacular). The phrase includes a translation of *gratia dei*, a phrase commonly used in the ninth century, as in S 1274 (858), S 329 (860) and various others. 6 then continues with a pious quotation which would fit better in a proem. Direct quotations from scripture are quite often found in contemporary texts, although usually no source is given, e.g. S 298 (847). Several slightly later charters, however, quote Solomon with an attribution: S 221 (901), S 472 (940) and S 505 (945). The clause recording the consent of ecclesiastical and lay councillors is rather longer than in most Latin charters, although S 346 (889) has a similarly expanded (though not identical) clause, as do the versions of the 854 decimation charter, and S 342 uses some of the same vocabulary. Æthelberht makes the grant on behalf of himself, his living friends, his father and his brother, the latter being buried at Sherborne. Although most charters were designed to bring spiritual benefits to the donor only, there are occasional reliable examples in which these are extended to other people, e.g. S 1274 (858), S 438 (937) and S 432 (937). Two dubious Mercian charters, S 193 (840) and S 197 (844), both from Bredon, include additional spiritual beneficiaries, and the former has the phrase *pro illius caros amicos*, which is very reminiscent of **6**.

The services remitted are common for the period. *Worldlices broces* is the equivalent of *ab omni secularium servitutum*, a widely used blanket phrase. Only military service and bridge construction are reserved, which seems to be in keeping with West Saxon practice at least until the reign of Æthelbald. From then on the building of fortifications began to be added to the list of reservations, though not consistently (see Brooks 1971, pp. 81–2). The first anathema is very much in keeping with ninth-century styles, and although the syntax is somewhat different from the Latin, almost all of the clauses used here are translations of adaptations of common Latin formulas, although once again there is more stress on the rewards possible in this life than is found in the Latin examples: 'geiece him ælmihti God eal god her on porlde. 7 his dagas gesundfulle' (Robertson: 'God Almighty shall increase all good things for him here in this world, and make his days prosperous').

The dating clause is fairly standard, with the equivalent of *in villa regali*, as in S 1862 (854). The use of *tacencircole* for 'indiction' is noteworthy; most of the vernacular charters which use this form of dating use the Latin word (e.g. S 1437, 313 and 427), but the Horton charter, **22** (dated 1061), which is almost identical in wording with **6**, uses *tacncircule* with the meaning of 'lunar cycle', and gives the correct calculation. The date given here corresponds to the year 863 in modern reckoning. The grant was made at Dorchester, but the following Easter the king was at Sherborne and was able to present the charter in person, with the addition of a memorandum and another set of witnesses. The laying of charters on the altar has already been discussed (see above, p. 17). The king's younger brothers were included among the spiritual beneficiaries on the second occasion, and another anathema was declared, in a form freer from Latin models than the first. The mention of mercy is not usual in anathemas; this must be the scribe's own rendering. Also at this time, the grant was made to last 'as long as God willed that the Christian faith should flourish [or increase] unshaken among the English'. This is an elaboration of an eighth- and ninth-century Latin phrase (Stenton 1918, p. 445 n. 57), although the Latin uses a verb meaning 'endure' (*perdurare, permanere*), so again the vernacular is more optimistic with *peaxan* (see below, pp. 35–6).

Incidentally, the confirmation of **6** provides useful and hitherto unnoticed evidence as to the beginning of the year at this period in West Saxon charters. It has been established that in the mid ninth century the indiction was changed simultaneously with the year, and that the year itself was changed at midwinter, either at Christmas or on 1 January (see Harrison 1973, p. 65, and *Framework*, p. 117 n. 17). In **6**, the main grant is dated 26 December 864, and the confirmation clause begins 'Then in the same year after this had been done at midwinter it came to pass that King Æthelberht on Friday, two days before Easter ...', implying that the day after Christmas and the following Easter fell within the same year. This must surely clinch the argument in favour of a Christmas change of year for this period in Wessex.

Both witness-lists are quite acceptable for the years 863 and 864. The first list contains names mostly familiar from other lists, whereas the second list, which the charter text declares to be a record of those who were present at Sherborne, contains a number of *ministri* who are otherwise unknown, and who may have been local dignitaries, as well as eight members of the Sherborne *familia*. The *Heahmund presbiter* who appears in the first list, and also in **3** and in S 332 (863), may well be the man who succeeded Ealhstan as bishop of Sherborne in 867 × 868. His appearance in S 332, an acceptable Kentish charter with no episcopal witnesses, might suggest that he was a member of the royal court rather than of the Sherborne foundation.

As a whole, **6** appears to be an authentic text. Its wording corresponds well to Latin formulas for the mid ninth century, and both witness-lists are consistent with the given dates. Linguistically also there are no anachronisms. The inflexional system is very well maintained throughout. Professor Whitelock called my attention to the retention of the spelling *ie*, as in *ieðnesse*, which does not appear in original texts after the mid tenth century. The spelling of proper names agrees with ninth-century West Saxon usage: for instance, the initial letter of the second element is retained (*-wulf, -helm*). The form *-breht* occurs, which is usually, though not exclusively, found in early sources, as in the first hand of the Parker manuscript of the *Anglo-Saxon Chronicle*. Manuscripts of Alfred's time show the same variation between broken (*ealra*) and unbroken (*alra*) forms. Occasionally the companion charter **22** has modernized the language used in **6**, as where 'mine þa liofestan lifiende frynd' was replaced by 'mire leofostra frenda' (and see below, p. 79).

One pecularity in the language of **6** is the use of *nymþe*, which is very unusual in early West Saxon, although it does occur in Mercian texts of a similar date (see *The Life of St Chad*, ed. R. Vleeskruyer (Amsterdam, 1953), p. 33). In **22**, *nymþe* is replaced by *butan*.

One last and minor point in favour of the authenticity of **6** is the plain cross which introduces the charter. As Dr Keynes has observed (1976, pp. 261–71) the use of chrismons as pictorial invocations only became common from 956. Chrismons introduce all the Horton texts except **22**, which opens with the same simple cross as **6**, thus confirming the dependence of the former on the earlier text. The full relationship of the two texts is discussed in the commentary on **22**.

7

King Athelstan grants ten hides (cassatae) *at Bradford Abbas, Dorset, to the* familia *of the monastery of Sherborne.*
A.D. 933

B. BL Add. 46487, 9r–10v: copy s. xii[med]

Ed.: Birch 695

Listed: Sawyer 422; Finberg, *ECW* 578

CARTA . X . HIDARUM APUD BRADEFORD .[a]

Flebilia fortiter detestanda titillantis[b] sęculi piacula . diris obscenę horrendęque mortalitatis . circumsepta latratibus . non nos patria indemptę pacis securos . sed quasi fetidę corruptelę in uoraginem casuros . prouocando ammonent . ut ea toto mentis conamine cum casibus suis – non solum despiciendo . sed etiam uelut fastidiosam melancolię nausiam abominando fugiamus . tendentes ad illud euangelicum . Date ∵ et dabitur uobis . Qua de re infima quasi peripsima quisquiliarum abiciens . superna ad instar pretiosorum monilium eligens animum sempiternis in gaudiis figens . ad nanciscendam melliflue dulcedinis misericordiam ∵ perfruendamque infinitę letitię iocunditatem . ego Æthelstanus rex Anglorum – per omnitonantis dexteram . totius Bryttannię regni solio sullimatus – quandam telluris particulam fideli Scireburnensis monasterii familię . id est . x . cassatarum ∵ in loco quem solicolę æt Bradan forda uocitant – libenter tribuo . eo tamen interposito tenore – ut unusquisque predicta ex familia . omni anno in cunctorum festiuitate sanctorum – quę semper fit[c] in kalendis Nouembris an'i'mę pro excessibus meę . integrum exceptis aliis orationum obsecrationibus – decantet psalterium ∵ adiectis insuper missarum celebrationibus indefessis . quatinus ante dictus clericorum grex – illam cum omnibus ad eam utilitatibus rite pertinentibus – liberaliter ac immutabiliter – sine iugo exosę seruitutis habeat . ac euo feliciter perfruatur ęterno .
Predicta siquidem tellus . his terminis circumcincta clarescit . Ærest on east healfe . of ættan pylles heafde . andlang lace . to mylenburnan . þonne andlang streames oþ gifle . þonne eft andlang streames oþ ennan pol . þanon andlang lace oþþa ealdan dic . þonne andlang dic – oþ hloscumbes heafud . þanon on ecge . andlang ecge ∵ oþ þa dic . þanon andlang dic . oþ ecgulfes treoþ . þanon east to ættan dene middepeardre[d] . andlang dene eft to ættan pylle . Si autem quod absit aliquis diabolica deceptus fraude – hanc meę liberalitatis breuiculam in aliquo elidere uel impugnare temptauerit ∵ sciat se die tremende districtionis ultima .

clara reboante archangeli uoce cum Iuda proditore – qui a satoris pio sato filius perditionis dicitur . ęterna dampnatione edacibus indicibilium tormentorum flammis arsurum . Huius namque a Deo dominoque Iesu Christo inspiratę atque inuentę uoluntatis scędula . anno dominicę incarnationis . dccccº . xxxºiiiº . regni uero michi commissi . ixº . indictione . vi . epacta . xxii . concurrente . i . septimis Februarii kalendis . luna . xxvi . in uilla omnibus notissima – quę Cippanham nominatur . tota optimatum pluralitate sub alis regię dapsilitatis ouanti – perscripta est . Cuius etiam inconcussę firmitatis auctoritas . his testibus roborata constat ⸭ quorum nomina subtus minulis[e] depicta annotantur.

+ Ego Æþelstanus totius florentis Bryttannię rex huius indiculi litterulas – cum signo sanctę semperque colendę Crucis corroboraui et subscripsi .
+ Ego Þulfhelmus Dorobernensis ęcclesię archiepiscopus consensi et subscripsi .
+ Ego Þulfstanus Eboracensis ęcclesię archiepiscopus consensi et subscripsi .
+ Ego Ælfƿine . episcopus consensi . et subscripsi
+ Ego Þeodred . episcopus consensi . et subscripsi .[f]
+ Ego Byrnstan . episcopus consensi et subscripsi .
+ Ego Ælfheah . episcopus consensi et subscripsi .[g]

+ Ego Oda .	episcopus	consensi
+ Ego Cyneferð .	episcopus	consensi
+ Ego Cenpald .	episcopus	consensi
+ Ego Þulfhelm .	episcopus	consensi
+ Ego Alfric .	abbas	consensi
+ Ego Eadƿine .	abbas	consensi
+ Ego Æþelnoþ .	abbas	consensi
+ Ego Aldred .	abbas .	consensi
+ Ego Osferð .	dux .	consensi
+ Ego Ælfƿold .	dux .	consensi
+ Ego Æþelstan .	dux .	consensi
+ Ego Uhtred .	dux .	consensi
+ Ego O`d´da	mi`n´ister .	consensi
+ Ego Buga .	minister .	consensi[h]
+ Ego Þulfhelm .	minister	consensi .
+ Ego Þulgar .	minister	consensi .
+ Ego Þulfsige .	minister	consensi .
+ Ego Þulfnoþ .	minister	consensi .
+ Ego Þulfmær .	minister	consensi .
+ Ego Þulfbold .	minister	consensi .
+ Ego Ælfnoþ .	minister	consensi .
+ Ego Eadric .	minister	consensi .

+Ego Æþelmund .	minister	consensi .
+Ego Ælfric .	minister	consensi .
+Ego Æþeric .	minister	consensi .
+Ego Þihtgar .	minister	consensi .
+Ego Ælfheah	minister	consensi .
+Ego Þulfnoþ .	minister	consensi .[i]

[a]CARTA... BRADEFORD. *rubric*   [b]*Glossed* id est fluctuantis . *Main text should read* totillantis *as in* 8, *but here it appears that the scribe's* o *was later emended to* i   [c]*For* sit   [d]*For* -peardne   [e]*Glossed* id est colore rubeo .   [f]*First column of subscriptions ends here, at bottom of folio*   [g]*Second column of subscriptions ends here, at bottom of folio*   [h]*Third column of subscriptions ends here.* Odda minister *is written out in full in* B; *all the following* minister *titles have been expanded from* m̄   [i]*Fourth column of subscriptions ends here*

For commentary on this charter, see that on **8** below, pp. 29–33.

8

King Athelstan grants five (or eight) hides (familiae) *at Stalbridge Weston, Dorset, to the church of Sherborne 'castle'.* A.D. 933

B. BL Add. 46487, 12r–13v: copy, s. xii[med]

Ed.: Birch 696 (incomplete)

Listed: Sawyer 423; Finberg, *ECW* 579

CARTA . VIII . HIDARUM APUD WESTONAM .[a]

Flebilia fortiter detestanda totillantis sęculi piacula . diris obscenę horrendeque mortalitatis circumsepta latratibus . non nos patria indeptę[b] pacis securos . sed quasi fetidę corruptelę in uoraginem casuros prouocando ammonent . ut ea toto mentis conamine cum casibus suis – non solum despiciendo – sed etiam uelut fastidiosam melancolię nausiam abominando fugiamus . tendentes ad illud euangelicum . Date [c] et dabitur uobis. Qua de re infima quasi peripsima quisquiliarum abiciens . superna ad instar pretiosorum monilium eligens . animum sempiternis in gaudiis figens . ad nanciscendam mellifluę dulcedinis misericordiam . perfruendamque infinitę letitię iocunditatem ; ego Æthelstanus rex Anglorum – per omnipatrantis dexteram . apice totius Albionis sullimatus . quandam ruris partem humili Scireburnensis castri ęcclesię libenter in loco quem solicolę æt Þesttune uocitant . id est . v . familiarum . ea tamen interiacente condicione . ut omni anno in kalendis Nouembris unusquisque ex familia – exceptis missarum orationumque[c] celebrationibus . quas ut indesinenter horis canonicis peragat fas est . integrum pro animę meę excessibus quoque animę Beorhtulfi comitis . spiritu et mente decantet[d] . tribuo . quatinus iam dicta uenerabilis congregatio . illam cum omnibus ad eam utilitatibus rite pertinentibus . sine iugo exosę seruitutis liberaliter ac ęternaliter habeat . spontanee quoque uoluntate deuotionis . Deo feliciter deseruiat beata . Predictum namque rus his terminis circumcinctum clarescit . Ærest of cirichylle on horgan sloh . þanon on beorh leage . þanon on pest mæd ufepearde . þanon on bydeburnan . þanon on anne mapulder . þanon on bilian pyrþe . spa forþ on hagan . þæt on beorreding mæd norþepearde . þanon on þa greatan ac . þæt forþ on hagan oþ stanbroc . þonon on hean pifeles hylle oþ þone ealdan peg . andlang peges oþ fildena pylle . þanon on þone ealdan hagan . þæt spa forþ ut on bealtunes ersc . nyþepeardne . þonon on æsc leage . of þam æsce forþ on hagan on gerihte ut on feld on anne stan . þæt spa forþ east andlang peges . eft on cirichylle . Si autem quod absit aliquis faculis inuidię successus – hanc meę liberalitatis singrapham elidere uel infringere conauerit ⸵ sciat se nouissima ac magna examinationis die . classica archangeli clangente salpice[e] – bustis[f] sponte patentibus . sonata[g] iam rediuiua propellentibus . cum Iuda proditore infaustoque pecuniarum compilatore . suis quoque impiissimis fautoribus Iudeis . sub ęternę anathemate maledictionis . edacibus innumerabilium tormentorum flammis – sine defectu periturum . Huius namque a Deo dominoque Iesu Christo – inspiratę atque inuentę uoluntatis scedula . anno dominicę incarnationis . dcccc°. xxx°iii° . regni uero gratis michi commissi . ix° . indictione . vi . epacta . xx[a]ii[a] . concurrente . i° . septimis Februarii kalendis . luna rotulantis astri . xx[a]vi[a] . in uilla celeberrima quę Cippanham nuncupatur . tota procerum generalitate sub ulnis regię excellentię congaudenti craxata[h] est . Cuius etiam radicatę auctoritas firmitatis . his testibus roborata constat . quorum nomina subtus literulis depicta cernuntur.

+ Ego Æþelstanus singularis priuilegii ierarchia preditus rex ⸵ huius indiculi apicellos . cum signo sanctę semperque amandę Crucis corroboraui et subscripsi .

+ Ego Þulfhelmus Dorobernensis ęcclesię archiepiscopus consensi et subscripsi

+ Ego Þulfstanus Eboracensis ęcclesię archiepiscopus consensi et subscripsi .

+ Ego Ælfpine . episcopus consensi
+ Ego Oda . episcopus consensi
+ Ego Byrstan . episcopus consensi

+ Ego Ælfheah .	episcopus	consensi
+ Ego Eadulf .	episcopus	consensi
+ Ego Cyneferþ .	episcopus	consensi
+ Ego Þeodred .	episcopus	consensi
+ Ego Cenƿald .	episcopus	consensi
+ Ego Ƿulfhelm .	episcopus	consensi
+ Ego Ælfric .	abbas	consensi
+ Ego Eadƿine .	abbas	consensi
+ Ego Æþelnoþ .	abbas .	consensi
+ Ego Aldred .	dux	consensi[i]
+ Ego Osferþ .	dux	consensi et subscripsi .
+ Ego Ælfƿold .	dux	consensi et subscripsi .
+ Ego Æþelstan .	dux	consensi et subscripsi .
+ Ego Æ⟨s⟩cbryht .	dux	consensi et subscripsi .
+ Ego Ælfstan .	dux	consensi et subscripsi .
+ Ego Odda .	minister	consensi et subscripsi .[k]
+ Ego Buga .	minister	consensi et subscripsi .
+ Ego Ƿulfhelm .	minister	consensi et subscripsi .
+ Ego Ƿulfgar .	minister	consensi et subscripsi .
+ Ego Æþelstan .	minister	consensi et subscripsi .
+ Ego Ælfheah .	minister	consensi et subscripsi .
+ Ego Ƿulfnoþ .	minister	consensi et subscripsi .
+ Ego Ƿulfmær .	minister .	consensi et subscripsi .[l]
+ Ego Ƿulfsige	minister	consensi .
+ Ego Ƿihtgar .	minister	consensi .
+ Ego Ælfric .	minister	consensi .
+ Ego Ælfnoþ .	minister	consensi .
+ Ego Æþeric .	minister	consensi .[m]
+ Ego Ælfsige .	minister	consensi et subscripsi .
+ Ego Ƿulfnoþ .	minister	consensi et subscripsi .
+ Ego Ælfheah .	minister	consensi et subscripsi .
+ Ego Eadric .	minister	consensi et subscripsi .
+ Ego Ælfred .	minister	consensi et subscripsi .[n]

[a] CARTA ... WESTONAM . *rubric deleted from text by points and a line drawn through it* [b] *For* indemptę [c] *Celebrationumque* [d] *Word omitted:* 7 has psalterium *here* [e] *Glossed* tubi [f] *Glossed* sepulcris. *In margin, in same hand as glosses,* hoc bustum uel sepulcrum [g] *For* somata [h] *Glossed* ka *over the* cr- [i] *First column of subscriptions ends here, at bottom of folio* [k] Odda minister *is written out in full in B; all the following* minister *titles have been expanded from* m̄ [l] *Second column of subscriptions ends here, at bottom of folio* [m] *Third column of subscriptions ends here* [n] *Fourth column of subscriptions ends here*

These two charters (**7** and **8**) call for a combined analysis, for they are intimately connected in style, wording and date. **7** records a grant of ten *cassatae* at Bradford made by King Athelstan to the *familia* of Sherborne monastery, with the stipulation that yearly on All Saints' Day they should sing the entire psalter for the king's soul. **8** is a grant by Athelstan of five *familiae* at Weston 'to the church of Sherborne castle', for which the psalter is to be said annually for the souls of the king and a 'Beorhtwulf comes'. Both grants are dated 26 January 933, at Chippenham.

The two charters employ similar formulas, with minor variations of vocabulary and sometimes phrasing. They open with the proem 'Flebilia fortiter detestanda . . .', used in all the charters issued by Athelstan between 23 March 931 and 26 January 933 (Keynes, *Diplomas*, p. 44 and n. 77). **7** has *titillantis*, glossed *fluctuantis*, in place of the correct *totillantis* as found in **8**; otherwise the two are almost identical. The royal styles differ somewhat in wording, though both versions are quite acceptable for the period. S 417 (932) has the phrase exactly as in **7**, while S 405 (930), S 419 (932) and others have the single difference of *omnipatrantis* (also used in **8**) in place of *omnitonantis*. S 421 (933) has the same version as **8**.

The same pattern occurs in the dispositive section, with such minor variations as *telluris particulam, clericorum grex* and *liberaliter ac immutabiliter* in **7**, where **8** has *ruris partem, venerabilis congregatio* and *liberaliter ac aeternaliter* (**8** also uses *familiarum* for land units, on which see below, p. 32). A few of the Sherborne phrases are unique: *ruris partem, immutabiliter, clericorum grex* and *venerabilis congregatio* are not found elsewhere in Athelstan's charters, although S 414 and 415 (931, neither of them reputable charters) come close with *venerabilis familiae*.

Conditions of a religious nature are found in other charters of the reign. In S 419 (932) a grant is made to the nunnery at Shaftesbury on condition that the nuns shall say fifty psalms and sing a mass daily for the king's soul. In S 418 (932) Alfred the thegn receives a grant on condition that he and his heirs will feed 120 poor people daily (a large burden on a modest estate). In both these charters, which are both diplomatically acceptable, the clause begins 'ea interiacente conditione, ut . . .', very close to **8**'s 'ea tamen interiacente conditione, ut . . .'. The corresponding phrase in **7** is not found elsewhere in this period. S 414 and 415 (931) also decree daily masses and 'sweetly sung psalms' for the souls of Athelstan and his father Edward, but their testimony is suspect. There are various other charters from this reign that ask for prayers, usually for the king, but sometimes also for his relatives (e.g. S 438 and 432).

The anathemas of **7** and **8** are variations of a type fairly common for the period, **8** being the more elaborate (see *Crawford Charters*, p. 72, for a list of examples). There is nothing questionable about the Sherborne variations except for the appearance in **8** of the word *syngrapha*, which would be more acceptable in a later tenth-century setting (ibid. p. 117). It is used in S 409 and 410 (931) and in S 404 (930), none of them reliable. However, it does appear in S 400 (928) and in S 399 (intended for 928), neither of them particularly suspect (other than in their use of *syngrapha*), and in three good charters of Edmund, S 473, 469 and 460 (all dated 940), and the word certainly fits well with the ornate language popular in the charters of this period.

The dating clauses in **7** and **8** are almost identical, and very elaborate.

The use of the year of grace, regnal year, indiction, epact, concurrent, day and month in Roman reckoning and lunar day is found in several charters of Athelstan, e.g. S 405 (930) and S 417 (932); see also *Crawford Charters*, p. 66. None has the 'luna rotulantis astri' of **8**, although S 405 and S 517–19 have 'luna rotigere vagationis'. In the final clause introducing the witness-list, the various phrases used by **7** and **8** are found in many contemporary texts (e.g. S 407, 416 and 434) in similar, sometimes identical combinations. **7** and **8** have differing forms of royal subscription, but both are paralleled elsewhere, **7** in S 1604 (931), S 434 (937) and S 438 (?937), and **8** in S 413 (931), S 425 (934) and others. There are minor variations in vocabulary, which is common practice in the diplomatic of the period.

The witnesses to both charters are entirely compatible with the year 933, and some of the bishops bracket the date very closely. Byrnstan was bishop of Winchester from 931 to November 934, Cenwald was elevated to Worcester in 930, and Eadulf, bishop of Crediton, who appears only in **8**, died in 934 (see O'Donovan 1972 and 1973). A Bishop Wulfhelm, who cannot be assigned to any particular see, occurs in both lists. He appears occasionally between 931 and 937, and may be the Wulfhelm who is named in the post-Conquest Hereford lists (O'Donovan 1972, pp. 41–2, and 1973, p. 107). The witness-lists are not identical: **7** has three names that do not appear in **8**, whereas **8** has six that are not found in **7**. **8** lists an Aldred *dux*, whose title is properly given in **7** as *abbas*. **8** has two *ministri* called Wulfnoth, only one of whom appears in other charters of the period.

There appears no reason to doubt the reliability of **7**. Its formulas are either paralleled exactly in other charters of the reign, or show small variations that are very much in keeping with the elaborate vocabulary popular at the time, and the witness-list fits the date closely. There are no detectable anachronisms. The stipulation for the psalter and masses to be offered for the king's soul, although somewhat uncommon, can be accepted. Sherborne was certainly a more likely candidate than some foundations for this sort of condition, since it was one of the two oldest West Saxon bishoprics, and one of the burial places of the West Saxon dynasty. The parcel of land at Bradford is recorded in Domesday Book as being one of the nine estates held by the bishop of Salisbury for the monks of Sherborne, and, if **11** is accepted as genuine (see below, pp. 41–3), was already in the monastery's possession by 998. The language used in the bounds is tenth-century. The bounds themselves have been traced by Grundy (1933, pp. 250–3), and follow the parish boundaries of Bradford Abbas to the south, west and north. To the east they include the west part of Castleton parish. Castleton is a fairly modern name for an area which was part of the town of Sherborne itself, and seems to have been made into a separate parish after 1824. At that date the area was known as Sherborne Wyke (Grundy 1933, p. 250). Grundy's identification is supported by the papal grants of 1126 and 1146, both of which refer to the estate as *Bradeford et Wica*. To the north the boundary comes within half a mile of the village of Over Compton, another Sherborne possession, although no charter or bounds have survived (see above, p. xxxvi), and to the south the bounds share a couple of landmarks with the boundary of Thornford, also owned by the monastery (**9**). Keen (1984, pp. 218–19 and Fig. 74) confirms Grundy's work, referring to later tithe maps.

It is much more difficult to come to any assessment of **8**, which betrays some obvious anachronisms inserted into what appears to be a genuine document. Professor Finberg suggests that **8** is a fabrication modelled on **7** (*ECW*, pp. 166–7), which is the simplest explanation, but one that leaves certain problems untackled. Laying aside the blatant mistakes for the present, it does not seem possible that **8** could have been composed by a later writer on the basis of **7** alone. In language **8** differs from its companion in a number of minor points, sometimes corresponding more closely to contemporary usage than does **7**. The witness-list includes more names than **7**, and all are in keeping with the year 933. The two ealdormen who witness **8** and not **7**, Æscbryht and Ælfstan, only appear as signatories elsewhere between the years 930 and 934. The episcopacy of Eadulf of Crediton, who appears only in **8**, ended in 934, when his successor's signatures begin. Although Aldred receives his correct title in **7** and not in **8**, this mistake is a common copyist's error, and could have originated at any time, perhaps when the cartulary was compiled.

In contrast to the apparent integrity of the underlying text, there are the unacceptable features. In the body of the grant, the estate is said to be of *v familiarum*, although the cartulary copyist headed the deed *CARTA VIII HIDARUM* ... In Domesday Book the estate is recorded as being of eight hides, and the same number is confirmed to the monastery in Æthelred's charter of 998 (**11**). *Familiae* was very occasionally used to denote a land unit, and is found in two Winchester charters of 749 (S 258 and 259: the former looks more reliable than the latter), but it is not found thereafter until Anglo-Norman times. It seems an unlikely choice either for a charter writer of Athelstan's reign or for a later forger. However, the form of the place-name in the text – *Þesttune* – is early, and only found in a few other tenth-century charters (*DEPN*, pp. 508–9).

Another obvious flaw in **8** is the use of *castrum* in the dispositive section, for Sherborne Castle was built by Bishop Roger of Salisbury *c.* 1138 (*Registrum Osmundi*, i. 235). Fowler in his study of medieval Sherborne suggests that *castrum* has here the meaning of 'town' (J. Fowler, *Mediaeval Sherborne* (Dorchester, 1951), p. 56), citing W. H. Stevenson's note on *castellis* (*Asser*, pp. 331–2). *Castellum* is found in two associated charters, S 517 and 536 (945 and 948), referring to Wallingford, probably in its capacity as a 'burh' (see Gelling, *ECTV*, p. 40), but the texts are doubtful, and there are no other examples. Moreover, there is no evidence that Sherborne was ever a 'burh'. *Castrum* is not found in any other charter of the period: indeed, there is very little variety in the vocabulary used in this context, either *in loco* or *in civitate* being almost always employed. *Castrum* could also be used of a monastery, but in this sense it is employed with a qualifier such as *Dei*, and usually in the plural (cf. Latham, *DML*, s.v. *castrum* 1.), but the wording in **8** does not fit this interpretation. To Professor Finberg (*ECW*, p. 167), *castrum* reveals the forger, implying that the text was forged between 1138 and the compilation of the cartulary some twenty-odd years later.

Also noteworthy is the appearance of Beorhtwulf as a spiritual beneficiary in partnership with the king. This is possibly the second ealdorman of the name, who witnesses as *comes* in 903 (S 367), as *dux* in a group of dubious Winchester charters dated 909 (S 375-8 and 381-3), and possibly as *comes* in 889 or 891 (S 347: see Whitelock 1979, pp. 85-6, for a discussion of this charter and of the two Beorhtwulfs). It seems likely that Beorhtwulf was the original recipient of the Weston estate, especially if the use of *comes* is taken into account: '... *comes* is greatly preferred to describe the beneficiary ... [in tenth-century texts]. This striking preference when speaking of the beneficiary suggests that *comes* was felt to express more warmly the personal relationship with the king making the grant' (Whitelock 1979, p. 98). **7** and **8** (initially a grant of five hides to Beorhtwulf) could well have been drawn up on the same occasion; there are several similar pairs of charters from Athelstan's reign and later (see Keynes, *Diplomas*, pp. 42-3). At a later date the Weston estate, increased to eight hides, might have passed to Sherborne together with the charter, quite possibly given or willed by Beorhtwulf himself, since his name is deliberately retained in the text, but anyway by 998 (see above). Later still, perhaps shortly before the cartulary was compiled, the text was altered to give the impression that Sherborne was the original beneficiary (see above, pp. xxiv-xxix, for a discussion of this being a possibly widespread practice), and Beorhtwulf's name was moved to the position of a spiritual beneficiary in acknowledgement of his part in the transactions. This scenario would account for the variation in hidage, Beorhtwulf's appearance and the untimely reference to Sherborne Castle.

The liturgical clause in **8** remains an unexplained item. It contains the same conditions as those imposed in **7**, in similar but not identical language. Whether the clause was included because the land was intended to revert to Sherborne after Beorhtwulf's lifetime, or whether it was added when the charter was altered can only be guessed at. There are some indications that the passage has been disturbed: a word has been omitted after *decantet*, and *tribuo* seems to have been misplaced from much earlier in the clause. The passage also contains the only visible copying fault to be found throughout the cartulary part of the manuscript (the deleted *celebrationumque*).

The boundary clause was examined by Grundy (1939, pp. 60-5), who found himself unable to locate the estate securely, either in Stalbridge Weston, the identification usually accepted (see Fägersten, *Place-Names of Dorset*, p. 37), or in Weston in Corscombe. More recently, the bounds have been re-examined by Cyril Hart, who has argued quite convincingly for Stalbridge Weston ('Some Dorset Charter Boundaries', *Proceedings of the Dorset Natural History and Archaeological Society*, lxxxvi (1965), pp. 159-60; map references are given here for many of the boundary marks). However, several of the landmarks cannot be precisely identified, and there is no way of determining whether the area outlined would equal five or eight hides. The language of the boundary clause would fit a pre-Conquest date.

9

King Eadred grants eight hides (cassati) *at Thornford, Dorset, to Wulfsige, bishop of Sherborne.* A.D. 903 [*for* ?953]

B. BL Add. 46487, 11r–12r: copy, s. xii^{med}

Ed.: Birch 894

Listed: Sawyer 516; Finberg, *ECW* 594

CARTA . VIII . HIDARUM APUD TORNEFORD .[a]

+ Oportet nos ergo fratres karissimi istum contempnere mundum . ut possimus sequi saluatorem nostrum . Caueamus ne perdamus uitam perpetuam propter uanam huius mundi gloriam. Quid enim sit hodie aspicimus . sed quid cras futurum sit unusquisque nostrum nescimus . Transeunt huius uitę dies uelut umbra . et incerta est hora unicuique nostrum quando reuertatur puluis in puluerem . et spiritus redeat ad dominum qui dedit illum . ut iudicetur secundum opera sua . Quam ob rem ego Eadred Occidentalium Saxonum rex pro amore Dei et pro remedio animę meę – et pro remissione peccatorum meorum do atque concedo meo dilectissimo ac fidelissimo Þulfsige episcopo aliquam partem terrę . hoc modo dicendum est octo cassatos in illo loco qui dicitur Ðornford . ita ut habeat atque possideat cum omnibus ad se pertinentibus – quamdiu in hac uita uixerit . et post obitum suum reddatur terra iam dicta sine aliqua contentione et lite ad refectionem familię Scireburnensis ęcclesię . et illud[b] ab omnium sęcularium rerum liberam esse concedo . nisi quod omni plebe commune est . expeditione et pontis instructione . et arcis munitione . et hoc sit tam firmiter constitutum omnibus diebus christianitatis quasi libertas illa constituta est quandiu[c] fides crescit in gente Anglorum . et qui hoc augere uoluerit . augeat Deus bona illius in regione uiuentium . Si autem aliquis diabolica fraude deceptus in magnis aut in modicis hoc infringere uel minuere temptauerit . sit anathematizatus ab omnibus fidelibus hic et in futuro sęculo . nisi ante satisfactione emendauerit .

+ Ego Eadredus rex huic[d] libertatem et donationem cum signo Sanctę Crucis firmaui .
+ Ego Oda archiepiscopus hoc firmando signum Sanctę Crucis impono .
+ Ego Þeodredus episcopus consensi et subscripsi .
+ Ego Ælfeah .   episcopus .

+ Ego Þulfhelm .   episcopus .
+ Ego Æðelstanus .   dux .
+ Ego Þulfric .   minister .
+ Ego Ælfheah .   minister .[e]
+ Ego Æðelric .   minister .
+ Ego Beorhtulf .   minister .
+ Ego Ælfheah .   minister .
+ Ego Þulfstan .   minister .[f]

Þis synd þa landgemæru . On east healfe on cumtun bricgge up on ða lace . oð ran pylle . of ran pylle . up on þone eastemestan holan peg up to hricgge . andlang hrigcges . pest be ecge on merc . þonon on lyngærstun easteperdne . þonon on slæp . þonne andlang streames on gifle oþ mylenburnna[g] ut scyt up on stream eft to cumtun bricgge . Annus dominicę incarnationis . dcccc . iii . indictio . xi .

[a] CARTA ... TORNEFORD . *rubric*   [b] *For* illam   [c] *For* quamdiu   [d] *For* hanc
[e] *First column of subscriptions ends here*   [f] *Second column of subscriptions ends here*
[g] *For* -burnan?

This text opens with what sounds like part of a Latin homily on the uncertainty of human life, a common theme of tenth-century proems, although this particular version does not appear elsewhere. S 1029, a spurious Peterborough charter dated 1060, has a proem that opens 'Oportet nos quos Deus praefecit . . .' and closes '. . . et secundum opera sua reddat unicuique', but otherwise there is little resemblance between the two. The use of *fratres* if taken as addressed literally to the recipients of the grant might indicate a date of composition after 998, when monks replaced the secular clerks (see below, p. 43), although it is not a word usually found in reliable charters with reference to monks.

The royal style belongs to the ninth century, and there is no record of Eadred being called 'Occidentalium Saxonum rex'. S 539, ostensibly a charter of Eadred dated 948, uses the style, but that text is in reality a corrupt copy of a charter of Æthelred I of Wessex. The dispositive clause would be quite usual were it not for the phrase 'reddatur terra . . . sine aliqua contentione et lite ad refectionem familię Scireburnensis ęcclesię'. The common procedure, except in the case of a lease, was to grant the land outright. There is a Worcester lease dated 849 (S 1272) which uses a very similar phrase: 'sine aliqua dissentione et sine conflictu reddatur ad supradictam aecclesiam . . .' The passage 'et hoc sit tam firmiter . . . in gente Anglorum' is a variation of one that is found in both eighth and ninth centuries (Stenton 1918, p. 445 n. 57). This particular wording occurs exactly in the Malmesbury version of the 844 decimation text (e.g. S 322), a copy of which must have been available at Sherborne. The Sherborne adaptation (**5**) omits the phrase 'quasi libertas illa constituta est'. *Crescere* in this context appears only in **9** and in the 844 decimation texts, although **6** (864) has *peoxa*, probably suggested by a Latin model (see above, p. 23). The anathema in **9** is also identical with that found in the 844 texts.

In the witness-list the form of King Eadred's subscription does not have a tenth-century parallel: it is more closely echoed in West Saxon charters of the mid ninth century, as for instance in S 315 (855). Apart from this, the witness-list is consistent with a date in Eadred's reign, and is limited to the years 946–51 by the witnesses of Eadred himself (946–55) and of Ælfheah, bishop of Winchester, who died on 12 March 951 (*ASC* MS A). The dating clause is placed most unusually after the witness-list and bounds, and is patently incorrect. The indiction (11) would fit 953, which might well be the date originally intended ('dccciii' miscopied from 'dcccliii'). 953 is the date given to the grant in one of the medallions in the Sherborne Missal (p. 383), although there is no way of knowing whether this was the scribe's own emendation or whether he had some other source, now lost (see above, p. xl). 953 would not fit with the appearance of Bishop Ælfheah, but historical consistency does not seem to have worried the composer of **9**. The boundary clause itself appears to be of pre-Conquest date. The landmarks follow the boundary of the parish of Thornford (Grundy 1938, pp. 87–9), confirmed by Keen (1984, p. 218 and Fig. 74). To the north the river Yeo divides Thornford from the Bradford Abbas estate as far as the *Mylenburna*, a landmark mentioned in both bounds.

Sherborne certainly possessed the Thornford estate by 1066 (in Domesday Book it appears among the bishop of Salisbury's holdings), and probably owned it already in 998 (**11**), but either the charter did not accompany the land or it was subsequently lost, for **9** cannot be considered in any way authentic. Only the witness-list and possibly the proem derive from a genuine charter of Eadred. The text's insistence on the estate reverting to the community suggests some connection either with Wulfsige III's division of estates between the monastery and the bishop or with the bishopric's move to Salisbury. The fact that Wulfsige I's name has been included as the first beneficiary suggests that a memorandum recording a connection between him and the estate at Thornford once existed.

10

King Edgar grants five hides at Oborne, Dorset, to God and St Mary. [A.D. 959 × 975]

B. BL Add. 46487, 10v–11r: copy, s. xii^{med}

Ed.: a. Birch 1308
 b. Robertson, *Charters*, no. 50, with translation

Listed: Sawyer 813; Finberg, *ECW* 611

CARTA . V . HIDARUM APUD WOBURNAM .[a]

In nomine domini Iesu Christi . Ic EADGAR cing cyðe on þisse bec þ is Cristes boc þ ic habba þa fif hyda æt Þomburnan agifen Gode 7 Sancta MARIA for me sylfne 7 for mine yldran ðe þar restat æt Scireburnan . Aðelbold cing . 7 Æthelbyrht cing . 7 ðis ic habbe idon for ure ealra saule lufon . to ecre reste . Gif hƿa beo sƿa dyrtig[b] þ þis abrece oððe apenden pylle ⋅ þas mine gife 7 sylene mid ænegum uncræfte þære stope atbredan þence oððe pille ⋅ ƿite he on domes dæge riht to agildanne beoforan Gode 7 eallum his halgum nymþe . bute he hit ær her on þorolde gebete . Ic EADGAR cyning mid þara halgan rode tacn ðis hate sƿiþe geornlice getrymman 7 gefæstnian. + Dunstan archiepiscopus Cantƿarubyri .

+ Ƿulsin episcopus .
+ Alfstan episcopus .
+ Eanƿulf . dux .
+ Ælfstan . dux .
+ Alhhard . abbas
+ Heahmund . presbiter
+ Huita . prępositus
+ Osmund . minister
+ Ƿulfhere . minister .[c]
+ Cyma .   minister .
+ Ƿulfred .   minister .
+ Ecgbreht .   minister .
+ Monnel .   minister .
+ Eadpulf .   minister .
+ Ƿistan .   minister .
+ Æþelpulf .   minister .
+ Ƿynsige .   minister .
+ Goda .   minister .[d]
+ Coenpald .   minister .
+ Ƿulfhelm .   minister .
+ Beocca .   minister .
+ Æþelmod .   minister .
+ Beorhnoð .   minister .
+ Hunred .   minister .
+ Ecgulf .   minister .
+ Æþelric .   minister
+ Ælfhere .   minister .[e]

[a]CARTA...WOBURNAM . *rubric*   [b]*For* dyrstig   [c]*First column of subscriptions ends here.* B *has* Osmund miñ; *all the following titles have been expanded from* m̄   [d]*Second column of subscriptions ends here*   [e]*Third column of subscriptions ends here*

10 has more the form of a memorandum than a charter, although it does contain an anathema and a witness-list. The grant, made for the spiritual benefit of Edgar and his two ancestors buried at Sherborne, Æthelbald and Æthelberht, was originally recorded in a gospel book, a well-known and not unusual practice (see Wormald 1957, p. 106 and n. 2, and Ker, *Catalogue*, p. 557). The gift might be of land, as here or in Robertson, *Charters*, no. 71 (?999), or of the book itself, as in ibid. no. 24 (*c*. 934), a memorandum similar to 10, both in form and phrasing.

There are few grounds of comparison with contemporary Latin charters: no proem, no royal style, no mention of taxes or public services. The anathema is not a direct translation of any in use at the time, although S 543 (949) and S 634 (956) contain formulas that could underlie the vernacular phrases.

Linguistically there is little out of place, although there are a few late forms in unstressed vowels (such as *habba* for *habbe*, *þara* for *þare*), which could result from late copying. *Aðel-* before a second element with a back vowel, e.g. *-bold*, is normal usage from the mid tenth century on. The Oborne estate is one of those reserved for the support of the monks in Domesday Book, and is also mentioned as in Sherborne's possession in 998 (11).

In the witness-list, the first two names belong to Edgar's reign, the next two probably do so, and the rest have been lifted from 6. Edgar's subscription 'mid þara halgan rode tacn ... gefæstnian' is also copied from Æthelbreht's in 6, though the latter shows the correct unstressed forms. The first three episcopal witnesses, Dunstan, Wulsin (Wulfsige) and Alfstan, do not help much in dating the charter. Dunstan was archbishop from 959 to 988. Wulsin, if he belongs to Edgar's reign, could be either the bishop of Cornwall, 959 × 963–980, or the bishop of Sherborne, 943–958 × 964. There were three bishops called Alfstan during Edgar's reign, at London, 961–995 × 996, Rochester, 946 × 964–995, and Ramsbury, 970–981. Dr Robertson suggests that Wulsin should be identified as the bishop of Cornwall and Alfstan as possibly the bishop of Ramsbury, since they sign together in this order in S 790 (973), which would limit 10 to the years 970 × 975. But it would be unwise to place much reliance on these episcopal witnesses, since the rest of the list, including the king's subscription, is clearly not part of the original text. All the names after Alfstan have been taken from 6. Dr Robertson suggests (ibid.) that this was a copyist's mistake, made perhaps when the cartulary was being compiled, and that the scribe confused the *Alfstan eps* of 10 with the *Alhstan eps* of 6. But this seems too charitable an explanation, for the scribe was careful enough to omit the names of the two athelings, Æthelred and Alfred, whose presence would have betrayed his borrowing immediately. Moreover, the king's title shows that the scribe had already drawn upon 6 before he became 'confused'.

It is far more likely that the original memorandum, which seems quite authentic, did not have a witness-list (see S 328, 1377 and Robertson, *Charters*, no. 24, for other examples without lists), but that a later copyist thought to make the text appear more regular, and added on a few names of approximately the right period, and then borrowed some more from **6** to achieve a suitable length. A medallion in the Sherborne Missal (p. 384) records that Edgar gave Oborne 'cum omnibus suis pertinentibus' to Sherborne in 970, but the source of this statement made *c.* 1400 is unknown. It would probably be unwise to give **10** any closer date than that of Edgar's reign.

11

King Æthelred grants Bishop Wulfsige permission to convert Sherborne into a Benedictine monastery, and confirms possession to the monastery of its lands (listed). A.D. 998

B. BL Add. 46487, 3r–4r: copy, s. xii^{med}

C. BL Cotton Otho A. xviii, fo. 132r: copy, s. xii^{i} (badly burned)

Ed.: a. Hearne, *Leland's Itinerary*, ii. 80–1, from B
    b. *Mon. Angl.*, i. 337 (no. 2), from Hearne
    c. Kemble 701, from Hearne and *Mon. Angl.*
    d. Thorpe, *Diplomatarium*, pp. 293–4
    e. *Anglia Sacra*, i. 170–1, from C

Listed: Sawyer 895; Finberg, *ECDC* 45; Finberg, *ECW* 614

Printed from B, with variants from *Anglia Sacra* (AS), and all legible readings from C

Anno ab incarnationis dominicę . dccccc^a nonagesimo octauo . ego Æthelredus totius Albionis Dei gubernante moderamine basileus suadente archiepiscopo Ælfrico cum^b consilio meorum episcoporum ac^c principum seu nobilium michique^d fidelium assistentium annui episcopo Wlsino^e ordinare monachicę conuersationis normam . castamque uitam et Deo amabilem secundum institutionem sancti patris Benedicti in cenobio Scireburnensis ęcclesię . ea ratione uidelicet ut quisquis successor ei aduenerit siue ^{f}pius siue crudelis non habeat^f facultatem male tractare res monachorum . sit pastor non tirannus gubernet ad fratrum utilitatem secundum pastoralem auctoritatem^g non ad lupinam rapacitatem . pascat suos et se sequentes^h . habeat ipse solus uictum inter fratres ^{i}sicut scriptum est^i . Principem populorum te constitui . esto in illis quasi unus ex illis . Regat ipse iuxta animarum et corporum utilitatem substantiam monasterii ita dumtaxat^k ut fratrum consilio non sit^l ignotum quicquid agatur^m . Et si forte^n quod absit euenerit ut pastor et grex discordantur^o . semper ^{p}ad examen archiepiscopi reseruetur . et ipse regi intimet^p ut iusta correctio sequatur . Et quia mos minime apud nos consentit ut^q in episcopali sede abbas constituatur . fiat ipse episcopus eis abbas et pater . et ipsi fratres 'obedientes ei sint sicuti filii' et monachi cum castitate et humilitate et subiectione ˢsecundum disciplinam almi patrisˢ nostri Benedicti . ut una brauium ęternę coronę accipere mereantur . 'Et quoniam sicut ait apostolus . nos sumusᵗ in quos fines seculorum deuenerunt . et multiplicato iam genere ᵘhumano . adeo ut perplures gratia inopięᵘ ruris non habentes ubi uel arando uel fodiendo ʷagriculturam exercentes uictum adipiscanturʷ . insuper et crescente philargiria non nullorum ˣut quisque rapiat sibi quod potuerit . optimumˣ duxerunt priores nostri ut omnis lis terminibus certis ʸadnulletur . ideoque territoria causa concordięʸ assuescereᶻ nuper inter mundanos ᵃ²cepere ut portionem quisque proprię tellurisᵃ² libere excolet . Quorum ego exampla imitatus rus predicti ᵇ²cenobii hac cartula annotariᵇ² censeo . hoc est in ipsa Scireburna centum agelliᶜ² in loco qui dicitur Stocland et predium ᵈ²monasterii sicut Wlsinus episcopus fossisᵈ² sepibusque girare curauit . deinde nouem cassatos in ᵉ²loco qui ab incolis Holancumbᵉ² nuncupatur . item in Halganstokeᶠ² . xv . in Þor⟨n⟩fordᵍ² . vii . in ʰ²Bradanford . x . in Þonburnaʰ² . v . in Þestunⁱ² . viii . in Stapulbreicgeᵏ² . xx . in Þulfheardigstoke . x . in Cumbtunˡ² . viii . in Osanstoke . ii . et mansamᶠ³ unam iuxta ripam maris ᵐ²quę dicitur ǣt Limᵐ² . Et quicquid Deus his auxerit ex donis fidelium continua securitate et iugi ⁿ²libertate possideant fratres inibiⁿ² degentes . tribus exceptis quę omnibus communia sunt scilicet ᵒ²expeditione . pontis arcisueᵒ² restauratione . tamen nulli debitores sint in rogi constructione ᵖ²eo quod monasterium hoc opusᵖ² indigere nouimus . Si forte quod absit hanc nostram donationem quispiam annullare temptauerit . et ad libitus proprios deflectere . sciat se ęquissimo iudici rationem redditurum . clangente tuba archangeli extremoᵠ² examine . ubi omnis ęquitas et iustitia Christo iudicante cunctis manifestabitur . Ego Æðelredusʳ² rex Anglorum hanc libertatem concedo sepedicto monasterio sub episcopo quęmcumqueˢ² elegerit semper regendo etᵗ² signaculo sanctę ᵘ²crucis + hanc munificentiam consigno coram his testibus .ᵘ² Ego Ælfricus archiepiscopus hoc ʷ²donum data michi benedictione firmaui . Ego Ealdulf archiepiscopusʷ² libens faui atque consensi . ˣ²Ego Wlstanus episcopus hoc idem affirmaui .ˣ² ʸ²Ego Ælpheagus episcopus consensum prebui .ʸ² Ego Wlsinusᶻ² episcopus ᵃ³ hoc meum desiderium ad perfectum usque perduxi .ᵃ³ Ego Ælfwinus episcopus hilari mente concessi . ᵇ³Ego Æthelward dux gratanter corroboraui .ᵇ³ Ego Æ`l´fric dux consentaneus fui . ᶜ³ Ego Ælfsige abbas . Ego Wlfgar abbas .ᶜ³ Ego Leofric abbas . Ego Godwine abbas . ᵈ³Ego Æðelmær . minister . Ordulf . minister . Þulfget .ᵈ³ minister . Brihtmær . minister . Leopine . minister . Brihtric . minister . ᵉ³Þulfnoð . minister .ᵉ³

KING ÆTHELRED

a nongentesimo AS   *b* de AS   *c* episcoporum ac *omitted* AS   *d* inque AS   *e* Wlfsino AS   *f...f* praesul crudelis si fuerit AS   *g* auth- AS   *h* servientes AS   *i...i* scriptum est enim AS   *k* duntaxat AS   *l* consilium sit AS   *m* quicquid aga[ ] *legible in* C   *n* quando AS   *o* discordent AS   *p...p* judex ... archiepiscopus se praebeat ... AS; ... archiep[.] reseru[ ] *legible in* C   *q* apud nos consent[. .] ut *legible in* C   *r...r* obedientes ei si[. .] sicuti f[ ] *legible in* C   *s...s* secundum disciplinam almi patr[ ] *legible in* C   *t...t* Et quoniam sic[.] ait apostolus . nos sum[.] *legible in* C   *u...u* [-]mano [. . .] ut perplu[. .]s [.]g[. .]nop[ ] *legible in* C; B reads grę, expanded here as gratia   *w...w* [-]cultura[.]xercentes [.]ict[.] adipisca[. .] *legible in* C   *x...x* ut quisque rapi[. . . . .] quod potuerit . opt[ ] *legible in* C   *y...y* adnulletur [. . .] q[. . . .]toria cau[. .] *legible in* C; AS *reads* territoriae causae creberrime   *z* adsuescere AS   *a2...a2* ut portionem quisque proprie telluris l[ ] *legible in* C; AS *reads* coepere in   *b2...b2* *legible in* C   *c2* agellos AS   *d2...d2* monasterii . sicut Wlfsin episcopus fos[ ] *legible in* C; Wlfsinus AS   *e2...e2* [. .]co qui ab incolis holanc[.]m[.] *legible in* C; AS *reads* agro *in place of* loco   *f2* -stoce AS   *g2* Thornford AS   *h2...h2* in hradanford . x in po[.]b[ ] *legible in* C; AS *reads* Hradanford   *i2* Westum AS   *k2* Stawilbrycge AS   *l2* 7 eumtum AS   *m2...m2* que dicitur æt lim[ ] *legible in* C; AS *reads* Ætbun   *n2...n2* [-]tate possi[. . . . .] f[. .] in *legible in* C   *o2...o2* [-]tione . pontis arcisue [ ] *legible in* C   *p2...p2* eo quod monaste[. . .] hoc o[ ] *legible in* C; AS *reads* monasteriis   *q2* in extremo AS   *r2* Ego Æthe[ ] *legible in* C   *s2* quod AS   *t2* . . .do que AS   *u2...u2* crucis [. . . . .]unificentiam consigno c[. . .] his testib[ ] *legible in* C   *w2...w2* dat[ ]dicti[. . .] firmau[. .] Ego Ead[.]ulf arc[ ] *legible in* C; AS *reads* denunciata *in place of* donum data michi   *x2...x2* Ego Wlfst[.]nus [. . .] hoc [.]dem adfi[. .]avi . *legible in* C; AS *reads* hoc adfirmavi   *y2...y2* Ego Ælfh[ ] *legible in* C; AS *reads* Ego Ælfheagus epsc. consului   *z2* Wlfsinus AS   *a3...a3* hoc meum desiderium a[. . . .]fectum usque per[ ] *legible in* C; AS *reads* concessi *for* perduxi   *b3...b3* Ego Æðelp[. .]d dux g[. . .]anter corrobor[ ] *legible in* C   *c3...c3* [.]g[.] Ælfsige abb[ ]abbas *legible in* C   *d3...d3* Ego Æðelmær m . Ordulf [ ]lfge[ ] *legible in* C; AS reads Osthulf   *e3...e3* Wlf[. .]ð . minister . *legible in* C; AS *reads* Wlfnad ... B *has* m̄ *throughout, expanded here to* minister. C *has* m̄ *except after* Wulfnoð, *when* minister *is written out in full*   *f3* B *has* massam   Square brackets indicate lacunae in MS. C. Where possible, illegible letters have been indicated by dots.

This is the foundation charter of Sherborne as a Benedictine monastery, and had pride of place in the cartulary on the original first folio. In it Æthelred confirms Bishop Wulfsige's installation of Benedictine monks at Sherborne, and provides that the bishop shall be abbot, and that the archbishop shall be judge in case of any dispute between abbot and community, presumably because the community could not seek redress from the local bishop, as would be the normal recourse. Then the charter names the possessions of the monastery, and declares them free of all except the three common dues.

The charter has an unusual opening: it begins with the date, followed by Æthelred's royal style. Although the great majority of Æthelred's charters begin with a proem, a few follow the same pattern as **11**, in particular S 862, dated 986. S 862 is a diplomatically acceptable text, and it is interesting to note that Dr Keynes links it to a group of charters of which several are associated with Glastonbury and Dunstan (*Diplomas*, pp. 48 and 94–5). According to the *Vitae* of both men, Dunstan was Wulfsige's patron, and the *Vita Wlsini* says that the archbishop was instrumental in Wulfsige's being appointed abbot of the monastery of Westminster (ch. iii). Another authentic charter, S 909 (1004), uses the same opening, as do several leases issued by Oswald of York (e.g. S 1343, dated 981). S 894, a spurious Westminster text (see above, p. xix), has been modelled on **11**, sharing the same opening and royal style. This charter also stresses the relationship between Dunstan and Wulfsige, which must have been Westminster tradition. The royal style used in **11** is not found exactly elsewhere, although other charters use very similar wording. Mentioning the advice and consent of the *witan* was not customary in late tenth-century charters, but there are other examples (e.g. S 842, 881 and 942).

The main body of the text records the details of Wulfsige's arrangements at Sherborne, and there are few diplomatic comparisons available. Two other foundation charters, S 792 (973) from Thorney and S 838 (981) from Tavistock, mention the Benedictine Rule, and list the possessions of their houses, but otherwise they have little in common with **11**, and neither charter is acceptable as it stands. However, **11** belongs to the group of Æthelred's charters which were issued to religious houses and 'represented not simply fresh grants of land but involved more complex matters – for example, definition of the privileges to be enjoyed by the new foundations ... Those responsible for drafting such documents would have had to abandon the conventional format of royal diplomas where necessary, in favour of a more individually distinctive text that took the particular circumstances of the transaction fully into account' (Keynes, *Diplomas*, p. 98). **11** would also fit into the group of late diplomas that could well have been 'drawn up in close co-operation with the beneficiaries, if not necessarily by the beneficiaries themselves' (ibid. p. 121). In this context, Wulfsige's attestation is rather suggestive: 'Ego Wlsinus episcopus hoc meum desiderium ad perfectum usque perduxi.'

11 reverts to normal diplomatic format towards the end of the text. The immunity clause, however, which frees the monastery lands from all save the three common burdens, contains a specific and unique immunity. The monastery is to owe no one the duty of constructing a *rogus*, since the monastery itself would have need of this service. *Rogus*, a pile of wood, beacon or fire (*RMLWL*, p. 441), is not found in use in England at this date, and does not occur elsewhere in the Anglo-Saxon charters, but in the context of the 990s, warning beacons may well have been part of a local defence system: in 998 for instance the *Anglo-Saxon Chronicle* records the Danish army as going 'everywhere into Dorset as widely as they pleased'. The clause is found in C as well as in the cartulary text, so it is unlikely to be a later interpolation (see above, p. xx).

The anathema is not found elsewhere, but it displays the flamboyant language of Athelstan's charters, and is reminiscent of the formulas found in texts such as S 416 (931) and **8** (933). The practice of borrowing formulas from earlier charters was not uncommon under Æthelred, especially in the first part of his reign (Keynes, *Diplomas*, pp. 85–6). The royal subscription that heads the witness-list is also unique, while acceptable for the period, and its content is comparable to equivalent formulas in S 911 (1005) and S 918 (on which see ibid. p. 263). The styles used in the rest of the list correspond to those found in such texts as S 876 (993), S 882 (995 for 994), S 888 (996), S 889 (996) and again S 911 (1005). Bishop Wulfsige's subscription with its note of personal concern is similar in tone to Abbot Wulfgar of Abingdon's 'hoc sintagma triumphans dictavi', in the confirmation of Abingdon's land and privileges in S 876 (993). All the names in the witness-list are acceptable for the given date, although the list itself is rather short (see ibid. p. 256 and Tables), and may well have been abridged during a recopying. The cartulary scribe was most probably using a copy rather than the original, since the witness-list is not presented in columns, nor is there a chrismon, which would have been appropriate for a charter of this date and type (see above, p. xxx). The witnesses in MS C are also presented within the text rather than in columnar form.

11 is not an easy text to assess, for it is not really a land grant, and its make-up is distinctly atypical. On the other hand, as has been mentioned, such charters form a recognizable sub-group among Æthelred's diplomas, and there is nothing in **11** to which objection should be taken on diplomatic grounds. Moreover there are several external points in its favour. We know from the *Vita Wlsini* that Sherborne was placed under the Benedictine Rule by Wulfsige, as happened at many houses in the late tenth century under the influence of the monastic reformers (see *ASC*, s.a. 964). Goscelin, who wrote the *Vita* and had access to Sherborne materials, says that he saw documents (*singula privilegia*: *Vita Wlsini*, ch. iv) concerning this. He had left Sherborne by 1078, so must have seen them by that date.

11 is often cited as proof that the actual reform of Sherborne took place in 998, but the charter does not support this interpretation. Instead it suggests that the change-over from a secular house to a monastic community was a gradual process, as would befit the work of a disciple of Dunstan. The lands confirmed to Sherborne include 'predium monasterii sicut Wlsinus episcopus fossis sepibusque girare curauit', which means that Wulfsige had already enclosed the grounds in accordance with the Rule. Wulfsige's subscription also suggests that his work is completed by the charter. Æthelred's dispositive word is *annui*, i.e. 'I have approved', with reference to the institution of monks, but he changes to the present subjunctive when arranging for the bishop to hold the office of abbot. This last arrangement, which was contrary to the Benedictine Rule, was certainly in effect at the beginning of the eleventh century (see **14**, below, p. 51). It is a provision most unlikely to have come from a later writer when, especially after the move to Salisbury, the concern of the monastery would presumably have been to move away from episcopal control. Sherborne achieved independence from Salisbury in 1122 (see above, p. xv), with the appointment of an abbot. It is clearly a sign of **11**'s authenticity and of the respect in which it was held that, despite the power-struggle between the bishop of Salisbury and the community of Sherborne, Wulfsige's arrangements were copied unaltered into the very cartulary that was designed to guarantee Sherborne's immunity from episcopal interference (see above, pp. xv–xvi).

It seems most probable that in **11** Wulfsige was officially separating the lands which were to support the monastery from those estates belonging to the bishopric, a division that apparently had not existed before. As has already been discussed (above, p. xv and Fig. 2), the monastic estates are all – with the exception of Holcombe – clustered around Sherborne, evidence of a deliberate selection. The lands named in **11** were as far as can be determined all possessions of Sherborne in 998. The list is not dependent on the foundation's possessions as given in Domesday Book, nor on the charters contained in the cartulary, although by and large these three sources agree as to the main bulk of the monastery's estates (see Fig. 1). Most of the estates named in **11** are covered by charters issued or at least dated before 998: Halstock (**3**), *Osanstok* (**4**), Lyme (**2**), Bradford (**7**), Weston (**8**), Thornford (**9**) and Oborne (**10**). The nine hides at Holcombe were nominally in the monastery's possession just a few years later (see **13, 14** and commentaries), but the community was forced to lease out the land, and by the time Domesday Book was compiled in 1086 the estate had been in lay ownership for twenty years. Of the lands named that have no surviving charters, Compton is recorded as a Sherborne estate in Domesday Book; *Wulfheardigstok* does not appear elsewhere, although it may well have been the *Stoche* recorded as a Sherborne estate in Domesday Book and later lists. The one hundred *agelli* at *Stocland* in Sherborne may be connected with the *Propeschirch et Stocland* mentioned in the 1146 privilege of Pope Eugenius III, and possibly with the nine hides in Sherborne held by the bishop for the monks as recorded in Domesday Book. Corscombe is not listed in **11**, but according to **15** it was leased out by Bishop Ælfwold during Edgar's reign for two lifetimes and not returned until Æthelric's episcopacy.

11 is the only Sherborne charter of which a second copy has survived, in Cotton Otho A. xviii (cited as MS C), in a hand of the first half of the twelfth century. In this manuscript the charter text is associated with two Bury texts, one of which also deals with the installation of monks in the place of secular clergy, and with a Worcester text whose nature suggests that the fragment of manuscript originated there. It seems very likely that the copy of the Sherborne text reached Worcester through Archbishop Wulfstan, a correspondent of Wulfsige's, within a few years of 998 (see above, pp. xviii–xix). MS C appears to have retained slightly purer forms of certain Anglo-Saxon names (see above, p. xx), which would support this hypothesis.

12

Bishop Wulfsige grants all the possessions of the former clerks of Sherborne to the monks of the monastery, as well as making other concessions. [A.D. 998]

B. BL Add. 46487, 4rv: copy, s. xii^{med}

Ed.: a. Hearne, *Leland's Itinerary*, ii. 81–2
 b. *Mon. Angl.*, i. 337 (no. 3), from Hearne
 c. Kemble 702, from Hearne and *Mon. Angl.*

Listed: Sawyer 1382; Finberg, *ECW* 615

In nomine domini[a] . Ego Wlsinus gratia Dei episcopus constituo et ordino sapientes monachos in matre ęcclesiarum Sanctę MARIĘ Scireburnię iussu et consilio regis Æðelredi . et hortatu Ælfrici archipresulis et omnium episcoporum et consensu principum totius Anglię expulsis clericis . Trado etiam eis territoria et possessiones quas habuerunt ab initio qui sancto loco deseruierunt ad gloriam et laudem Dei . et ad honorem et reuerentiam antecessorum et successorum meorum . et unum cassatum in ipsa uilla . et omnem decimam episcopii[b] eiusdem uillę in omnibus rebus . et decimum agrum in tota uilla in decimam . et . xxiiii . carucarum onera de silua per omnes annos . Statuo eis ad remedium animę meę et regum et pontificum et principum et ęcclesias et terras liberas a regali exactione et a tributis in omni ciuitate et mercatu . Si quis hęc permutare uoluerit ⁖ excommunico eum a regno Dei . Data Lundonie indictione . xi . presente rege coram omni concilio .

[a] *Coloured initial but no rubric. The text follows on from* **11** *with no gap*   [b] *Sic*

This text records that Wulfsige set monks at Sherborne in the place of secular clergy, and transferred to the monks the lands and possessions of the latter: he added to these 'one hide in that same town', i.e. Sherborne; all the tithes (*omnem decimam*) of the bishop in the same town in all things; 'decimum agrum in tota uilla in decimam': '(the produce of) every tenth acre in the whole town as tithe'; and twenty-four cartloads of wood every year.

 Charters and leases granted by bishops during this period often do not employ charter format, though a witness-list is usual, and anathemas are quite common. **12** has very little in the way of formulas, and what it has is hardly acceptable. Wulfsige declares the grants free 'a regali exactione et a tributis in omni ciuitate et mercatu'. The latter phrase is not found in contemporary texts, nor would it be legally possible for Wulfsige himself to declare the lands free of all services. The anathema is more like a casual bow to convention than a serious attempt at a diplomatic formula. But what really clinches the document's unacceptability is the dating clause – 'Data Lundonie indictione . xi . presente rege coram omni concilio' – a formula impossible for the Anglo-Saxon period, but revealing strong Anglo-Norman influence. The indiction was presumably intended to indicate 998 as the year in which **12** was issued. The omission of a witness-list, and clearly there was not intended to be one, is most unusual in a Latin charter, and is again reminiscent of Anglo-Norman writs. The charters issued by Bishop Oswald in Latin were always witnessed at least by his *familia*.

12 raises the question of the monastic holding of tithes. According to G. Constable (*Monastic Tithes from their Origin to the Twelfth Century* (Cambridge, 1964), pp. 57–83), the holding of tithes by monasteries, although theoretically indefensible until the eleventh century, was a continental practice in the tenth, and he suggests that English monasteries followed suit. There are only two examples from this period in England (S 1448, dated ?963, and S 1423, dated 1016 × 1023), but both mention the practice as if it were well known. The *Vita Wlsini*, ch. xviii, mentions that Wulfsige gave tithes to the Sherborne monks: 'decimas et dimidiam iugerum carucam que de episcopo fratribus monasterii sui concesserat'. The passage is placed very awkwardly in the middle of a description of church ornaments, and is probably an interpolation. Although the passage claims less for the community than does **12**, it is possible that the two are in some way connected – as with other Sherborne charters, the move from Sherborne to Salisbury may have led the community to strengthen various claims by producing an appropriate document. It is certainly possible that Wulfsige might have bestowed tithes on Sherborne, and **12** may embody the tradition of such a gift, but in terms of diplomatic it is obviously spurious.

13

A writ of Bishop Æthelric to Æthelmær concerning various lands (listed) which should have contributed to the shipscot *to be collected by the bishop, and mentioning a threat to the community's ownership of the estate of Holcombe Rogus, Devon.* [A.D. 1002 × 1014]

D. Paris, Bibl. Nat. lat. 943, 170v: copy, s. xi[in]

Ed.: a. Kemble 708
  b. Brotanek, *Texte*, pp. 33–49
  c. Förster, *Themse*, p. 784
  d. Harmer, *Writs*, no. 63, with translation

Listed: Sawyer 1383

+ Æþelric bisceop gret Æþelmær freondlice 7 ic cyþe þæt me ys þana æt þam scypgesce[ote][a] þus micelys þe mine foregengan on

BISHOP ÆTHELRIC 47

ealles folces[b] gepitnysse æt Nip[.......][c] an æt Bubbancumbe 7 tpa æt Apultune . vii . æt Upcerl[e] [d]v . æt Cliftun[e] . æt Hipis[ce][d] æt Tril tpa æt Þyllon an . æt Buchæmatune . v . æt Dibberpurðe þreo æt Peder[...][e] þære abbuddyssan an . Þises ys ealles þana þreo 7 þritig hida of ðam þrim hund hidun þe oðre bisceopas ær hæfdon into hyra scy[re][f] 7 gif hyt þin pilla þære þu mihtest eaðe gedon Þ ic hyt eal spa hæfde[f] git us man s[ege]ð Þ þe ne moton þæs purðe beon æt Holancumbe þe þe hpilon ær hæfdon[f] þonne þolie i[c] þus miceles ealles 7 ealle[s] þæs þe mine foregengan hæfdon Þ syndon tpa 7 feopertig hida .

[a] I have followed Harmer's supplied readings except as indicated. Her edition notes variant readings from earlier editions   [b] D appears to read polces   [c] Harmer supplies -antune hæfdon. However, the lacuna in the manuscript would accommodate a longer phrase, and several characters are partially legible which cannot be fitted into Harmer's phrase   [d-d] Harmer reads . vi . æt Cliftun[e] æt Hipis[ce fif], but D reads v . fairly clearly, in which case the number to be supplied after Hipis[ce] would be siex or . vi . to make up the bishop's total of missing hides; Kemble and Brotanek read v ., Förster has vi   [e] Several letters are illegible at the end of the line: Harmer has a full discussion of this lacuna in Writs, p. 485   [f] Harmer supplies a full stop and new sentence here

This writ is the only text printed here which does not come from the cartulary. In it Æthelric, bishop of Sherborne, asks for the aid of Æthelmær in restoring the shipscot from certain estates that had been included in the 300 hides allotted for that purpose to each diocese. He adds that he fears that they are also about to lose Holcombe, in which case he will be forty-two hides short. Text and translation have been printed and very fully discussed by F. E. Harmer (*Writs*, no. 63, pp. 266–70 and 482–6). The pontifical in which the writ has been preserved was written between 960 and 990, and was certainly at Sherborne at the beginning of the eleventh century, for it contains a list of Sherborne bishops up to Æthelric, as well as the writ, both copied in hands of s. xi[in] (see Ker, *Catalogue*, no. 364). The writ is on the verso of the last leaf of the manuscript, and is very badly rubbed, particularly at the right-hand margin.

In language and style, with its formal opening, and the shift from third to first person, the writ is undoubtedly authentic. It must have been composed after 1002 (the date of Æthelric's succession) and before the settlement recorded in **14**, which can be dated 1007 × 1014 (see Harmer, *Writs*, p. 268, and below, p. 50). The emphasis on the collection of shipscot, urgent enough to warrant the intervention of the ealdorman, would suggest a date close to 1008 (see ibid. pp. 266–7; see also C. W. Hollister, *Anglo-Saxon Military Institutions on the Eve of the Norman Conquest* (Oxford, 1962), pp. 108–15, for a more detailed account of these arrangements). All the places mentioned in the writ except *Niwantune* and *Holancumbe* have been identified certainly or tentatively as being in Dorset, mostly within the three hundreds assigned to Salisbury for the provision of ships (Sherborne, Yetminster and Beaminster; Harmer, *Writs*, pp. 267 n. 2 and 483–6). *Niwantune*, the most likely place-name expansion of Niw-, has not been satisfactorily identified. Both Maiden Newton and Sturminster Newton have been suggested (ibid. pp. 483–4), but neither falls within the relevant hundreds, and Newton is an extremely common name. The identity of *Holancumbe* is less of a problem. An estate at Holcombe is mentioned in several Sherborne documents, in **11**, where it is assessed at nine hides, as in **13**, and in **14** and **17**, where the hidage is not given. There is no reason to suppose that more than one Holcombe is involved, and the fact that **17** was decided in the Devon court, as well as the connection between **17** and the entry for Holcombe in the Exeter Domesday (see below, p. 60), firmly links the estate with Holcombe Rogus in Devon (the identification suggested by Robertson, *Charters*, p. 448).

Chaplais has argued (1966, pp. 17–18) that as **13** 'consists of a statement regarding the rights of Æthelric's own bishopric, the bishop should be regarded as the beneficiary of the writ rather than as its originator', and suggests that **13** is the written record of an oral declaration, and that no document was in fact sent to Æthelmær. This interpretation is based on his understanding of the writ: 'The royal writ–charter, which is a notification – to the official suitors of the shire-court – of a royal grant of lands and liberties, may have started as a purely oral declaration made by the king or on his behalf, the keeping of a written record of such a declaration being left to the beneficiary.' While not wishing to challenge this general interpretation, I am not sure whether it applies to **13**, which is a complaint and a request for action by the ealdorman: 'This amounts in all to thirty-three hides which are lacking from the three hundred hides that other bishops had for their diocese. And if thou wert willing, thou couldst easily bring it about that I had it in the same way' (Harmer, *Writs*, p. 270). The appeal may have been made orally in the shire-court, although it is not addressed to such a gathering (as are many of the examples printed by Harmer), but it seems an unlikely form to have chosen to preserve as a title to the bishop's rights; one would expect a beneficiary to have formulated a more positive record. There are a few other non-royal writs, such as that addressed by Archbishop Wulfstan to the king, informing him that he has consecrated the archbishop of Canterbury (ibid. no. 27), or that addressed to the shire-court of Berkshire by Bishop Siwerd, then co-adjutor to the archbishop of Canterbury (ibid. no. 3), but these also witness to grants or benefits bestowed. To my mind, **13** is better understood as pointing to a substratum of administrative documents that must have existed in the late pre-Conquest period, letters exchanged between officials concerning immediate affairs, which may have borrowed the format of more weighty documents, but had no particular testatory powers in themselves.

14

The community at Sherborne leases the estate at Holcombe Rogus, Devon, to Edmund Ætheling for his lifetime, in return for twenty pounds. [A.D. 1007 × 1014]

B. BL Add. 46487, 16v: copy, s. xii^med

Ed.: a. Thorpe, *Diplomatarium*, p. 300
   b. Kemble 1302
   c. Robertson, *Charters*, no. 74, with translation

Listed: Sawyer 1422; Finberg, *ECDC* 50

Her sputelaþ on þisum geprite þ Eadmund æþeling bæd þone hyred æt Scireburnan þ he moste ofgan þ land æt Holancumbe ; ða ne dorste se hyred hym þæs pyrnan . ac cpæþon þ hy þæs pel uðon . gyf se cing 7 se bisceop þe heora ealdor pæs þæs geuðon . Ða gepærþ hym . 7 se æþeling 7 se prafost 7 þa yldostan munecas comon to þam cinge 7 him fore cyddon 7 his leafe bædon . 7 þ ærende abead Þulfstan archebisceop . Ða cpæð se cing þ he nolde þæt þ land mid ealle ut aseald pære . ac þ hi elles spilce foreþord þorhton þæt þ land eft in to þære halgan stoþe agifen pære to þam fyrste þe hym ealle gepurde . Ða gepearþ hi þæt se Æþeling sealde þam hyrede . xx . punda pið þam lande ælspa hit stod mid mete 7 mid mannon 7 mid ællon þingon . 7 bruce his dæg . 7 ofer his dæg eode þ land eft in to ðære halgan stoþe mid mete 7 mid mannon 7 mid eallum þingum spa spa hit ðonne pære . Ðises þæs to gepitnesse Þulfstan archebisceop . 7 Lyfing bisceop . 7 Æþelric bisceop . 7 Æþelsie bisceop . 7 Eadric ealdorman . 7 Æðelmer ealdorman . 7 Æþelfand Æþelmeres suna . 7 Leofsuna abbud æt Cernel . 7 Ælfget Hengþes suna . 7 Sipærd . 7 Brihtric reada . 7 ealle þa ildostan ðægnas on Dorsæton . 7 Ealdpine preost . 7 Þulfric preost . 7 Lofþine æþelinges disc þen . 7 Ælfget 7 Ælperd his cnihtas . 7 ealle þege oþre hired men .

This text records the settlement of a dispute between Edmund Ætheling and the Sherborne community over the possession of the estate at Holcombe: it has been printed with a translation and full discussion by Robertson (*Charters*, pp. 146–9 and 392–4). It has also been discussed in reference to **13** by Harmer (*Writs*, pp. 269, 482 and 485–6).

There is no reason to doubt the authenticity of this text. Lawsuits, disputes and leases were very often recorded in the vernacular (see Robertson, *Charters, passim*). They usually followed no fixed pattern, unlike the writ, but often included a witness-list with a distinctly local flavour, as here. The language in **14** is well suited to the early eleventh century, with very little miscopying. In the last phrase, 'þege oþre hiredmen' (for which Robertson reads 'þe geoþre . . .'), **14** is using *þæge* for 'they' or 'those'. Although the form was formerly assumed to come from ON *þeir*, a list of examples collected by Max Förster all come from the south-west (*Zur Geschichte*, p. 75 n. 1), and **14** adds yet another instance from Wessex, giving additional support to D. Hofmann's questioning of the assumption of Scandinavian origin (*Nordisch-englische Lehnbeziehungen der Wikingerzeit*, Bibl. Arnamagnæana xiv (Copenhagen, 1955), pp. 213–14).

The date of the settlement is determined on the one hand by the subscription of Eadric as ealdorman, a title he received in 1007 (*ASC*), and on the other by the appearance of the bishops Lyfing and Æthelric. Lyfing was nominated to Canterbury in 1013 (*ASC*), but although he began to head the list of bishops, signing after Wulfstan, archbishop of York, in charters of 1013 and 1014, he does not seem to have received the pallium until some time in 1014 or 1015, first attesting with the title of archbishop in 1015 (S 934: see Keynes, *Diplomas*, Table 3).[1] Since the list in **14** is so short, and confined (with the exception of Wulfstan) to bishops of the south-west, it is not possible to say whether Lyfing's appearance at the head of the bishops indicates that he had already been nominated to Canterbury or not.

Dr Robertson suggested that **14** should be dated 1012 (*Charters*, p. 393), as she argued that the Bishop Æthelsi[g]e who signs **14** is a mistake for Ælfsige of Winchester, and 1012 would be the only year in which Ælfsige (whose predecessor Æthelwold signs until 1012) and Æthelric of Sherborne could appear together. But the dates of Æthelric's death (his last dated attestation being in 1011) and of the succession of the next bishop of Sherborne, another Æthelsige, are not easily determined. A Bishop Æthelsige of no definite see appears in 1009 (S 922) and 1011 (S 924), and it has been suggested that he held the see of Cornwall between Ealdred and Burhwold (see Sawyer, *Burton*, p. 63, and Keynes, *Diplomas*, p. 264 and n. 64). It is very likely, as Keynes suggests (ibid.), that the Æthelsige who appears in S 922 and 924 is the same man as the Æthelsi[g]e of **14**; and if one accepts his assignment to Cornwall this would give **14** a *terminus ante quem* of 1012, since Burhwold had succeeded there by 1012 (S 929). It would also imply that at Sherborne Bishop Æthelric was succeeded by Æthelsige by the same date, 1012 (S 929). It would be a coincidence that in the short period 1011 × 1012 a Bishop Æthelsige of Cornwall died and another Bishop Æthelsige succeeded to Sherborne, but a quite possible one.

However, there is another possible interpretation of the witness-lists, which is that there was only one Æthelsige. It would be most unlikely that he held Cornwall formally and was then translated to Sherborne

---

[1] There is something questionable about the list in S 934, since it includes the subscription of Ælfhun, bishop of London. Ælfhun's successor to London, Ælfwig, was consecrated at York on 16 February 1014, *ASC* MS D, shortly after Swegn's death. Dr Keynes suggests that this was done before it was realized that Ælfhun might return from Normandy, and that Ælfhun's appearance in S 934 means that he was reinstated. Professor Whitelock, however, implies that Ælfwig held the bishopric from February 1014 (*Bishops of London*, p. 31). Neither bishop appears again until Ælfwig signs in 1018.

upon Æthelric's death: there are no known translations between sees at this period except to the archbishoprics. Dunstan was once thought to have been translated from Worcester to London, but in fact he held both sees in plurality (Whitelock, *Bishops of London*, p. 21). Æthelsige might, however, have been an assistant bishop assigned to the south-west, perhaps more particularly to help Æthelric, in whose company he always signs and whom he succeeded (an arrangement which would parallel Asser's position a century earlier). In this case the date of Æthelric's death and Æthelsige's succession to Sherborne can only be determined by Æthelsige's appearance in **15**, dated 1014, where he is almost certainly bishop of Sherborne, leaving **14** with the same date as its *terminus ante quem*.

It is interesting to note that the Sherborne community is headed in **14** by the *præfost* rather than an abbot: Wulfsige's arrangement was still in effect.

15

King Æthelred grants thirteen (or sixteen) hides (mansiunculae) *at Corscombe, Dorset, to the monastic community at Sherborne.* A.D. 1014

B. BL Add. 46487, 4v–6r: copy, s. xii[med]

Ed.: a. Hearne, *Collections*, pp. 444–5
    b. Kemble 1309
    c. Pierquin, *Recueil*, pt 5, no. 47

Listed: Sawyer 933; Finberg, *ECW* 617

CARTA . XVI . HIDARUM APUD CHORISCVMBAM .[a]

⚜ Annuente Dei patris ineffabili humanę proli clementia . qua annullato primi protoplasti piaculo . ammirabile quoddam mundo decus ęternę consortem maiestatis filium mittere dignatus est . qui terrenę condolens fragilitati custoditę per uirginei pudicitiam flosculi . affatu angelico uirginis claustra subintrans . nouę incarnationis misterium se ostentando dedicauit . ostendens se dictis uerborum . factisque miraculorum quibus deifice pollebat dominum totius mundi creatorem . curans omnium imperanti sermone infirmitates egrotationum . tandem quadrati pro nobis perferens supplicia ligni . iugum hereditarię mortis absumens . diu longeque interdictę reserauit limina portę . Pro cuius inenarrabilis glorię recordatione ego ÆTHELREDVS gratia Dei sullimatus rex et monarchus totius Albionis . ruris quandam particulam tredecim uidelicet ab incolis estimatam mansiunculis . in loco qui dicitur Corigescumb ad cenobiale monasterium quod solicole regionis illius Scireburnan uocitant liberam preter arcem . pontem . expeditionemque in perpetuum ius libenter admodum concedendo . scedulam istam annotare mandaui . Hanc uero prefatam terram . xvi^{cim} . ut prefati sumus cassatis consistentem . quondam Alfpoldus episcopus rege EADGARO consentiente duorum hominum tempus de ipso monasterio accommodauit . sed sequens post illorum uitę terminationem successor Æthelricus uocamine episcopus recte redintegrauit . necessitudineque postea cogente . ob malorum infestationes direptionesque Danorum duci Eadrico traditione perpetuali tribuit . Labentibus denique annorum curriculis ׃ quidam predicti monasterii famulus nomine Wlfgarus . fauente amicorum amminiculo . multo auri argentique pretio . illam terram ab ipso comparauit Eadrico . atque pro animę suę remedio – supra memorato concessit cenobio . Si autem tempore contigerit aliquo – quempiam hominum aliquem libellum ob istarum apicum adnichilationem in palam producere . sit omnimodis ab omnibus hominum ordinibus condempnatus . omnique abolitus industria ueritatis . cuiuscumque regum fuerit tempore perscriptus . Si quis uero contra hoc decretum machinari uel infringere aliquid temptauerit . ni prius digna satisfactione cessauerit aut emendauerit . penalis eum deglutiat tartarorum interitus . Acta uero est presens pergameni scedula . anno dominicę incarnationis millesimo . xiiii^{mo} . indictione uero . xii^{ma} . Istis terminibus supradicta terra circumgyrata est . Ærest on ærne dene . þanone on hornes beorh . ðanone on leas ende . þanone on miclan corf . on miclan cruc middeþearne . þanone andlanges hricges on hlydan pol . þanone on syres^b ford . ðanone on þone hagan . þanone on breopoldesham . ðanone on byssan broc . þanone on lyfdic . ðanone on lyc hagan on grenan peg . þanone on focgan crundel . þanone on trynd leapege . þanone on earna leapege . þanone forð andlanges herpaðes eft on ærne dene . Ista kartula illorum testium testimonio est corroborata . quorum hic uocabula litteris uidentur karaxata .

+ Ego Æðelred gubernator sceptri huius insulę hanc nostri decreti breuiunculam alme crucis notamine muniens roboraui .
+ Ego Þulfstan archiepiscopus   corroboraui .
+ Ego Lyfing episcopus   confirmaui .
+ Ego Ælfsige episcopus   consolidaui .
+ Ego Æðelsige episcopus   conscripsi .
+ Ego Beorhtpald episcopus   conquieui .
Ego Eadric   dux .^{c}
Ego Ælfric   dux .^{d}
Ego Leofpine   dux .

Ego Uhtred	dux .		
Ego Æðelmær	dux .		
Ego Godric	dux .[e]		
Ego Eadmund .	clyto .		
Ego Eadþig .	clyto .		
Ego Eadþeard .	clyto .		
Ego Ælfred .	clyto .[f]		
Ego Beorhtræd	abbas	libenter	annotaui .
Ego Þulfgar	abbas	humiliter	consensi .
Ego Ælfsige	abbas	benigniter	subarraui .
Ego Ælfnoð	abbas	grataner	muniui .
Ego Brihtmær	abbas	clementer	subscripsi .[g]
Ego Ulfkytel .	minister .		
Ego Sigeferð .	minister .		
Ego Godþine .	minister .		
Ego Ælfgar .	minister .		
Ego Odda .	minister .[h]		
Ego Æðelþeard .	minister .		
Ego Þulfgar .	minister .		
Ego Ælfmær .	minister .		
Ego Þulfþerd .	minister .[i]		

[a] CARTA ... CHORICVMBAM . *rubric in* B   [b] *Sic* B; *a miscopying of* fyres: *see* **16**   [c] *First column of subscriptions ends here, bottom of fo.* 5   [d] *Second column of subscriptions ends here, bottom of fo.* 5   [e] *Third column of subscriptions ends here*   [f] *Fourth column of subscriptions ends here*   [g] *Fifth column of subscriptions ends here*   [h] *Sixth column of subscriptions ends here*   [i] *Seventh column of subscriptions ends here*

Both **15** and **16** deal with an estate at Corscombe. **15** records that the land had been leased out by Bishop Ælfwold with King Edgar's consent, and that on its return in the time of Bishop Æthelric the community had been forced by Danish depredations to transfer the estate to Eadric, ealdorman of Mercia. Then Wulfgar, a *famulus* of the monastery, had bought the estate and given it back to the foundation, of which gift **15** is implicitly a royal confirmation.

The proem used in **15** is quite acceptable, its first recorded use being in 987 (Keynes, *Diplomas*, p. 89 and n. 23). The royal style is almost exactly matched by that of S 862 (986): 'Pro cuius inenarrabilis gloriae recordatione, ego Æthelredus gratia dei sublimatus, rex et monarchus totius insulae Brittaniae ...' *Albionis* (see S 841: 982 and S 921: 1009) is an acceptable variant.

Æthelred's charters are well known for their narrative estate histories, and occasionally, as in **15** and S 882 (995), mention Danish ravages. **15** fits well into the narrative group described by Keynes (ibid. pp. 96–7). The dispositive clause is not remarkable, except in its similarity to the equivalent clause in S 934, a charter from Abingdon dated 1015, which shares other features with **15** (see below, and above p. 50 n. 1). The amount of land in the dispositive clause is given as *tredecim* hides, which is to be preferred to the 'XVI' of the rubric and the narrative section. **16**, which covers the same estate with an additional parcel of land, gives the amount as 'XVI', and is probably the source of confusion in **15**.

A warning against the production of other charters is fairly common for the period. **15**'s version is paralleled in S 872 (988), and other such provisions are noted in Keynes, *Diplomas*, pp. 88 and 201 n. 176. The anathema proper is unique to **15**, but is well fitted in style and content to the period. There is little that is noteworthy about the dating clause except for the use of *pergamenum* to describe the substance on which the document was written. *Pergamenum* is not otherwise found in charter usage (except in **20**: see below, p. 69), but it does occur in Ælfric Bata's *Colloquia Difficiliora* (in *Early Scholastic Colloquies*, ed. W. H. Stevenson and W. M. Lindsay, Anecdota Oxoniensia, Mediaeval and Modern Series xv (Oxford, 1929), p. 28), a text almost contemporary with **15**. The royal subscription is similarly unremarkable. However, the whole passage from *Acta uero est* to *muniens roboraui* is found with precisely the same wording, but with a different date and bounds, and with Cnut substituted for Æthelred, in **20**, a Horton charter dated 1033. **20**, which looks in every way like a genuine product of Cnut's reign (see below, p. 73), presumably came into Sherborne's possession in 1122, when the two houses were amalgamated, but it is quite possible that **20**, being a grant to a layman, was drawn up at Sherborne, and that **15** served as a partial model (see Keynes, *Diplomas*, p. 115 n. 108). It is also possible, though perhaps less likely, that the shared passages are not directly related, and merely reflect the well-documented continuity of formulas between the reigns of Æthelred and Cnut (ibid.).

The witness-list in **15** is correct for 1014, and must have been issued after Æthelred's return from Normandy in the spring (*ASC* MSS C, D and E). Lyfing is still signing as bishop, and so had not yet received the pallium. The atheling Athelstan does not sign, which could mean that **15** was issued after his death on 25 June (see Keynes, *Diplomas*, p. 267), or that he was already too ill to attend the court. As Dr Keynes has pointed out (ibid. p. 115 and n. 108), the list is unusual in that the abbots are given verbs of subscription, a practice not found in Æthelred's reign except here and in S 934 (1015: on this list see above, p. 50 n. 1). S 935 (1016) has *consensi* after all the names in its list, bishops, abbots, *duces* and *ministri* alike, but the list has obviously been tampered with, and is not good evidence. A little later S 979 (1023 × 1032) from Athelney has its two abbots signing with *muniui* and *subarraui*, showing that the practice was known in Cnut's reign.

The boundary clause has been discussed by Grundy (1935, pp. 130–5), who has traced it to outline the modern parish of Corscombe, excluding Benville and Tollor Whelme (the latter being included in the expanded bounds of **16**).

16

King Cnut grants sixteen hides (mansae) *at Corscombe, Dorset, to the monastic community at Sherborne.* A.D. 1035

B. BL Add. 46487, 6r–7v: copy, s. xii[med]

Ed.: a. Hearne, *Collections*, pp. 445–6
   b. Kemble 1322

Listed: Sawyer 975; Finberg, *ECW* 623

ALIA CARTA DE CHORISCVMBA .[a]

✠ Omnia qui[b] hic humanis considerantur obtutibus tam preterita tam etiam presentia necnon futura festinando iugiter de die in diem sine ulla dilatione declinant ad ruinam rapidissimoque cursu annorum cum mensibus temporalia siquidem tempora fugitiuis incessanter horis properant ad finem . Quapropter dispensanti domino omnia regnorum terrę regna . ego CNUT rex Anglorum sollicita mente cogitando perscrutaui profuturum ac necessarium esse cum his transitoriis ac minime mansuris diuitiis perpetua atque iugiter perseuerantia cęlorum premia adquirerem . Iccirco tali memoria instructus – atque meorum utique antecessorum roboratus exemplis aliquam terrę partem . id est . xvi . mansas in loco qui uulgari[c] dicitur CORIGESCUMB . famosissime familiarie uenerabilium fratrum in illo sancto ac celeberrimo loco Scireburnensis ęcclesię libenti animo Deo omnipotenti et sanctę MARIĘ semper uirginis . hilari uultu menteque preclara concedo pro redemptione animę meę et criminum meorum absolutione cum omnibus bonis ad mensam cenobialis uitę fratribus Deo seruientibus largitus sum ⁓ quatinus illi famuli Dei apud altissimum Deum semper fundant preces . et cotidie flagitant Deum in psalmodiis et missarum celebrationibus pro facinoribus meis . ut post obitum meum per misericordiam Dei et per eorum sancta suffragia possim ad regna cęlorum peruenire . Et si umquam contigerit quod absit ante uel sero aliquis hominum siue episcopus – siue laicus – hanc meam regalem donationem et elemosinam infringere uel minuere conauerit ⁓ sit a consortio Christi ęcclesię et collegio omnium sanctorum ʻsegregatus ⁓ʼ et ʻinʼ inferni barathrum demergatur . Sit autem prenominata terra libera ab omni mundiali grauedine . exceptis quod omnibus commune est pontis arcisue instauratione . His namque confiniis prefatum rus circumgyrata est .
Ærest on hornes beorg . Of þam beorge on leas ende on corf get . Of þam gete on cruc middeþeardne . þonne of cruc on ðone smalan

hricg . andlang hricges on hlyda pol . Of þam pole andlang streames on fyrs ford . Of þam forda andlang readan hyrstes to hlype gete . Fram hlype gete to þam colpytte . Fram colpette to þam healfan treope . þanone forðrihtes on bropoldes heal . 7 þanon on staford upp ongean stream . Of þam streame on stocchylle . Of stocchylle on fogga crundel eastpeardne . Of þam crundele forð be pyrtruman on þone fulan slo . Of þam slo forð be pyrtruman on brum dun middepearne . Of brum dune on murtes pyll . Of murtes pylle ongean stream on tollor æpylman . Of þam æpylman on cotte dene . Of cotta dene on rupan beorg . Of þam beorge on rigcumb middepeardne . Of rigcumbe on gyrd lea middepeardne . Of gyrd lea on þone stanigan peg . Of þam pege on þone pæter pytt . Of þam pytte on coccelmæres dene . Of þære dene on earne dene . Of earna dene eft on hornes beorg . Scripta est autem hęc singrapha . anno dominicę incarnationis millesimo . xxxv^o . indictione uero . iii . his testibus consentientibus quorum nomina subter prenotata cernentibus clare patescunt.

+ Ego Cnut singularis priuilegii ierarchia preditus rex huius acumen indiculi cum signo sanctę Crucis corroboraui .
+ Ego Ælfgeofu regina hanc largitionem benigniter subarraui .
+ Ego Æþelnoð Doruernensis archiepiscopus consensi et subscripsi .
+ Ego Ælfric Eboracensis archiepiscopus consentaneus fui .
+ Ego Ælfpine   episcopus   humiliter consensi .
+ Ego Br⟨i⟩htpold   episcopus   adquieui .
+ Ego Brihtpine .   episcopus   adsignaui .
+ Ego Godpine .   dux   confirmaui .
+ Ego Leofric .   dux   consolidaui .
+ Ego Ælfpine .   dux   muniui .[d]
+ Ego Ælfpine .   abbas .
+ Ego Æþelpeard .   abbas .
+ Ego Ælfpig .   abbas .
+ Ego Ælfric .   abbas .
+ Ego Ælfpig .   abbas .
+ Ego Æþelpig .   abbas .
+ Ego Stigand .   presbiter .
+ Ego Eadpold .   presbiter .
+ Ego Smelt .   presbiter .
Ego Osgod .   minister .
Ego Toui .   minister .
Ego Ðored .   minister .
Ego Boui .   minister .
Ego Urki .   minister .[e]
Ego Ælfget .   minister .

KING CNUT

Ego Siþerd .	minister .
Ego Þulnoð .	minister .
Ego Þinus .	minister .
Ego Æþelmær .	minister .
Ego Scirpold .	minister .
Ego Odda .	minister .
Ego Ordgar .	minister .
Ego Ælfgar .	minister .
Ego Ecglaf .	minister .
Ego Eadþold .	minister .
Ego Eadþig .	minister .
Ego Godþine brytæl .	minister .
Ego Godric .	minister .[f]

[a]ALIA ... CHORISCVMBA . *rubric in* B   [b]*For* que   [c]*For* uulgariter   [d]*First column of subscriptions ends here*   [e]*Second column of subscriptions ends here*   [f]*Third column of subscriptions ends here.* B *has* m̄ *throughout, expanded here to* minister

16 has nothing in common with **15** except for its concern with Corscombe and a possible relationship with **20**. However, large portions of its text coincide word for word with an Athelney charter, S 979, which has lost its dating clause and boundaries, but whose witnesses limit it to 1023/4 × 1032. The two charters share the same text, with appropriate adjustments of place- and proper names, from the beginning of the proem to the end of the dispositive clause, '... ad regna cęlorum peruenire'. The anathemas are quite distinct, and S 979 lacks mention of liberties and reservations. The charters also employ the same style of regnal subscription, although their witness-lists are not otherwise related.

Diplomatically, the formulas of both are acceptable. The proem is not found elsewhere, but language and sentiments fit well with the period, and S 1010 (1045) has a very similar passage. The dispositive clause is again unique, but similar expressions are found in S 921 (1009) and S 967 (1033). The clause asking for prayers on the king's behalf is unknown elsewhere in Cnut's charters, although he was a pious man. However, a similar request occurs in S 867 (933), and Cnut's charters are strongly influenced by those of his predecessors. The anathema has echoes in both S 967 (1033) and S 976 (1035); but a closer parallel is to be found in S 298 (843), an original charter which might have Sherborne connections (see Chaplais 1965, pp. 57–8).

Many of Cnut's charters have a short immunity and reservation clause like the one in **16**: for instance, S 1384 (1018) and S 957 (1020). The dating clause has only one peculiarity, the use of *singrapha*, which is not found elsewhere in contemporary texts, although it occurs both earlier, in 1005 (S 910), and later, in 1044 and 1046 (S 1004 and 1014). It also appears in two other Sherborne charters, **4** and **8**, the first spurious and the second dubious. The final clause is of a common pattern, and very close in wording to that in S 921 (1009).

The witness-list is very full and completely acceptable for 1035. The appearance of Ælfwine, bishop of Winchester, indicates a date after his accession on 1032 (*ASC* MS E), and Cnut himself died in November 1035. The list is almost identical with, though somewhat shorter than, that of **20**, the Horton charter of two years earlier, and again raises the question of a Sherborne scribe making use of the Horton document after 1122. But it seems extremely unlikely that a twelfth-century scribe would have known enough to omit Ælfmær of Selsey (who died in 1032: see below, pp. 72–3), Brihtwig of Wells (who died in 1033: *ASC*) and Duduc the priest (who succeeded Brihtwig the same year), all of whom sign **20**, and to include Smelt, who only appears in one other charter (S 982) and in Domesday Book.

The textual coincidences with the Athelney charter S 979 are not a problem if one accepts the existence of a royal writing office. There are many such correspondences in the charters of Æthelred's reign, which, as Dr Keynes has shown, are consistent with such an organization (see *Diplomas*, esp. pp. 134–53), and it is reasonable to assume that Cnut adopted the office together with the other instruments of English royal government, since there is considerable continuity in the diplomatic formulas of the two reigns.

16 makes no mention of the earlier Corscombe grant recorded in **15**. Either **15** was not effective in securing the estate for the foundation, or **16** was issued to provide a firm title to the extra piece of land now included in the estate, the area of Tollor Whelme (see the discussion of the bounds by Grundy 1935, pp. 136–9). Thirty years later (TRE) Sherborne had lost Tollor Whelme, and the Corscombe estate was valued at ten hides less one virgate, almost the same amount listed as the original grant from Cuthred in the Faustina A. ii text.

There is one area in which **16** is open to criticism: the insistence with which the grant is made to the monastic community. There may well be a case for arguing that some alteration has been made to the text to emphasize that the land belonged to the monastery rather than to some other party. **15** states that Corscombe had been a Sherborne possession before Wulfsige III's episcopacy, when the estates of the monastery were separated from those of the bishopric (**11**, and see above, p. xxvi). Possibly the question of who owned the Corscombe estate was raised when the episcopal seat was moved to Salisbury, and the text was emended to strengthen the claim of the community (see above, pp. xxiv–xxix, for a discussion of this practice), although Domesday and the subsequent history of the estate show that the monastery retained ownership. Apart from this aspect, the overall appearance of the text and the appositeness of its witness-list strongly suggest that **16** has an authentic base. That both **15** and **16** exist is another point in favour of **16**, since it is difficult to imagine a motive for the later forgery of either, if the other was already available.

17

Agreement between Bishop Ælfwold and the community at Sherborne, and Care, Toki's son, regarding the estate at Holcombe Rogus, Devon. [A.D. 1045 × 1046]

B. BL Add. 46487, 23rv: copy, s. xii^{med}

Ed.: a. Thorpe, *Diplomatarium*, pp. 346–7, with translation
  b. Kemble 1334
  c. Robertson, *Charters*, no. 105, with translation

Listed: Sawyer 1474; Finberg, *ECDC* 62

Her cyð on þisum geþrite hu þa forþord wæron geþorhte on Excestre æt foran Godwine eorle ⁊ æt foran ealra scire betwyx Alfwolde bisceope ⁊ þam hirede æt Scireburnan ⁊ Care Tokies suna æt þam lande æt Holacumbe . Þ þæs þ hi wurdon sehte þæt þa gebroðra eallæ geodon of þam lande butan anum . se is Ulf gehatan þe hyt becweden þæs . Þ he hyt hæbbe his dæg . ⁊ ofer his dæg ga þæt land swa swa hit stent mid mete ⁊ mid mannum unbesacun ⁊ unbefliten in to þam halgan mynstre to Scireburnan . Þyses is to gewitnesse Godwine eorl . ⁊ Alfwold bisceop on Dorsæton . ⁊ Lyfing bisceop be norðan . ⁊ Ælfwine abbud on Bucfæsten . ⁊ Sihtric abbud on Tæfingstoce . ⁊ Odda . ⁊ Ælfric his broðor . ⁊ Ordgar ⁊ his twegen gebroðra . Ælfgær ⁊ Escbern . ⁊ Dodda cild . ⁊ Alon . ⁊ Æþelmær Cola sunu . ⁊ Osmær . ⁊ Leofwine æt Exon . ⁊ Ælfweard Alfwoldes sunu . ⁊ Wiking ⁊ Ælfgær æt Mynheafdon . ⁊ Wulfweard æt Winesham . ⁊ Hunewine Heca sunu . ⁊ Ælfwig æt Hægdune . ⁊ Godman preost . ⁊ Lutsige on Wiht ;· ⁊ se þe þis awendan wylle oþþe ætbredan wænce wære halgan stowe ." si he awend fram Gode on domes dæg ⁊ fram eallum his halgum . ⁊ si he besenct on middan þam weallendan bryne helle wites mid Iudan Cristes læwan a ecelice fordemed . butan^a he hit her ær þe deoppor gebete ;· Þyssera gewrita syndon twa . an ys æt Scireburnan . ⁊ þæt oþer æt Cridiantune . sprecaþ buta an : –

^abuton *altered to* butan

This, like **14**, has been printed with translation and full discussion by Robertson (*Charters*, pp. 200–3 and 447–9), and it deals with the estate at Holcombe which the bishop and community of Sherborne were struggling to retain in **13** and **14**. Presumably the outcome of **14** was that Holcombe passed with the rest of Edmund's estates to his successor Cnut, who rewarded one of his followers with the estate, either outright or in leasehold: perhaps the latter, since in **17** Sherborne's ultimate ownership is apparently not questioned. The names of those involved, Care, Toki and Ulf, are Scandinavian. Toki may well be the same man who as *minister* witnesses S 971 and 963 (1031) and **21** (1042), all of which concern lands in Devon, and possibly also witnesses S 967 (1033), an Abingdon charter. It is not clear whether Care was one of the brothers on the estate, but it looks probable, in which case Ulf was also Toki's son, and since Ulf had been willed the estate, Toki must have died some time after 1042. **17** certainly sounds like an inheritance wrangle. As Robertson has pointed out (*Charters*, p. 448), the Exeter Domesday originally recorded the estate at Holcombe Rogus as held TRE by Ulf, presumably the same man as the Ulf named in **17**. At some time during or after the Conquest Sherborne must finally have lost possession of the estate, which by 1086 was in Norman hands (DB, Exon. i. 299 v).

17 states that two copies of the agreement were made, one being kept at Sherborne and one at Crediton. This supports Robertson's argument that it was Holcombe in Devon that was in question, as does the fact that the matter was decided in the Devon court (see also Harmer, *Writs*, pp. 485–6).

Linguistically **17** is very acceptable as mid-eleventh-century Old English. It consistently preserves *Ælf-* before a front vowel (*Ælf-ric*), and goes to *Alf-* before a back vowel (*Alf-wold*). The only passage resembling normal diplomatic in **17** is the anathema, which is a free translation of a Latin formula found in S 1014 (1046) and S 1058 (1052 × 1053). The witness-list looks like an authentic record of a shire court, with many local names: for example, Ælfwine, abbot of Buckfast (whose only other appearance is in Domesday Book), Leofric of Exeter, Ælfgar of Minehead and Wulfwerd of Winsham. Lyfing, although called bishop *be northan*, is more likely to have been present in his capacity as bishop of Crediton and Cornwall, which sees he held in plurality with Worcester. Robertson (*Charters*, p. 449), suggests that 'Lutsige' of Wight is a mistake for 'Wulfsige', but a version of the same name appears in a Hampshire charter a few years later as 'Lutrise' (S 1024, dated 1053: see Finberg, *ECW* 170). The Anglo-Saxon minuscule *s* and *g* could easily be misread as *r* and *s* by someone unfamiliar with the script, but it much less likely that two scribes should independently misread 'Wulf-' as 'Lut-'. The prefix is very uncommon, but Lutting occurs in two other texts: p. 158, line 171 in the *Liber Vitae* of Lindisfarne, ed. H. Sweet in *The Oldest English Texts*, EETS 73 (London, 1885); and p. 17 in the *Liber Eliensis*, ed. E. O. Blake, Camden Third Series xcii (London, 1962); and the same element appears in *Luttes crundele*, in the bounds of a Somerset estate in S 265 (757 × 758).

The date of **17** is determined by the appearances of Ælfwold, bishop of Sherborne, who succeeded to the bishopric in 1045 or 1046 (his predecessor witnesses for the last time in 1045: S 1007, 1008 and 1012; and Ælfwold first appears in 1046: S 1014), and of Lyfing, who died on 23 March 1046 (*ASC*). Robertson's objection to the appearance of Sihtric, abbot of Tavistock, has been answered by Knowles (*HRH*, p. 72).

There is no reason to suspect **17** of being anything other than what it seems. By the time the cartulary was compiled the estate had been lost; it is not mentioned in the 1126 papal letter nor in Faustina A. ii. The community, however, obviously wished to remember what they had once possessed and fought for; and they may also have retained some hope of making future use of the document.

CHARTERS OF HORTON ABBEY

18

King Eadwig grants fifteen and a half hides (mansae) *at Ipplepen, Dainton and Abbotskerswell, Devon, to Æthelhild,* nobilis femina. A.D. 956

B. BL Add. 46487, 30rv: copy, s. xii[med]

Ed.: Birch 952

Listed: Sawyer 601; Finberg, *ECDC* 32

Ðis is seo boc to Iplanpenne 7 to Doddingtune 7 to Cærspylle ðe Eadƿig kyning gebocode Æþelhilde on ece yrfe: –[a]

☩ In nomine domini nostri Iesu Christi. Igitur apostolicis dictis nos congrue parere oportet . qua in epistola nos pie monet ꝫ ut inquit ipse suprema uoce amet proximum qui diligit Deum . et hoc itaque ab utriusque sexu propagatum esse perhibetur . Propter quod ego EADƿIG gentis Anglorum ceterarumque per gyrum nationum basileus . cuidam nobili feminę uocitatę nomine Æþelhild . xv . mansas[b] et dimidiam duobus in locis illic ubi uulgariter dicitur Iplanpen 7 æt Doddintune 7 æt Cærspylle perpetualiter concedo . Amodo cum securitate nostrum donum uita comite sibi usurpet . se obeunte cuicunque uoluerit in carisma perenne impertiat . cum campis – pascuis – pratis – siluis . Hęc tellus a cuncto sit immunis seruitio – nisi pontis – et arcis – et expeditionis iuuamine . Si quis uero minuerit hanc meam donationem . sciat se reum omni hora uitę sue et tenebrosum tartarum non euadere . Istis terminis ambitur predicta tellus . Ðys synd þa landgemæra to Ipelanpænne 7 to Doddingtune 7 to Cærspylle . Of mæscumbe on landscore an horsa tor . Þonon on streame oþ [c]eoþ of eoþ on pen[c] . Of pænne on riht landscore on lyttlan tor . Þonon on landscore to langan dene . Þonon an landscore to þære linde . Of þære linde to þam beorge . Þonon to odding torre on landscore to mædercumbe . 7 Cærspellan landscore on þa lace . of þære lace on spiþredes stan . Þonon on herepað to poggan pylle . Þonon on

herpað on þa rode . of þære rode on herpað oþ þa laca . Þonne up be streame on mædercumbe on þa pic . þe þarto hyrþ . 7 æt bitelanpyrþe an hiþisce . 7 æt bromleage an hiþisce .
Acta est autem hęc donatio anno ab incarnatione domini nostri Iesu Christi . dcccc . lvi . indictione . xiiii .

+ Ego Eadpig rex Anglorum indeclinabiliter concessi .
+ Ego Eadgar eiusdem regis frater consensi .
+ Ego Oda archiepiscopus cum signo Sanctę Crucis roboraui .
+ Ego Ælfsinus presul sigillum agię Crucis impressi .
+ Ego Cenpold   episcopus   consignaui .
+ Ego Oscytel   episcopus   subscripsi .
+ Ego Osulf .   episcopus   confirmaui .
+ Ego Byrhthelm   episcopus .   conclusi .
+ Ego Æþelstan .   dux .
+ Ego Eadmund   dux .
+ Ego Byrhtþerþ[d]   dux .
+ Ego Aþelmund   dux .[e]
+ Ego Ælfere   dux .
+ Ego Æþelsige   dux .
+ Ego Ælfsige   minister .
+ Ego Þulfric   minister .
+ Ego Æþeleard   minister .
+ Ego Ælfheah .   minister .
+ Ego Ælfgar .   minister .
+ Ego Byrhtfer⟨t⟩h .   minister .[f]

[a]Ðis ... yrfe: – *rubric in* B   [b]B *reads* mensis   [c...c]*Written in one word in* B   [d]*For* Byrhtferþ   [e]*First column of subscriptions ends here*   [f]*Second column of subscriptions ends here.* B *has* m̄i *throughout, expanded here to* minister

This is the earliest of the Horton charters, a grant by King Eadwig of lands in Devon to the noble woman Æthelhild. The text and witness-list show no suspicious features. The charter belongs to the second group of diplomas issued by Eadwig in 956, perhaps around 13 February (see Keynes, *Diplomas*, pp. 54–6 and Fig. 4). The invocation is a common type, found both alone and followed, as here, by a pious reflection. Close examples are S 573 (955 × 956) and S 628 (956). The proem does not appear elsewhere in Eadwig's charters (other than in S 600), but this is not unusual. The royal style is similar in vocabulary to the formulas found in S 611 (956) and several others. The clauses of disposition and conditions of tenure are all found in contemporary charters (e.g. in S 590, 592, 624 and 636). The anathema is found almost word for word in many of Eadwig's charters (ibid. p. 64 and n. 117), as is the dating clause (e.g. S 591 and 618). The witness-list, Keynes's criterion for assigning the diploma to Group Two (ibid. Fig. 4), is completely correct for 956.

18 is a grant to a lay person, with no mention of a subsequent regrant to an ecclesiastical body, which is very much in its favour, since to forge a charter in this form would be of little gain to the church holding or claiming the lands concerned. In fact the only question raised by **18** is its correspondence word for word with S 600, with which it forms a subgroup (ibid. p. 64). S 600 is another grant made by Eadwig to Æthelhild, this time of twenty hides at Droxford in Hampshire, preserved in the cartulary of the Old Minster, Winchester. The two texts are identical except for odd words and the place-names and bounds. The witnesses occur in identical order, although S 600 has a duplicate entry for Bishop Cenwald, and **18** has omitted the second Ealdorman Æthelstan, missing from several Group Two diplomas, and the second Ælfheah *minister*, also an intermittent witness in this group. The identical formulas and lists show that a single draftsman was responsible for both texts (ibid. p. 64). Presumably the grants were made to Æthelhild at that particular session of the court, and two charters were issued because the estates concerned lay in two different counties, and dispersal of the estates at a later date would be simplified by separate title-deeds. It is possible that there was a general rule of thumb that estates in different counties should be dealt with in different charters; there are other such pairs in S 597 and 588, grants of lands in Oxfordshire and Warwickshire respectively made to Ælfhere *comes*, and S 612 and 613, grants to Beornric of estates in Wiltshire and Hampshire (although S 720 may be an exception, depending on whether one places *Ernlege* in Warwickshire or Worcestershire).

Dr Keynes has pointed out to me that **18**, like all the Horton charters preserved in the cartulary, is introduced by a vernacular rubric which is very probably a copy of an endorsement of the original document. Translated, the rubric reads: 'This is the title-deed to Ipplepen and Dainton and [Abbots]kerswell which King Eadwig granted by charter to Æthelhild in perpetual inheritance.' It is not known who Æthelhild was, although she must have been of good family to have been called *nobilis*. She may well be the Æthelhild mentioned in S 1376, another charter from the Winchester cartulary, dated 975 × 978. The woman who is mentioned in and who witnesses S 1376 was the widow of Ælfsige, and the mother of Ælfwine, who was conducting the transaction; she is probably to be identified with the Æthelhild commemorated in the New Minster *Liber Vitae* (ed. Birch, p. 58), the wife of the *comes* Ælfsige. There is no mention of a husband in **18** and S 600, and indeed the proem would be more appropriately addressed to a single person, but Æthelhild could either already have been widowed in 956, or alternatively have married and been widowed between 956 and 975 × 978. It seems a possible identification. There is an Ælfsige who appears in several charters between 946 × 947 and 956, called variously *miles* (S 544 and 556), *discifer* (S 591) and *meus fidelis* (S 597), but whether any of these are connected with Æthelhild can only be conjecture.

The bounds contained in this charter have been discussed briefly by F. Rose-Troup in 'Anglo-Saxon Charters of Devonshire' (*D&CN&Q* xvii (1932–3), pp. 55–8). The identification of *Cærswylle* with Abbotskerswell is confirmed by the occurrence of *mædercumbe* and *woggan wylle* in the bounds, recognizable as Maddercombe and Ogwell in Abbotskerswell. *Ipelanpænne* and *Doddingtune* are clearly Ipplepen and Dainton, but where in any of these places the actual lands lay cannot be determined by the bounds. *Bitelanwyrth* is identified in *PN Devon* (i. 526) as Bittleford in Widdecombe, and the same source suggests Brimley in Bovey Tracy for *Bromleage* (i. 467), although this is not so secure an identification, as it is a common formation, and there are at least two other Brimleys in Devon. Only the estate at Abbotskerswell is mentioned in Domesday Book (Exon. i. 184r) as belonging to Horton, with an assessment of one and a half hides, although both the papal privileges mention that Sherborne (by then joined with Horton) claimed land there and at Brimley. It is quite possible, considering its position at the end of the boundary clause, that the passage '7 æt Bitelanpyrþe an hipisce . 7 æt Bromleage an hipisce .' was not part of the original charter text, but was added later when these estates were acquired.

19

King Æthelred grants one hide (mansa) *at Seaton, Devon, to Eadsige,* minister. A.D. 1005

B. BL Add. 46487, 27v–29r: copy, s. xii[med]

Ed.: a. Kemble 1301
    b. Pierquin, *Recueil*, pt 5, no. 43

Listed: Sawyer 910; Finberg, *ECDC* 48

Ðis is þære anre higde boc æt Fleote þe Æðelred cingc gebocod Eadsige his gerefan on ece yrfe .[a]

✠ In nomine cosmi saluatoris et humani generis redemptoris Iesu Christi domini nostri qui solus cum patre et spiritu sancto regnum tenet inmortale . Ego Æðelred diuina dispositione gentis Angligenę et diuersarum nationum industrius rex – uni meo ministro nuncupato uocamine Eadsige . unam mansam perpetualiter concedo . in illo loco ubi anglica appellatione dicitur æt Fleote . pro eius placabili pretio . id est . c . mancusas[b] in auro purissimo . [c]en in suo uiuere[c] cum prosperitate semper istum exenium obtineat . et post se cum perpetuo cyrographo cui uoluerit ęternaliter derelinquat . Sit autem predictum rus liberum ab omni mundiali obstaculo cum omnibus quę ad ipsum locum pertinere dinoscuntur . tam in magnis quam in minimis rebus . campis . pascuis . pratis . siluis . sine expeditione . et pontis . arcisue instructione . Si quis uero tirannica inflatus potestate infringere temptauerit huius nostri decreti cyrographum ׃ sciat se

coram Christo et angelis eius in tremendo examine rationem redditurum . nisi hic prius emendare satagerit . Istis terminis ambitur predicta tellus .
Þis syndon þære anre higde landgemæro to Fleote . Ærest up of þære sæ on scypcumb . up þonne on scypcumb on þæne bydel æcer suðepeardne . Of þam bydel æcere up on Þ slæd besuðan dyrnan leage on gerihte to berhamme . up þanon on berham suðepeardne on þæne hricgpeg . Of þam hricgpege . norþ on readan peg ufepeardne . Of readan pege norþ andlang hricges on bitun liege . Of bitun liege pest andlang peges on gerihte to crymelhamme up on þa dic on ðone herpoð . pest þonne on herpoð of cumbpeges heafod . adune þænne on cumbpeg on horegan ford . of horegan forde adune on strem on nyðeran stanford . of nyðeran stanforda norð be þæs yrþlandes foton on gerihte to litegan hlosstede . of litegan hlosstede on hreodmæde lace . of hreodmæde lace on Axan . of Axan eft ut on sæ . 7 seo mædrædon beniðan dic betpeonan cealdan lace 7 cullig . Anno dominicę incarnationis millesimo quinto . scripta est huius munificentię singrapha his testibus consentientibus quorum nomina inferius karaxata esse uidentur .

+ Ego Æðelredus totius Brittannię monarchus meę largitatis donum agie Crucis taumate roboraui .
+ Ego Æðelstanus eiusdem regis filius plaudens consensi .
+ Ego Ecgbriht   clito   testis   fui .
+ Ego Eadmund   clito   testimonium   adhibui .
+ Ego Eadric   clito   non   abnui .
+ Ego Eadpig   clito   non   rennui .
+ Ego Eadgar   clito   non   negaui .
+ Ego Eadpeard   clito   faui .
+ Ego Ælfgyfu regina stabilitatem testimonii confirmaui .
+ Ego Ælfricus Dorobernensis ęcclesię archiepiscopus signo Sanctę Crucis subscripsi .
+ Ego Þulfstan Eboracensis ęcclesię archipresul consignaui .
+ Ego Ælfheah .   episcopus .   roboraui .
+ Ego Aþulf .   episcopus .   consignaui .
+ Ego Ordbyrht .   episcopus   adquieui .
+ Ego Lyfing .   episcopus   subscripsi .
+ Ego Godpine .   episcopus   non rennui .
+ Ego Æþelric .   episcopus   confirmaui .
+ Ego Ælfhelm .   episcopus   conclusi .
+ Ego Ælfhun .   episcopus   testis fui .
+ Ego Alfpold .   episcopus   non negaui .[d]
+ Ego Germanus .   abbas .

+ Ego Ælfsige .   abbas .
+ Ego Þulfgar .   abbas .
+ Ego Kenulf .   abbas .
+ Ego Eadnoþ .   abbas .
+ Ego Ælfþeard .   abbas .
+ Ego Byrhtþold .   abbas .
+ Ego Æluere .   abbas .
+ Ego Godeman .   abbas .[e]
+ Ego Ælfric .   dux .
+ Ego Ælfhelm .   dux .
+ Ego Leofþine .   dux .
+ Ego Æðelmær .   minister .
+ Ego Ordulf .   minister .
+ Ego Þulfgeat .   minister .
+ Ego Þulfheah .   minister .
+ Ego Ulfcytel .   minister .
+ Ego Eadric .   minister .
+ Ego Æðelric .   minister .
+ Ego Sigþerd .   minister .
+ Ego Sigered .   minister .
+ Ego Leofþine .   minister .[f]
+ Ego Æðelmær .   minister .
+ Ego Byrhtric .   minister .
+ Ego Aðelþold .   minister .
+ Ego Leofþine .   minister .
+ Ego Æþelþeard .   minister .
+ Ego Æþelþine .   minister .
+ Ego Godric .   minister .
+ Ego Ælfgar .   minister .
+ Ego Æþelþeard .   minister .
+ Ego Leofric .   minister .
+ Ego Þulfgar .   minister .
+ Ego Byrhtric .   minister .
+ Ego Leofnoð .   minister .[g]

[a] Ðis is ... yrfe . *rubric in B*   [b] B *reads* mancuras *in error*   [c...c] *Text corrupt; it should have here a phrase such as* quamdiu vivat *or* ut ipse vita comite   [d] *First column of subscriptions ends here, bottom of 28v*   [e] *Second column of subscriptions ends here, bottom of 28v*   [f] *Third column of subscriptions ends here*   [g] *Fourth column of subscriptions ends here*

This charter, also a grant to a lay person, is short and unelaborate compared with many of the same decade (see Keynes, *Diplomas*, pp. 95–8). It opens with a short invocation echoed, though not exactly, S 893 (999), and partially in S 882 (995); and there are others equally brief. The royal style is also unique in this form, but it employs the flamboyant vocabulary of the period, and S 851 (983) and S 938 (undated) use comparable expressions.

The practice of mentioning the price paid for the land is first found, in Æthelred's reign, in 1002 (ibid. pp. 107–8), and continued intermittently for the rest of the reign (ibid. p. 108 n. 72). The clause outlining the liberties of the estate is very close to that in S 858 (985), and other related formulas can be found in S 864 (987) and S 882 (995), although it derives ultimately from a mid-tenth-century formula (ibid. p. 114 n. 102). The anathema also has an earlier base (ibid. pp. 64–5 and n. 119), and does not appear in this form elsewhere in Æthelred's charters, although S 881 (998) is fairly close. The dating clause of S 881 also resembles that in **19**, although S 843 and S 892 (998) come even closer, both using the distinctive phrase *munificentiae singrapha* and omitting the indiction, as does **19** (see *Crawford Charters*, p. 117 n. 46, and Keynes, *Diplomas*, p. 232).

The witness-list opens with a royal subscription that is not duplicated in this reign, although there are many approximations to it in contemporary charters. The closest is again in S 892, and S 887 (996) and S 907 (1014) also contain similar phrases. The exact phrase is found in an early charter of Cnut, S 977 (1021). The elaborated forms of attestation used for the nobility of church and state are a fairly common feature of Æthelred's charters: other examples with comparable vocabulary include S 883, 902 and 916, but S 911 (which like **19** was issued in 1005) is particularly close.

The list itself is a very full one, and is compatible with the date. Episcopal signatures would limit it to the years between 1002 (Ælfhelm of Dorchester succeeded then, as did Æthelric of Sherborne and Wulfstan of York) and 1005, when Archbishop Ælfric died (*ASC*). The atheling Ecgbriht does not sign after 1005, and is presumed to have died shortly thereafter, whereas Edward's signatures first appear in that year (Keynes, *Diplomas*, Table 1). 'Eadric clito' must be a mistake for Eadred, who usually signs in this position. The list in **19** clearly belongs to the period before the changes that took place in the composition of the *witan* in 1005/6 (ibid. pp. 209–13), since it includes Ælfhelm *dux* and Wulfgeat and Wulfheah *ministri*, the unfortunates whose downfall is recorded in the *Anglo-Saxon Chronicle* (s.a. 1006).

Eadsige the beneficiary does not appear among the witnesses of Æthelred's charters. In the rubric he is called a reeve, and in *ASC* MS A, s.a. 1001, 'Eadsige, the king's reeve', together with 'Kola, the king's high-reeve', led an English army against the Danes at Pinhoe, Devon. The English were put to flight, and many fell, but it is possible that Eadsige survived. However, reeves are frequently-mentioned during this period (Keynes, *Diplomas*, p. 198 n. 165), and the names may be just a coincidence.

The land conveyed by **19** was at least partly in Horton's possession by 1066, when Domesday Book records that the church held half a hide at *Fleote* (Seaton). The bounds have been traced by J. B. Davidson ('Seaton before the Conquest', *Transactions of the Devonshire Association* xvii (1885), pp. 193–8), who found that they outlined the eastern half of

Seaton parish, including a strip of meadowland in the neighbouring parish of Colyton (both in Devon). Seaton is a comparatively new name for the area, not appearing until 1126 (in the papal privilege of that year). By 1086 the land was gelded at half a hide, a favourable assessment which Davidson suggested was arranged by Ordulf, perhaps as the founder of Horton. By 1066 Horton had also acquired the western half of the parish, which included the village of Beer, also gelded at half a hide. In the privilege of 1126 Seaton and Beer are named, and the papal text of 1146 includes Beer, Seaton and their saltworks, as well as the fisheries of Fleet and Beer.

The charter as a whole presents an authentic appearance. It contains no discernible anachronisms or other suspicious features, and it shows no particular similarities with the two other Sherborne charters of Æthelred's reign. As with **18** and the other Horton charters except **22**, there has been no attempt to write in an ecclesiastical beneficiary, and the rubric was very probably copied from an endorsement on the original charter. Translated it reads: 'This the title-deed to one hide at Fleet which King Æthelred granted by charter to Eadsige his reeve in perpetual inheritance.'

20

King Cnut grants seven hides (mansae) *at Horton, Dorset, to Bovi, minister.* A.D. 1033

B. BL Add. 46487, 26r–27v: copy, s. xii^{med}

Ed.: a. Kemble 1318
  b. Pierquin, *Recueil*, pt 5, no. 50

Listed: Sawyer 969; Finberg, *ECW* 622

Þis ys þæra . vii . hida land boc to Hortune þe Cnut cining gebocode Bouige hys huskarle on ece yrfe . Nu sputelaþ hit her þæt Boui mid his scette aperede þæt land fore scet . on ealre scire gepitnysse .[a]

✠ Regnante imperpetuum Deo et domino nostro Iesu Christo . Cum cuius imperio hic labentis seculi prosperitas in aduersis successibus sedulo permixta et conturbata cernuntur . et omnia uisibilia atque desiderabilia ornamenta huius mundi ab ipsis amatoribus cotidie transeunt . ideo beati quique ac sapientes cum his fugitiuis seculi diuitiis ęterna et iugiter permansura gaudia cęlestis patrię magnopere adipisci properant . Iccirco ego Cnut rex Anglorum ceterarumque gentium in circuitu persistentium gubernator et rector . quandam mei proprii iuris portionem . vii . terrę mansas illo in loco ubi iamdudum solicole illius regionis nomen imposuerunt HORTVN – meo fideli ministro quem noti atque affines BOVI appellare solent . confirmo hereditatem . quatinus ille bene perfruatur ac perpetualiter possideat . quamdiu Deus per suam mirabilem mis⟨eri⟩cordiam uitam illi et uitalem spiritum concedere uoluerit . deinde namque sibi succedenti cuicumque libuerit cleronomi iure hereditario derelinquat . ceu supra diximus in ęternam hereditatem . Maneat igitur hoc nostrum immobile donum ęterna libertate iocundum . cum uniuersis quę rite ad eundem locum pertinere dinoscuntur . tam in magnis quam in modicis rebus – in campis – pascuis – pratis – siluis – riuulis – aquarumque cursibus . excepto quod communi labore quod omnibus liquide patet . uidelicet expeditione pontis constructione . arcisue munitione . Si autem tempore contigerit aliquo quempiam hominum aliquem antiquiorem librum contra istius libri libertatem producere ׃ pro nichilo computetur . Si quis autem tetri demonis instinctu hoc nostrum decretum infringere uoluerit ׃ sit ipse a sanctę Dei ęcclesię consortio separatus . et infernalibus ęternaliter flammis cum Iuda Christi proditore cruciandus . nisi hic prius digna satisfactione penituerit . quod contra nostrum deliquit decretum . Acta uero est presens pargameni[b] scedula . anno dominicę incarnationis . millesimo . xxxiii . indictione uero . i . Istis terminis supradicta terra circumgirata est . Ærest cealdan broc scyt on þinburnan . Of þinburnan on mapoldor lea middeþeardne . Of mapoldor lea innan east lea . Vt of east lea on þæt[c] slæget . Of þam slægete[d] on suð beara suþeþeardne[e] . Of suð beara on linleaga mor . Of linleage more . on þa gemearcodan lindan . Of þære gemearcodan lindan on bisic[f] garan be þære norh ecge . Of bisic garan on þone norþ heal . Of þam norþ heale . on blacan dune . Of þære dune on ciddes beara . Of ciddes beara on þa haran[g] stanas . Of þam haran stanon andlang blacan dune ecge norþ on þa haran apoldran . Of þære apoldran suþ on þone mere on þona haran piðig . Of þam piðige pest on pænecan pyrþ on þa beorgas . Of pænecan pyrðe on suþ heal suþeþeardne . Of þan heale on holan broc . Of þan broce to rupan leges gete . Of þan gete on hyrn . Vp andlang hyrn ׃ on þone mearc hagan . Of þam hagan . on þone readan þeg . Of þam þege . on heara þulfrices gemære . Of þam landgemære andlang streames eft on cealdan broc . Ista cartula illorum testium testimonio est corroborata . quorum his uocabula litteris uidentur caraxata : –

+ Ego CNVT gubernator sceptri huius insulę hanc nostri decreti breuiunculam alme Crucis notamine muniens roboraui .
+ Ego Æþelnoð Doruernensis archiepiscopus consensi et subscripsi .
+ Ego Ælfric archiepiscopus corroboraui .

+ Ego Brihtƿold episcopus confirmaui .[h]
+ Ego Ælfƿine   episcopus .
+ Ego Brihtƿig .   episcopus .
+ Ego Ælfmær   episcopus .
+ Ego Lyfing   episcopus .
+ Ego Brih⟨t⟩pine .   episcopus .
+ Ego Æþelƿeard .   abbas .
+ Ego Ælƿig   abbas .
+ Ego Ælfric   abbas .
+ Ego Ælfpig .   abbas .
+ Ego Æþelƿig .   abbas .
+ Ego Godƿine .   dux .
+ Ego Leofric .   dux .
+ Ego Ælfƿine .   dux .
+ Ego Duduc .   presbiter .
+ Ego Eadƿold .   presbiter .
+ Ego Stigand .   presbiter .
+ Ego Godƿine .   presbiter .
+ Ego Ƿulfnoþ .   presbiter .
+ Ego Þored   minister .[i]
+ Ego Osgod .   minister .
+ Ego Toui .   minister .
+ Ego Urki .   minister .
+ Ego Ælfgar .   minister .
+ Ego Ælfget .   minister .
+ Ego Æþelmær .   minister .
+ Ego Siƿerd .   minister .
+ Ego Ƿulfnoð .   minister .
+ Ego Ƿinus .   minister .
+ Ego Scirƿold .   minister .
+ Ego Eadƿold .   minister .
+ Ego Ælfgar .   minister .
+ Ego Ƿihtnoþ .   minister .
+ Ego Ecglaf .   minister .
+ Ego Odda .   minister .
+ Ego Ordgær .   minister .
+ Ego Æþelmær .   minister .
+ Ego Leofric .   minister .
+ Ego Eadƿig .   minister .[k]

[a]Þis ys . . . geƿitnysse . *rubric in* B   [b]*For* pergameni   [c]*Interlineated* lin læge mor   [d]*Interlineated in* acs hirste   [e]*Interlineated in* þa þiƿgas   [f]*For* biric   [g]*Interlineated on* þa hara apolþore   [h]*First column of subscriptions ends here, bottom of 27v*   [i]*Second column of subscriptions ends here*   [k]*Third column of subscriptions ends here*

The commentary on this charter follows **20A**

20A

A Middle English version of the bounds of the estate at Horton, Dorset, conveyed to Bovi in **20**

B. BL Add. 46487, 24v–25r: copy, s. xiii^2

Listed: Sawyer 969

Istis terminis supradicta terra circumgirata est .[a]

Erest chealde brok scyt on Winborne . Of Winborne on mapeldure lea midewarde . þanne on east lea . vt of east lea linlege mor on þat slea3et . Of þan slea3iet on suth beare in okhurste suthward on þe wiþe3es . Of suth beare on linle3e mor . Vt of linle3e more on þe imerekede linde . Of þan imerekede linde on burches gore bi þare norþh egge . Of burches gore ⸱ on þane north heale . Of þan norþ hele on blake dune . Of þare dune ⸱ on cheddes bere . Of cheddes bere ⸱ on þe hore stones on þe hore apeldore . Of þan hore stonen ⸱ andlang blake dun egge north on þe hore apeldore . Of þare apeldore ⸱ suth on þane mere on þane hore wiþeh . Of þan hore wiþe3e ⸱ [b]west on wiþehlake heafde to wiþehlakeuorde . Sutþe to weggeleawe norþ ende . and suthe in to þare dich to kinges crofte in þat water þwrthouer to walerondes crofte . And sutþe under gorbuerge þat slad in to sluth an suthe anlang sluth in to þane sondieuord . and suthe þane hole wei in to trockes dich . of trockes dich in þat water anlang watere to ballardesham . sutþe to þan lange þorne . an suthe in þane okstub . an suth in þe hwite croftes dich . and suthe to ones þorne . and swo uorþ þa 3estrode to kinges hei3es hurne[b] . swo on penecan pprþe on þe buereges . of penece ppurþe ⸱ on sut heal suthward of þan heale on hole broc . of þan broke to ruan leges 3ete . of þan 3ete on hurn . up andlang hurne on þan mer ha3an . of þan ha3an ⸱ on þane rede wei . of þan weie on hore wluriches imere . of þan londimere anlang streames eft on chealden brok .

[a] Istis ... est . *rubric in* B   [b–b] *This passage is not found in the earlier version of the bounds*

20 is the first of the Horton charters entered in the cartulary, following the Latin charter of Henry I, in which Sherborne and Horton are amalgamated. It is introduced by a vernacular rubric, which falls into two parts. The first has the form of a straightforward endorsement, like those introducing the other Horton charters: 'This is the title-deed to Horton which King Cnut granted by charter to Bovi his housecarl in perpetual inheritance.' The second part ('Nu sputelaþ hit ... on ealre scire gepitnysse') is a formal statement that reads like the précis of a vernacular memorandum of the sort that recorded such matters as the settlements of disputes at shire meetings (see **14**, and many other examples in Robertson, *Charters*; and see also Harmer, *Writs*, pp. 449 and 459, on *sputelung*). Some of the language is obscure, but a possible translation would be: 'Now it is declared here [in this document] that Bovi defended that land successfully at law with his money in payment of tax due on it, the whole shire being witness.' (Both Professor Whitelock and Professor Stanley agree that this is the most likely meaning.) Whether this payment was part of his taking possession of the estate, or whether there had been some dispute over the taxes, is unclear. But certainly the note implies that he was accepted as the legal owner, which is probably why it was copied into the cartulary, perhaps from an endorsement to the charter, or from an accompanying note.

The invocation and proem do not occur elsewhere in the eleventh century, although various charters, such as S 951 (1018) and S 978 (1033), express the same sentiments. A ninth-century Worcester charter (S 217, dated 880 for 887) has the same formulas almost word for word. The royal style is identical with that found in S 966 (1032), and very similar to those found in S 954 (1019) and S 961 (1024); and the same formula and variants also occur in Æthelred's charters. The wording of the grant itself is unexceptionable, and the phrase 'meo fideli ministro ... solent' is closely echoed in S 961 (1024). The short excursus on possession for life and heritability afterwards is common in charters of the period: this clause is similar to one found also in S 961, and to a shorter version occurring in S 902 (1002).

A clause guarding against the production of an earlier *libellus* is found in many contemporary texts, as for instance in S 977 (1021 × 1023). The formula used in **20** is a variation of one current in Æthelred's charters (see Keynes, *Diplomas*, p. 88 n. 20, and **15** above), and is also used in S 961 (1024). The anathema appears with only minor variations in S 977. The clause containing the date and indiction appears in exactly the same form in **15** (see above, p. 52). The royal subscription, also found in **15**, is not found elsewhere in Cnut's charters, although it is very similar in language to many of his attestations (see, for example, S 961).

The witness-list is very full and almost identical with that of **16** (see above, p. 56), although it belongs to a slightly earlier date, as can be seen by the appearance of Brihtwig, bishop of Wells, who died on 12 April 1033 (*ASC*, and see Robinson, *Wells*, p. 51), and of Duduc the priest, who succeeded Brihtwig as bishop on 11 June of the same year. A date in or after 1032 is indicated by the signature of Bishop Ælfwine, almost certainly the 'king's priest' who became bishop of Winchester in 1032 (*ASC* MS E). There was a bishop of the same name at Elmham who may have survived until 1032, depending on whether 'Elfrigus episcopus' in S 971 (1031) was intended to be Ælfric, Ælfwine's successor at Elmham, or Ælfwig of London. However, at this period the bishops of Winchester usually appear at or near the head of the list, as in **16** or **20**, so that is probably the case here too. A problem is presented by the appearance of Ælfmær, who can only be the bishop of Selsey. Elsewhere Ælfmær's last signature appears in 1031 (S 963 and 971), and his successor Æthelric signs for the first time in an Abingdon charter dated

1032 (S 964), alongside his namesake of Dorchester, so there is no possibility of confusion. The date of 1032 for S 964 is supported by the witness of Ælfwine the priest, who became bishop of Winchester later that year. Bishop Æthelsi[g]e, who heads the episcopal signatures in S 964, must be meant for Ælfsige II of Winchester, who died the same year. S 964 may not be entirely reliable, and the date is oddly phrased ('xxxii post mille'), but the witness-list looks very sound (see Gelling, *ECTV*, p. 65, and Keynes, *Diplomas*, p. 11 n. 16). One possible explanation for the appearance of Ælfmær in the witness-list of **20** is that the charter text may have been drawn up slightly later than the grant was made. It has already been suggested (see above, p. 54, and Keynes, *Diplomas*, p. 115 n. 108) that the grant to Bovi, made in the regular way at a full meeting of the *witan*, may actually have been drawn up as a charter at Sherborne, which would account for the textual echoes between **20** and **15**. It is conceivable that the grant was made in 1032, while Ælfmær of Selsey was still alive, but that the charter itself was not written until early in 1033, perhaps after the tax settlement recorded in the rubric, and that the scribe mistakenly used the actual date, rather than the date at which the grant was enacted.

Apart from this discrepancy and the unusual proem, **20** is an acceptable text. A strong argument in its favour is that it is addressed to a layman with the stipulation that it should be left to any one of his heirs. The rubric which precedes the text, and which can hardly be anything but a copy of notes contemporaneous with the charter, is also very persuasive evidence.

The bounds of Horton included in the charter were discussed by Grundy (1936, pp. 124–9). The cartulary also contains a second set of bounds for the estate, printed above as **20A**. It was copied into the manuscript in a hand of s. xiii[med] after other additional material at the end of quire 3, before the bulk of the Horton texts, which occupy quire 4 (see above, p. xvii). **20A** displays many Middle English spellings: for example, *cheddes bere* for *ciddes beara*, *chealde* for *cealdan* and *londimere* for *landgemære*. It also uses the ME 3, as in *slea3iet*, *ha3an*, etc. The Anglo-Saxon letter þ appears throughout the text, including the landmarks found only in **20A**. The Anglo-Saxon letter *p* appears only in the words *penecan pprþe* and *penece ppurþe*: elsewhere *w* is used. These bounds have not been printed before, and were not referred to by Grundy.

The bounds in **20**, according to Grundy, outline the modern parish of Horton, with the exception of a stretch between the edge of the black down and the 'hollow brook' close to Mannington, where the bounds diverge. They contain no mention of the river Crane (which outlines the parish here), and they also include the tumuli (*beorgas*) which Grundy identified as those lying half a mile inside the parish boundary. Grundy did not include or discuss the interlineated marks. Two of these, *linleage mor* and *on þa hara apolþore*, occur in the main text a few lines after the interlineation. *In þa piþgas* may be related to *on þona haran piþig* several lines later in the text, but *in acs hirste* appears nowhere else. They seem to be written in a hand identical with or very similar to the hand of the main text. The interlineated marks have been incorporated into the body of the thirteenth-century version, in the same positions in which they occur in **20**, and with as little relevance.

The bounds in **20A** follow those in **20** almost word for word, except for a passage containing about sixteen extra landmarks (*b . . . b*), which has been added at the place which Grundy describes as 'possibly a very vague line of delimitation' (1936, p. 128). Several of the additional marks indicate small agricultural developments: *kinges crofte, walerondes crofte, ballardes ham* and possibly *kinges heiȝes hurne* (? corner of the king's enclosure). This suggests that new settlements had taken place in that area between the composition of **20** and **20A**. However, the later boundary still does not coincide with the present parish boundary; although none of the new marks can be traced in surviving place-names, there is no mention of the river Crane, and the tumuli (*buereges*) still form part of the estate bounds.

Horton was refounded as a monastery some time before 1066, or before 1061 if **22** is accepted, and in Domesday Book this is recorded as Horton property (DB, i. 78v). Bovi, identified in the rubric as a housecarl, appears as a witness in three other charters: S 955 (1019), S 961 (1024) and **16**. All his appearances are made at transactions concerning lands in Dorset, which suggests that he might have retired there after leaving active service at court.

21

King Edward grants half a hide (mansa) *at Littleham, Devon, to Ordgar*, minister. A.D. 1042

B. BL Add. 46487, 29r–30r: copy, s. xii^{med}

Ed.: a. Kemble 1332
    b. Davidson 1883
    c. Pierquin, *Recueil*, pt 5, no. 53

Listed: Sawyer 998; Finberg, *ECDC* 59

Ðis is þære healfan hyde land boc æt Littlanhamme þe Eadpeard kyng let gebocygeun Ordgare his þegne on ece yrfe .[a]

☧ In nomine domini nostri Iesu Christi .
Omnis quidem susceptio et datio passionum[b] terrarum melius litterarum exemplis confirmanda sit ne in posterum aliquis testamenti confirmationem ignorans presumptionis peccatum uel direptionis incaute crimen incurrat . Qua de re ego EADWARD rex regali fretus dignitate aliquam terram cuidam fideli meo ministro uocitato nomine ORDGAR – unum dimidium mansam in loco ubi dictum est Littleham ⸭ cum sylua ad se pertinente in australi parte in hereditatem perennem impendere curaui . Sit uero

predictum rus ab omni sęculari grauedine expers . nisi expeditione pontis arcisue munitione . Quicumque hoc decretum minuere seu transmutare satagerit ꞉ noscat se reum esse in die iudicii coram Christo et sanctis eius . Terra autem ista his terminibus circumdatur . Ðis syndon þære healfan hide landgemæro æt Lytlanhamme .
Ærest on Exanmuðan . þonne up on stryem . be norðan lydepicnæsse on þone norþran mere . up andlang riðan of þone æpylm . þanone east rihte to hafocys setle . þanone east rihte to þan hricgpege . andlang þæs hricgpeges . on þa ealdan dic . east andlang þære dic of þære pega gelæto be norðan þam fulan landa . þanon norð on þone grenan peg on auan ford . of þam fordan up andlang stryemes on þone sele . of þam sele norð on þone grenan peg to þam slæde . east up andlang þæs slædes to þære plegin stope . þonne to þan herpaðe . andlang þæs herpaðas to fugelis beorh dune . andlang þære dune to fuhgeles beorhge . fram þam beorhge suð to ellepurðie . þanon to þan broce . adun þonne andlang þæs broces eft ut on sæ꞉ − Acta est autem hęc prefata donatio anno ab incarnatione domini nostri Iesu Christi . millesimo . xl . ii . indictione . x .

+ Ego Eadweard rex Britannię totius Anglorum monarchus hoc agię Crucis taumate roboraui .
+ Eadsige Dorobernensis ęcclesię archiepiscopus eiusdem regis principatum et beniuolentiam sub sigillo Sanctę Crucis conclusi .

+ Ego Ælfgyfu	reg⟨i⟩na	humillima adiuui .
+ Ego Ælfpine	episcopus	assensum prebui .
+ Ego Byrhtpold .	episcopus	dictando titulaui .[c]
+ Ego Dudoc .	episcopus .	consolidaui .
+ Ego Lyfing .	episcopus .	dignum duxi .
+ Ego Godpine .	dux .	
+ Ego Sigperd .	dux .	
+ Ego Leofric .	dux .	
+ Ego Sigperd .	abbas .	
+ Ego Ælfpine .	abbas .	
+ Ego Odda .	minister .[d]	
+ Ego Ordgar .	minister .	
+ Ego Ælfgar .	minister .[e]	
+ Ego Godpine .	minister .	
+ Ego Æþelric .	minister .	
+ Ego Toky .	minister .	
+ Ego Toui .	minister .	
+ Ego Dodda .	minister .	

+ Ego Ælfperd .   minister .
+ Ego Osmær .   minister .[f]

[a]Ðis is . . . yrfe. *rubric in* B. *In* gebocygeun, *the copyist has* misread an *a as* u [b]*For* possessionum. *A connective has also been omitted here* [c]*First column of subscriptions ends here, bottom of 29v* [d]minister *abbreviated here as* miñ, *all the following as* miñ [e]*Second column of subscriptions ends here* [f]*Third column of subscriptions ends here*

This grant, of what seems a very small piece of land, is the first surviving charter issued by Edward after his accession following Harthacnut's death on 8 June 1042 and before his coronation the next year (*ASC* MS A, C and D, s.a. 1043; E, s.a. 1042); the next charter is dated 1043 (S 999), and then (discounting the spurious S 1000) six charters were issued in 1044. This circumstance may account for some of the peculiarities of **21**.

The charter opens with an invocation, common in Edward's charters, followed by a proem stressing the importance of recording grants in writing. Two other diplomas, S 1012 (1045) and S 1014 (1046), make the same point, but it is a charter from the beginning of Cnut's reign, S 1388 (1016), which comes closest to the thought expressed in **21**. The royal style is not found elsewhere in the eleventh century, but the phrase 'rex regali fretus dignitate' occurs in three dubious charters from the Codex Wintoniensis purporting to be from the reign of Egbert of Wessex (S 272, 273 and 276). Though all are spurious as they stand, the second may contain some genuine material (see Whitelock, *EHD*, p. 185 n. 4). In other charters, however, Edward occasionally uses royal styles of a similarly short pattern, such as 'divina adridenti gratia' (S 1017).

In many of Edward's charters there is a clause stating that the grantee shall enjoy the land as long as he lives and leave it free to whomsoever he wishes, as in S 1008 (1045) or S 1022 (1050). In **21** the phrase is very much shorter, and does not appear elsewhere, although it is reminiscent of one found in a charter of Æthelred, S 900 (1002). The phrase covering the liberties of the estate is again unparalleled, and much shorter than the usual formula. The word *gravedine* is not found elsewhere in eleventh-century diplomatic except in **16** (1035). The anathema, like so much else of this text, does not appear elsewhere in Edward's charters, nor in earlier eleventh-century texts, although the theme is very common in contemporary documents. Faint echoes of the wording appear in S 1664 (1003), S 927 (1012) and S 1034 (1061).

The royal subscription, in contrast, is well known; it is commonly used by Cnut (e.g. S 962 and 963), and in a longer version by both Cnut and Æthelred (e.g. S 910 and 957). This fits in well with **21**'s position right at the beginning of Edward's charters: in his later grants he developed his own royal style. The witness-list is in accord with the date of 1042. Sigweard was abbot of Abingdon until 1044, when he was consecrated suffragan bishop of Canterbury (*ASC*). As Professor Barlow has pointed out (*Edward the Confessor* (London, 1970), p. 75), the court represented here was with only one exception inherited in its entirety from Edward's Scandinavian predecessor (the exception,

Osmær, only appears in three other charters, also concerned with Devon and Cornwall: **17**, S 1003 and 1004). The grantee, Ordgar, is a regular charter signatory from 1031 to 1049. In S 1003 (1044) he is called *nobilis*, and in S 1226 (*c.* 1043), not an acceptable text, he is called 'Ordgarus Devonensis'. In **17** he is called the brother of Ælfgar and Æscbearn, and is almost certainly related to the Ordgar who founded Tavistock Abbey (see Finberg 1943).

The estate at Littleham, although assessed at half a hide, has been identified by Davidson as having very much the same boundaries as the modern parish of Littleham, amounting to roughly 3,000 acres (Davidson 1883, pp. 150–6). Davidson suggested that the very favourable assessment was probably due in large part to the uncultivated and unprofitable state of the land, and was not uncommon in Devon, although he could also have suggested, as he did in the case of Fleet (see **19** above), that Ordgar secured a low assessment for his own benefit and the future benefit of the Church. By 1086, if not before, the estate was in the possession of Horton (DB); an owner TRE is not given, but it may very well already have been owned by the monastery in 1066. It may have passed to Horton as a bequest from Ordgar, probably *c.* 1050, judging by the date of his disappearance from the witness-lists.

There seems no reason to suspect **21** of being a forgery, for the grant is addressed to a layman, the estate concerned is not very valuable and the brevity of the formulas and their uncommon wording are easily accounted for by the charter's position at the beginning of Edward's charter series. The author may well have been trying to find new wording suitable for the new reign, although it was not until later that Edward's diplomas were to develop their own recognizable style. The rubric (probably taken from the charter's endorsement: see above, p. xxiii) can be translated 'This is the title-deed to half a hide at Littleham which King Edward permitted to be granted by charter to Ordgar his thegn in perpetual inheritance'.

22

King Edward grants liberties to the holy foundation at Horton, Dorset. A.D. 1061

B. BL Add. 46487, 31rv: copy, s. xii[med]

Ed.: a. Thorpe, *Diplomatarium*, pp. 380–8, with translation
    b. Kemble 1341
    c. Robertson, *Charters*, no. 120, with translation

Listed: Sawyer 1032; Finberg, *ECW* 627

Ðis is se freols ðe Eadpeard cyngc 7 Eadgyð seo hlæfdige geuðon in to þam haligum mynstre æt Hortune Criste to lofe 7 Sancta MARIAN 7 eallon Cristes halgon .[a]

+ Regnante in perpetuum domino nostro Iesu Christo . ⟨R⟩ixiendum[b] urum drihtne hælendum Criste on ecnysse ðam heahstan 7 þan untosprecen`d´lican ealra þinga 7 ealra tida scyppend . se þe manegum þingum his mihtum setteð 7 pealdeþ . Eac spylce þam up ahafenlican 7 þam unasecgendlican rice Þ ðe he þises lifes eadignysse 7 gesælignesse nænigum þingum ne forlæte ; For þan ic Eadperd Engla landes cyngc mid Godes gyfe 7 mid minra pitena geþeahte 7 ræde ic forgyfe þisne freols in to þære haligan stope æt Hortune Gode to lofe 7 Sancta MARIAN to purðmynte ðe seo stope ys fore gehalgod . 7 me on gemende ys mid þisum eorðlicum þingum þa ecanlican gestreon to begytende . Sicut Salomon dixit . Redemptio animę proprię diuitię . Spa spa Salomon cpæð . Þ þe sceoldon mid urum spedum urum saplum þa ecan gesælignysse begytan . For þan ic cuðlice mid geþeahte geþafunge 7 leafe ealra minra biscope 7 eorla 7 butan ðan ealra minra selostra pitena – ic forgef þisne freols for mine agene saple 7 for mire[e] leofostra frenda . Þ eall Þ land þe lið in to þan haligan mynstre æt Hortune – Þ hyt sy fæstlice 7 unapendedlice a ecelice gefreod ealra cynelicra 7 ealdordomlicra þeopdoma . ge þeoffengces ge æghpylcere uneaðnesse ealles poroldlices broces . buton fyrdsocne 7 burhgeþeorce 7 bricggeþeorce . Gif hpa þanne si Þ he hine for Godes lufon to þam geeadmedan pylle Þ he þas mine gyfe geycan pylle oððe gemenig fyldan ∴ geyce him ælmihtig God eall god her on porolde . 7 his dagas gesundfullie . Gif ðonne hpylc mann to þam geþristlæce oððe mid deofles searpum to þam bespicen sy – Þ he þis on ænegum þingum lytlum oððe mycelum þence to abrecende oððe to apendenda pite he þonne Þ he þæs riht agyldende sy beforan Cristes þrymsettle . Þonne ealle heofonpara 7 eorðpara on his andperdnysse beoð onstyred 7 on hrerede buton he hyt ær her on porolde mid rihte gebete . Ðis þæs gepriten on þam geare þe þæs agan fram Cristes acennednysse . an þusend geara 7 an 7 sixtig geara . 7 an þam tacncircule Þ seofanteoþe gear . Ic Eadperd cyngc mid þære halgan Cristes rode tacne þis het spiþe geornlice getrymman 7 gefæstnian þisne freodom on ælmihtiges Godes naman . 7 on ealra his halgena . Ic fæstlice bebeode . Þ hine nænig minra æfterfyligendra eft ne onpende ne on nænigum dælum læssum ne on marum hyne ne onpyrdon . ac þes freols a ecelice forð þurhþunige spa lange spa God pylle Þ Cristen geleafa mid Angelcynne untosceacan purþe . ealra þæra[d] poroldcundra hefignyssa þa her beforan genemnede syndon . 7 se hæbbe[e]

[a] Ðis is . . . halgon . *rubric in* B   [b] *A space has been left in the MS. for a large capital letter*   [c] *For* mine   [d] þære *altered to* þæra   [e] *The text ends here at the bottom of 31v. The next folio is missing from* B

22 shares an almost identical text with **6**. Where **6** granted liberties to all the possessions of Sherborne in 864, **22** does the same for Horton in the same words, with the date 1061. In some places the text has been adapted: the names of the church and its dedication have been changed, the reference to dead relatives has been omitted, the exemption from constructing fortifications has been withdrawn, and the confirmation has been shortened and rewritten in the first person to match the rest of the charter. But essentially it is a repetition of the ninth-century text in eleventh-century form.

As has already been discussed (see above, pp. 22–4), there is little doubt that **6** is authentic, and the original text: the question that remains is when and why it was adapted to fit Horton. The obvious answer would be when Sherborne acquired the smaller house in 1122; it would have been a logical move for the older house to adapt its own best charter of liberties so that its privileges could be extended to the new acquisition. However, the linguistic evidence favours an eleventh-century date, for where **22** has a phrase independent of **6** it is in good late Old English. This is so with 'Gode to lofe ... gehalgod', 'þæt eall þæt land ... Hortune', 'Ic Eadþerd cyngc ... getrymman 7 gefæstnian' and 'Ic fæstlice bebeode ... hyne ne onþyrdon'. There are the occasional signs of late copying, but no more than is usual throughout the cartulary.

In two instances **22** has better readings than the earlier text: *uneaðnesse* for *ieðnesse*, and *gesundfullie* for *gesundfulle*. **22** has *ealdordomlicra þeopdoma* in place of the *alra domlicra þeopdoma* of **6**. This could be a misinterpretation of the earlier charter, although ninth-century formulas tend to support *ealdordomlic* (e.g. S 204, with *regalium et principalium*), and either version makes sense.

These points may mean that **22** was made from a better copy of the original of **6** than was available to the cartulary scribe, or it may indicate that the scribe of **22** was as careful to correct the errors he found in his model as he was to bring it up to date, and to make it correspond in all details to its new use. Occasionally the language as well as the spelling have been updated, as have technical points, such as the replacement of *ældormanna* with *earla*, and *Þestsaxne cyning* with *Englalandes cyngc*. The use of *fyrdsocn* in place of *fyrde 7 brycge peorces* may also be to conform with later usage, for the former first occurs in two late tenth-century leases of Oswald (S 1362 and 1366). This sort of careful reworking is strongly suggestive of an authentic eleventh-century use.

A peculiarity of both texts is the use of the word *tacncircul*, the only two instances in which the word is recorded (Harrison, *Framework*, p. 117). In **6** the calculation shows that it is meant for 'indiction', whereas in **22** the accompanying numeral is for the lunar cycle. Both have been correctly calculated. The scribe of **6** was apparently determined to use no word of Latin, but there is no known Old English word that specifically means indiction (all the vernacular texts in Robertson, *Charters*, that have an indictional date use the Latin *indictio*; Byrhtferth's *Manual*, vol. 1, ed. S. J. Crawford, EETS 177 (London, 1929), p. 120, calls it *þone circul þe hatte Indictionalem*). *Tacncircul* could be translated 'signified circle', a suitable equivalent of *indictio*. However, the scribe who was adapting the text of **6** to produce **22**, misunderstood it. Why he did so is not clear, for the combination of incarnation and indiction was the most commonly used dating apparatus throughout the period, but perhaps the uniqueness of *tacncircul* led him to think that it must have meant some unusual cycle. The lunar cycle would certainly fit this description as far as diplomatic usage goes. I have only found this cycle in one other charter – S 830, a Devonshire text of Edward the Martyr, which appears genuine, and which is assigned to the year 976 by *anno domini*, indiction, concurrent, epact, nineteen-year (lunar) cycle and regnal year.

It is most unfortunate, in speculating when **22** was produced, that the folio bearing the witness-list is missing from the cartulary, for this might have afforded solid evidence one way or the other, and the following argument lacks corroboration. By all the available internal signs, **22** is a genuine eleventh-century adaptation of the earlier Sherborne text. The linguistic evidence clearly supports this argument, but even more convincing to my mind are the small adjustments, such as the change from ealdorman to earl, and the addition of fortress work. There is also the omission of the high altar ceremony, which eleventh-century contemporaries would not have accepted unless it had taken place, but which twelfth-century editors would surely not have scrupled over. But why should such a borrowing have come about? Perhaps the Horton monks, since they belonged to a relatively new foundation (see above, pp. lvii–lxi), could not have produced a solemn charter in Latin, but they could certainly have contrived an Old English text. In the cartulary the text is introduced by a rubric that states that the liberties were granted by Edward and his queen Edith: perhaps – the most simple explanation – the king and queen were visiting Sherborne, and the grant was made and drawn up there. Æthelbert's grant was found to have a suitable text, and was used as a model; since the other two Sherborne charters of liberties, **1** and **5**, are spurious, they may well not have been available for copying in 1061. We do not know Edward's movements for that year, but it is interesting that both the other 1061 charters deal with West Country lands – the first estate in Devon, the other in Somerset (S 1033 and 1034); both documents are suspect, but probably embody genuine grants. The rubric to **22**, like the other Horton rubrics, appears to have been copied from an endorsement to the charter, re-emphasizing the impression of authenticity given by the text. It reads: 'This is the charter of freedom which King Edward and the Lady Eadgyth gave to the holy monastery of Horton, in praise of Christ and St Mary and all the saints of Christ.'

APPENDIX 1

This text is taken from BL Cotton Faustina A. ii, 25rv. The script is a fairly legible gothic *textura*, belonging to s. xiv². Some of the place-names are unrecognizable, and it is sometimes impossible to know whether the scribe intended to write *u* or *n*: in cases of doubt the letter is printed in italics. *C* and *E* are also written identically in several instances, but the context indicated what was intended in all but one case, that of *Erutecoune* (25v, line 9), which could be read either *Erute-* or *Crute-* (see above, pp. xlvii–xlviii). For discussion of the text, and for place-name identifications, see above, pp. xxxvii–xl and xli–l). Abbreviations have been expanded throughout, except those at the end of place-names. The manuscript has *hid'* invariably (*hyd'* in the first instance).

Incipiunt nomina regum eiusdem ecclesie fundatorum.[a]

Kenewalc rex dedit lanprobi de . c . hydis . Edgarus rex dedit Woburnham de . u . hidis . Athulfus rex dedit Bradford' Cerdel et Algerstoke et getemynst' de[b] . u . hidas de xxxui . hidis et Nutherburie et Ethelbaldingham Athertus rex dedit libertatem de . c . xl hidis . et Cernel de xii . hidis et Tauistoke de . uiii . hidis et Stapulbrige de . xx . hidis et Cuncton' de . uiii . hidis . Kenfulsus rex dedit pidel de . u . hidis et lym de . i . hida . Et [c]Tauistoke de[c] Cuthredus rex dedit in lydene . xii . hidas . et Coruscumbe de x hidis et aput[d] menedip . xxu . hidas . Kenefulsus . rex dedit Snarstok de . ui . hidis et talre de . uiii . hidis et Wegentesfunte et Aueltune de xxx . hidis et Erutecoune de xxxui . hidis . et Wytecumbe et Wlueue . Offa rex dedit Poterne cum pertinenciis suis . Egbertus rex dedit iuxta Cernel . x . hidas . et Power de . uii . hidis iuxta flumen quod dicitur Woch . et . x . iuxta Pedriduñ . et Albambruth . de . uii .[e] hidis . Et in henangre . xii .[f] hidas . et kelk . xii . hidas . Et Ros et macor de . xuiii . hidis . et in Chesterbled . x . hidas et in winurod . xu . hidas . Sigeberhtus rex dedit Boselingtone de . u . hidis Et in est canne . uii . hidas . Ine rex dedit iuxta prediau . uii . hidas . Et Conbusburie de xx hidis . Gerontuis[g] rex dedit macuir de . u . hidis iuxta thamar . Ethelredus rex dedit atforde et clethangre Ethelredus rex dedit et restituit Corescumbam in oblatum et postea Cunitus eum restituit.

a Incipiunt ... fundatorum . *enlarged title*   *b* *Expuncted by two dots underneath*   *c* ... *c* *deleted by a line of red ink*   *d* *For* apud   *e* *Could be* uii *or* iiii   *f* *Sic, corrected from* ?xxii   *g* *The stroke denoting* i *is over the third minim*

APPENDIX 2

The hypothesis that Sherborne was founded on a British monastic site,[1] and that there was perhaps even some continuity between the two religious institutions,[2] has its origin in the opening statement of Faustina A. ii: *kenewalc rex dedit Lanprobi de . c . hydis*. It is a historical possibility. The Anglo-Saxon settlers, once converted, recognized the British as Christians like themselves, although this did little to allay hostilities, and the early missionaries from the continent made various attempts to assert their authority over the British clergy. Most of the Anglo-Saxon churchmen had little to do with the British Church, before or after Whitby, but there were exceptions. Wine, bishop of Winchester, even consecrated Ceadda as bishop with the help of two British bishops some time in 664 × 665.[3] There was undoubtedly some continuity of ecclesiastical sites between the two nations, but hard evidence is scarce, and it would therefore be a welcome addition to the sparse collection of facts if Sherborne could be shown to have enjoyed such a continuity.

This would require clear topographical evidence connecting the site of a British church or monastery named *Lanprobi* with the site of the English monastic foundation at Sherborne. But first the reliability of the Faustina statement must be considered. The main portion of the text does seem to have been derived from a pre-900 list of grants to the foundation at Sherborne, with a few later additions, and appears to embody some trustworthy information (see above, pp. xl–li). Post-900 donors' names appear at the beginning (Edgar) and at the end (Æthelred and Cnut) of the text, and probably derive from the surviving charters. Cenwalh would therefore seem to be out of place. There are various possible reasons for this: the record of his gift might have come from a different source from the main body of the text, or his name might have been shifted deliberately to the head of the list as a position of honour, because his gift was the largest, or the most important, or had the prestige of the greatest antiquity. There is no indication other than this position, which may or may

---

[1] S. Baring-Gould and J. Fisher, *The Lives of the British Saints*, 4 vols (London, 1907–13), iv. 127, and Finberg, *Lucerna*, p. 98.
[2] Barker 1980, pp. 229–31, and 1982, pp. 77–8.
[3] O'Donovan, 'Studies in the History of the Diocese of Sherborne', unpubl. Ph.D. thesis, Cambridge University (1972), pp. 41–2.

not be relevant, that the late fourteenth-century scribe equated *Lanprobi* with Sherborne.

There is no mention of *Lanprobi* in the version of this list preserved in the Sherborne Missal medallions (see above, p. xliv). Cenwalh is included among the kings who gave grants by charter, and to his grant of liberties (based on the charter text **1**) is added the record of a grant of *Wycam cum omnibus suis pertinenciis*. This most probably refers to the area linked with Bradford in post-Conquest sources, known as Sherborne Wyke until the early nineteenth century (Grundy 1933, p. 250; and see above, p. 31). It later formed part of the modern parish of Castleton, which includes lands to the north, west and east of the town of Sherborne, and must have taken its name from the eastern part, where the Norman castle was sited. However, Sherborne Wyke must have lain to the west of the town, close to Bradford Abbas, where it is still remembered in the name of Wyke Farm (OS ST 601145). There is no way of judging now whether the Missal scribe omitted a mention of *Lanprobi* which might have been in his exemplar (as he probably omitted some of Æthelwulf's and Æthelberht's gifts: see above, p. xlii), or whether the Faustina scribe added *Lanprobi* independently of his exemplar.[4] The two scribes could have had different, though very closely related, exemplars, only one of which contained the reference to *Lanprobi*; or yet another possibility could be that the Missal scribe substituted *Wycam* for *Lanprobi*, either because he equated the two estates, or because he did not recognize the name *Lanprobi* as referring to any place-name in the vicinity, and wanted to include *Wycam* as an estate that was owned by Sherborne but not covered by any particular charter (in the same way as he appears to have added *Abbatistocam* to his text). None of this leaves us much enlightened on the main issue.

The form of the name *Lanprobi* is the best indication that Faustina A. ii is transmitting a tradition of some weight. It consists of the Brittonic *lann*, 'enclosed cemetery', combined with a personal name which should also be Brittonic,[5] and must have originated at a time and place where Brittonic rather than Old English was spoken. It is very similar to the Cornish place-name *Lanbrebois* (DB), formed of *lann* plus the Old Cornish personal name 'Propus', the church there being dedicated to St Probus. In the case of *Lanprobi* there is a philological problem with the '-i'

---

[4] There is one small indication that this might be the case: whereas throughout the text 'hide' is spelled *hid*', in the case of *Lanprobi* alone it is spelled *hyd*'.

[5] See O. J. Padel, 'Cornish Names of Parish Churches', *Cornish Studies* iv/v (1976–7), pp. 15–27.

ending, which looks like the Latin genitive form, although there is no grammatical justification for this in the Faustina text; all the other place-names are in the vernacular. 'Probi' is not a likely form for a Brittonic name: it should be 'Probus', the '-us' being an integral part of the name.[6] However, it may be unnecessary to stress this difficulty, for the text is very late and must have been recopied at various stages. The important facts seem to be the Brittonic origin of the place-name, and its ecclesiastical connotation. Moreover, one could argue that it must have been an ecclesiastical centre of some importance for its name to have been recorded at all by the conquering nation.

The exact location of *Lanprobi* is open to question. If it was indeed a grant from Cenwalh, then both the form of its name and its gift to Sherborne suggest that it most probably lay somewhere in the lands controlled by Cenwalh west of Selwood, at the time a natural boundary between the older West Saxon lands of the diocese of Winchester and the new conquests of the seventh century. Exactly what these conquests comprised is hard to define: estimates include various combinations of Dorset west of Selwood and all or parts of Somerset and Devon.[7] *Lanprobi* does not survive as a place-name in any of these areas, but the size of the grant, and its position at the beginning of the Faustina A. ii list, suggest that it was seen as very important to Sherborne, and that the scribe may have understood it to be the foundation grant of the Saxon monastery, in which case one would look for it in the vicinity of Sherborne.[8] A chapel dedicated to St Probus did exist close to the town of Sherborne, the only references to it appearing in the twelfth century. It is recorded in a papal bull of 1163 as the *capella s. Probi* belonging to the church of St Mary Magdalene, next to the castle built in 1138, which lay well outside the town to the east.[9] It is probably to be identified with one of the two chapels (unnamed) mentioned as belonging to the same church in the earlier bull of 1146, confirming the possession of the monks of Sherborne.[10] This latter document also names as belonging to the monastery 'Propeschirche et Stocland cum siluis et pratis ...', which could well be intended to indicate the lands that went with the *capella*, for the bull first lists the various churches,

[6] I am most grateful to Mr Padel for his explication of the philology.
[7] Stenton, *Anglo-Saxon England*, pp. 63–4; W. G. Hoskins, *The Westward Expansion of Wessex*, Department of English Local History, Occasional Papers xiii (Leicester, 1960), pp. 10–17; and P. Hunter Blair, *Roman Britain and Early England, 55 B.C.–A.D. 871* (London, 1963), pp. 208–10.
[8] A point also made by Barker 1982, p. 80.
[9] *Mon. Angl.*, i. 339.
[10] Holtzmann, *Papsturkunden*, no. 51.

e.g. 'Ecclesiam de Bradeford cum capellis et aliis appenditiis suis', and then names the estates separately, 'Woburna, Torneford, Bradeford . . . cum omnibus pertinentiis suis'.

Katherine Barker[11] and Laurence Keen[12] identify this *Stocland* with that named in the clause 'in ipsa Scireburna centum agelli in loco qui dicitur stocland' in the charter of 998 (**11**), and Keen makes a further identification with some forty-eight acres of meadowland contained in ten fields lying to the east of the castle, called *Stokland* in various medieval and later sources, suggesting that the 'hundred little fields' could gradually have been dispersed until only ten retained the original name, or, alternatively, that they were originally strips which were later enclosed.[13] Barker envisages a much larger area, which she equates with the forty-three hides held by the bishop of Salisbury as Sherborne's successor in 1086 (DB, i. 77r; the Exeter Domesday gives the amount as forty-seven hides). If the *Stocland* of 998 is to be identified with the lands associated in the twelfth century with *Propeschirche*, Barker's siting of the estate is not convincing, for the sizes of the two areas do not correspond, nor is there any obvious reason why the monastery should have been given clear title to an estate in 998 that in 1066 appears as the bishop's most important holding. The area outlined by Keen looks more realistic in size, although again the Domesday evidence does not quite fit his hypothesis, since it records the monks as holding only twenty acres of meadowland (DB, i. 77r).

However, problems in locating *Stocland* do not detract from the fact that close to Sherborne Castle was a chapel dedicated to St Probus. Recent excavations have revealed burials below the twelfth-century castle levels, and Keen suggests that this is the site of *Lanprobus*.[14] Barker focuses on the *Propeschirche et Stocland* links, and suggests that *Propeschirche* was an area of land to be identified both with the *predium* of 998 and with the 100 hides at *Lanprobi*, and that this was the original monastic enclosure granted by Cenwalh, in which the monastery of Sherborne was then founded. As corroborating evidence she cites the town plan of Sherborne, which shows in parts a curvilinear shape reminiscent of Irish monastic enclosures.[15] Her argument has recently been challenged by David Hinton, on the grounds that the

---

[11] Barker 1982, pp. 82–4 and Fig. 7.3.
[12] Keen 1984, pp. 211–12.
[13] Ibid.
[14] Ibid.
[15] Barker 1980, pp. 229–31. Although our conclusions differ, I am very grateful to Mrs Barker for allowing me to see her work in typescript, and for some stimulating conversations.

enclosure proposed at Sherborne would be far larger than other known Irish examples, and that the curvilinear features could have quite other and much later origins.[16]

After all this, there is no hard evidence to link *Lanprobi* with the site of the Saxon monastery. The castle area is a more attractive alternative for the site of *Lanprobi*, and would explain the dedication to St Probus; yet the chapel is not mentioned until the twelfth century, and its association with the castle could suggest a later foundation.

However, it is worth looking at the problem from another angle. When Sherborne was chosen as the seat of the new bishopric in 705, it must have been considered a suitable location. New bishoprics appear to have been centred on an ecclesiastical foundation already in existence and possessing at least some endowments.[17] In 705 there were probably only a few acceptable foundations west of Selwood. Exeter, in existence as a Saxon foundation probably by *c*. 680,[18] was too far to the south-west to be suitable. Wells had a minster by s. viii^2 (S 262, 766 for ?774), and was traditionally founded by Aldhelm *c*. 700; it should have been suitably placed *vis-à-vis* access to the various areas of the south-west.[19] Glastonbury, only a few miles away, was established as a Saxon ecclesiastical foundation by s. vii^2, and received several grants of land in that half century.[20] However, it was not chosen as the new episcopal seat, its endowments and relatively central position being outweighed by some other factor (possibly its periodic inaccessibility in the marshes). Sherborne was chosen, despite being so close to the eastern edge of the new bishopric. It must therefore have existed as an ecclesiastical foundation prior to 705, and a foundation date some time in Cenwalh's reign (643–72, but after 648) would be quite appropriate: before that would probably be placing it too early in the Saxon advance. Thus there are good reasons for accepting the evidence offered by **1**, Faustina A. ii and the Sherborne Missal that Cenwalh played an important part in Sherborne history, possibly as the monastery's founder. Moreover, it is worth recalling Cenwalh's connection with Bishop Wine, whose British episcopal associates most probably came from west of Selwood. They would have been in a position to pass on to the Anglo-Saxons the original names of important British

---

[16] 'The Topography of Sherborne – Early Christian?', *Antiquity* lv (1981), pp. 222–3.

[17] Keen 1984, p. 209.

[18] G. W. Greenaway, *Saint Boniface* (London, 1955), pp. 8–9.

[19] W. Rodwell, 'From Mausoleum to Minster: the Early Development of Wells Cathedral', in *The Early Church in Western Britain and Ireland*, ed. S. M. Pearce, BAR British Series cii (1982), p. 52.

[20] E.g. S 227, 236 and 239.

settlements in the area. But if *Lanprobi* is to be identified with Sherborne, why is its name absent from the surviving charters, and especially from **1**; and if the 100 hides at *Lanprobi* were the foundation grant of land for Sherborne, why did the author of **1** bother to forge a relatively useless charter of liberties when he could have provided a charter for a genuine and very prestigious grant of land? Could the link between the British *Lanprobi* and the Saxon Sherborne foundation have been forgotten by the eleventh and twelfth centuries, despite the proximity of St Probus' chapel, and only have been preserved by chance in some obscure note later resuscitated in Faustina A. ii?

On the other hand, if *Lanprobi* was not in or near Sherborne, its location is a mystery. No *lann* place-names survive outside the Cornish and Welsh-speaking areas. But for the association with Cenwalh and the existence of the chapel of St Probus, one would look for it beyond the Tamar.

INDEXES

In these indexes *w* is substituted for *p, and th* for *ð* and *þ*. Personal names are given as they occur in the texts, with all the spelling variations noted in brackets. Square brackets [ ] contain editorial comments. Charters are referred to by their numbers, in bold type; other references are to the pages of the introduction and the commentaries.

1 INDEX OF PERSONAL NAMES

This is an index of names and titles rather than of individuals. References to laymen with the same name and rank are grouped together. Ecclesiastics have been identified as far as possible, and where two or more bishops of a see had the same name, they have been distinguished by the numbers conventionally assigned to them.

Ælfgar (Ælfgær), *minister*, **15**, **16**, **18**, **19**, **20** *bis*, **21**
— of Minehead, **17**; 60
— brother of Ordgar and Æscbeorn, **17**; 77
Ælfgeat (Ælfget), *minister*, **16**, **20**
— *cniht*, **14**
— son of Hengthe, **14**
Ælfgifu (Alfgeofu, Ælfgyfu), queen, **16**, **19**, **21**
Ælfgyth (Ælfgyva), ? abbess of Barking, lxi n. 126
Ælfheah (Ælfeah, Ælfheagus, Ælpheagus), bishop [of Wells], **7**, **8**
— bishop [of Winchester I], **9**; 36
— bishop [of Winchester II], **11**, **19**; xx
— *minister*, **7**, **8** *bis*, **9** *bis*, **18**; 63
Ælfhelm, bishop [of Dorchester], **19**; 67
— *dux*, **19**; 67
Ælfhere (Ælfere, Æluere), abbot, **19**
— *dux*, **18**
— *comes*, 63
— *minister*, **6A**, **10**
Ælfhun, bishop [of London], **19**; 50 n. 1
Ælfmær, bishop [of Selsey], **20**; 58, 72, 73
— *minister*, **15**
Ælfnoth, abbot, **15**
— *minister*, **7**, **8**
Ælfred (Alfrid), *clito*, **15**
— bishop of Sherborne, lviii
— *minister*, **8**
— thegn, 30
— *see also* Alf-
Ælfric (Alfric), archbishop of Canterbury, **19**; 67
— archbishop [of Canterbury], **11**, **12**
— archbishop of York, **16**, **20**
— bishop of Elmham, 72

— abbot [? of Pershore], **16**, **20**
— abbot, **7**, **8**
— *dux*, **11**, **15**, **19**
— *minister*, **7**, **8**
— brother of Odda, **17**
— Bata, 53
— the Homilist, xix
Ælfsige (Ælfsine), bishop [of Winchester II], 50, 73
— bishop [of Winchester I], **18**
— bishop [of Winchester II], **15**
— abbot, **11**, **15**, **19**
— *comes*, 63
— *miles, discifer*, 63
— *minister*, **8**, **18**
Ælfstan (Alfstan), bishop [of London, Rochester or Ramsbury], **10**; 38
— bishop, *see* Ealhstan
— *dux*, **6A**, **8**, **10**; 32
— *minister*, **3A**
Ælfthryth, wife of King Edgar, lix, lx
Ælfweard (Ælfwerd, Ælwerd), abbot [of Glastonbury], **19**
— *minister*, **21**
— cniht, **14**
— son of Alfwold, **17**
Ælfwig (Ælwig), bishop of London, 50 n. 1, 72
— abbot of Westminster, xix
— abbots [of Bath and ?], **16** *bis*, **20** *bis*
— of Haydon, **17**
Ælfwine, bishop of Elmham, 72
— bishop [of Lichfield], **7**, **8**
— bishop [of Wells], **11**
— bishop [of Winchester], **16**, **20**, **21**; 58, 72, 73
— abbot of Buckfast, **17**; 60

INDEX OF PERSONAL NAMES

Ælfwine (*cont.*):
— abbot [probably of New Minster, Winchester], **16**, **21**
— *dux*, **16**, **20**
— *minister*, **21**
— son of Æthelhild, 63
Ælfwold (Alfwold, -wolde, Alwold), bishop [of Crediton II], **19**
— bishop of Sherborne, **15**, **17**; xxxv n. 46, xliv; 44, 53, 60
— *dux*, **7**, **8**
— father of Ælfweard, **17**
Ælla, *minister*, **5**; 17
Æscbeorn (Escbern), brother of Ordgar and Ælfgar, **17**; 77
Æscbryht, *dux*, **8**; 32
Æscmund, *minister*, **6B**
Æthelbald (Athelbald, -bold), king, **4**, **6**, **10**; xl, xlii, xlix; 12, 23, 38
— *filius regis*, **3B**; 10
— *dux*, **3A**; 10
— *minister*, **5**
Æthelberht (Æthelbreht, -byrht, Athelbertus, Athertus), king, **4**, **6**, **10**, App. 1; xxxv n. 45, xxxvii, xl, xlii, xliv, lii; 2, 12, 18, 23, 24, 38, 80, 84
— *dux*, **3A**
Æthelfand (? for Æthelweard), son of Æthelmær, **14**
Æthelgar, bishop of Crediton, lv n. 105
Æthelheah, *presbiter*, **6B**
Æthelheard (Ætheleard), king, xlvii
— *minister*, **3B**, **18**
Æthelhild (Ethelhylde), *femina nobilis*, **18**; xxxi, xxxvii, lxii; 62, 63
Æthelmær (-mer), *dux*, ealdorman, **13**, **14**, **15**; 47, 48
— *minister*, **11**, **16**, **19** bis, **20** bis
— father of Æthelfand, **14**
— son of Cola, **17**
Æthelmod, bishop [of Sherborne], **2**; 5
— *minister*, **6A**, **10**
Æthelmund (Athel-), abbot, **5**
— [*praefectus*], **2**; 5
— *dux*, **18**
— *minister*, **6B**, **7**
Æthelnoth, archbishop of Canterbury, **16**, **20**
— abbot [possibly of Westminster], **7**, **8**
— [*praefectus*], **2**; 5
Æthelred (Ethelredus) I, king, App. 1; xxxvii, xliii, li; 35
— II, king, **11**, **12**, **15**, **19**, App. 1; xxviii, xxxii, xxxvii, xl, xliii, li, lv; 41–3, 53, 54, 58, 67, 68, 72, 76, 83
— *filius regis*, **3A**, **6A**, **6B**; 38
— *minister*, **5**
Æthelric (Ætheric), bishop of Selsey, 72–3
— bishop [of Sherborne], **13**, **14**, **15**, **19**; xviii, lvi, lvii; 44, 47, 48, 50, 51, 53, 67

— *princeps*, **3B**
— *dux*, **5**
— *minister*, **6A**, **7**, **8**, **9**, **10**, **19**, **21**
Æthelsige (-sie), bishop [of Sherborne], **15**; 50, 51
— bishop, **14**; 50
— *dux*, **18**
Æthelstan, *filius regis*, **19**; 54
— *dux*, **7**, **8**, **9**, **18**; 63
— *minister*, **8**
— *see also* Athel-
Æthelweard (-ward), abbot [of Glastonbury or possibly Malmesbury], **16**, **20**
— *dux*, **11**; xx
— *minister*, **15**, **19** bis
Æthelwig, abbot, **16**, **20**
Æthelwine, *minister*, **19**
Æthelwold (Athel-), bishop of Winchester, 50
— *minister*, **19**
Æthelwulf (Ætheluulf, -wlfus, Athulfus), king, **3**, **4**, **5**, **6**, App. 1; xxi, xxxvii, xl, xlii, xliv, xlix, li, lvi; 9, 12, 15, 17, 18, 84
— *princeps*, **3B**
— *dux*, **5**
— *minister*, **6A**, **6B**, **10**
Aldhelm, bishop of Sherborne, xx, xxi; 12, 87
— bishop [of Sherborne], **4**
Ald- *see* Eald-
Alexander I, king of Scotland, xviii
— II, pope, xviii
Alfred (Ælfred), king, xxxix n. 52, xliii, xlvi, li, liv; 9, 24
— *filius regis*, **3A**, **6A**, **6B**; 38
— *frater regis*, **6**
— *see also* Elf-
Alh- *see* Ealh-
Alnod, xxxv n. 46, xliv
Alon, **17**
Arfast, bishop of Elmham, xviii
Asser, bishop of Sherborne, xlvi, liv; 15, 50
Athelstan (Æthel-), king, **7**, **8**; xxxi, xl, xlvii, lii, lvii; 16, 29–31, 33, 34
Athulf, bishop [of Hereford], **19**

Babba, *minister*, **6B**
Baldwin, archbishop of Canterbury, xxxix n. 51
— abbot of Bury, xviii
Benedict, St, **11**
Beocca, *minister*, **6A**, **10**
Beorht- *see* Byrht-
Beornric, 63
Beornstan (Byrn-, Byr-), bishop [of Winchester], **7**, **8**; 31
Bovi (Bouige), *huskarle*, **20**; 71–4
— *minister*, **16**, **20**; xvii, lx
Briwere, William, bishop of Exeter, xxxix n. 51

INDEX OF PERSONAL NAMES

Bruynyng, Robert, abbot of Sherborne, xxi, xxxvii
Buga, *minister*, **7**, **8**
Burhghelm, *presbiter*, **6B**
Burhgred, *minister*, **6B**
Burhwold, bishop of Cornwall, 50
Byrhtferth (-ferh, -werth), *dux*, **18**
— *minister*, **18**
Byrhthelm (Beorht-), bishop [of Wells, London or ? Selsey], **18**
— abbot, **5**; 17
Byrhthere (Beorhtere), brother of Bishop Alfred, lviii
Byrhtmær (Briht-), abbot [? of New Minster, Winchester], **15**
— *minister*, **11**
Byrhtmund (Beorht-), *minister*, **6B**
Byrhtnoth (Beorht-, Beorh-), *minister*, **6A**, **10**
Byrhtred (Beorhtræd), abbot [of Glastonbury], **15**
Byrhtric (Beorht-, Briht-, Heorht-), king, xlv
— *minister*, **6B**, **11**, **19** *bis*
— *reada*, **14**
Byrhtwig (Briht-), bishop [of Wells], **20**; 58, 72
Byrhtwine (Briht-, Brih-), bishop [of Sherborne], **16**, **20**
Byrhtwold (Beorhtwald, Brhtwold, Briht-), bishop [of Ramsbury], **15**, **16**, **20**, **21**
— abbot [? of Malmesbury], **19**
Byrhtwulf (Beorhtwulf, -ulf), *comes*, **8**, **21**; 30, 33
— *diaconus*, **6B**
— *minister*, **9**
Byrhtwyn (Beorhtwne), lviii

Care, son of Toki, **17**; 59, 60
Ccadda, bishop, 83
Cenwalh (Cenwalch, -uualch, Coenuualh, Kenewalc, Kenvvalchus), king, **1**, App. 1; xxxvii, xli, xliii, xliv; 2–3, 18, 83–7
Cen- *see also* Coen-
Ceofa, *minister*, **6B**
Ceolheah, *minister*, **6B**
Ceolhelm, *minister*, **6B**
Ceolmund, *diaconus*, **6B**
— *minister*, **5** *bis*; 17
Ceolred (Cyrred), *minister*, **6B** *ter*
Ceolwulf, *minister*, **6B**
Ceorl, *princeps*, **3B**
— *dux*, **5**
Cerdic (Cær-), [*praefectus*], **2**; 5
Chaucer, xviii
Cnut (Cnuitus, Cunitus), king, **16**, **20**, App. 1; xviii, xxviii, xxx, xxxvii, xl, xliii, xlvi, lx; 54, 57–9, 67, 71, 72, 76, 83

Coenwald (Cenwald, -wold), bishop of Worcester, **7**, **8**, **18**; 31, 63
— *minister*, **6A**, **10**
Cola (Kola), high-reeve, 67
— father of Æthelmær, **17**
Cuthred, king, App. 1; xl, xli; 58
— *minister*, **6B**
Cuthulf, *minister*, **3A**
Cyma (Kyma), *minister*, **3A**, **6A**, **6B**, **10**
Cyneferth, bishop [of Rochester], **7**, **8**
Cyneheah, *minister*, **3A**, **5** *bis*
Cynelaf, *minister*, **6B**
Cynemund, *minister*, **6B**
Cynewulf (Kenefulsus, Kenfulsus), king, **2**, App. 1; xxxix, xl, xlii, xlv, xlix; 5
— *minister*, **3A**
Cyrred *see* Ceolred

Denegils, *minister*, **6A**
Dodda, *minister*, **6A**, **21**
— *cild*, **17**
Dudda (Duda), *minister*, **5**, **6B**
Duduc (Dudoc), bishop [of Wells], **21**; xlvi; 58, 72
— *presbiter*, **20**
Dunstan, archbishop of Canterbury, **10**; xviii, li, lv; 38, 41–3, 51

Eadberht, *diaconus*, **3**; xl; 9, 11
Eadgar, *clito*, **19**
— *see also* Edgar
Eadgyth, queen, **22**; 80
Eadmund, king, 30
— *ætheling*, *clito*, **14**, **15**, **19**; 49, 59
— *dux*, **18**
Eadnoth, abbot [of Ramsey], **19**
Eadred, king, **9**; xxii; 35, 36
— (Eadric), *clito*, **19**; 67
Eadric, ealdorman, **14**; 50, 53
— *dux*, **15**
— *minister*, **7**, **8**, **19**
Eadsige (-sith), archbishop of Canterbury, **21**
— *gerefa*, *minister*, **19**; 67, 68
Eadweard *see* Edward
Eadwig (Edwaynus), king, **18**; xxxviii, liii; 62, 63
— *clito*, **15**, **19**
— *minister*, **16**, **20**
Eadwine, abbot [? of Evesham], **7**, **8**
Eadwold, *presbiter*, **16**, **20**
— *minister*, **16**, **20**
Eadwulf (-ulf), bishop [of Crediton], **8**; liii, lv; 31, 32
— *minister*, **6A**, **6B**, **10**
Eahmund *see* Heahmund
Ealdberht (Ald-), *minister*, **3B**
Ealdred (Aldred), bishop of Cornwall, lv n. 102; 50
— abbot, **7**; 31, 32

INDEX OF PERSONAL NAMES

Ealdred (*cont.*):
— *dux* (error for abbot), **8**
— *minister*, **3A**
Ealdwine, *preost*, **14**
Ealdwulf (Eadulf), archbishop [of York], **11**; xx
Ealhferth, *minister*, **6B**
Ealhhard (Alh-), abbot, **6A, 10**
Ealhstan (Alh-, Ælfstan), bishop of Sherborne, **5**; 9, 24
— bishop [of Sherborne], **3A, 3B, 6A, 6B, 10**
— *minister*, **3B, 5, 6B** bis
Eanred (-ræd), *minister*, **5**; 17
Eanwulf (Eanulf, -uulf), *dux*, **3A** bis, **5** bis, **6A, 6B, 10**
— *princeps*, **3B**
— *minister*, **6B**
Eardulf, *minister*, **6B**
Ecgbald, bishop [of Winchester], **2**; 5
Ecgbriht (-breht), *clito*, **19**; 67
— *minister*, **6A, 6B, 10**
Ecgheard, *minister*, **3A, 5**
Ecglaf, *minister*, **16, 20**
Ecgstan, *minister*, **6B**
Ecgulf, *minister*, **3A, 6A, 10**
Edgar (Eadgar, Edgarus), king, **10, 15,** App. 1; xxxvii, xl, xliii, li, lviii, lx; 12, 38, 39, 83
frater regis, **18**
— *see also* Eadgar
Edward (Eadward, -weard, -werd), the Elder, king, liv; 15, 30
— the Martyr, king, lxi; 80
— the Confessor, king, **21, 22**; xv, xvii, lx, lxi; 76, 77, 79, 80
— *clito*, **15, 19**; 67
Egbert, king, App. 1; xlii, xlvii, xlviii, li, lv, lvi; 10, 76
Escbern *see* Æscbeorn
Esne, *minister*, **3A**
Eugenius III, pope, xvi, xxxii

Forthhere, bishop of Sherborne, xiv, xlviii, liv; 2
Freanwulf, *dux*, **4**

Geraint (Gerontius), king of Cornwall, App. 1; xli, xlviii
Germanus, abbot, **19**
Goda, *minister*, **6A, 10**
Godeman (Godman), abbot [of Thorney], **19**
— *preost*, **17**
Godric, *dux*, **15**
— *minister*, **16, 19**
Godwine, bishop [of Lichfield or Rochester], **19**
— abbot, **11**
— *presbiter*, **20**

— *eorl*, **17**
— *dux*, **16, 20, 21**
— *minister*, **15, 21**
— *brytæl, minister*, **16**
Goscelin of St Bertin, lviii–lx; 43
Gregory [I], pope, **5**

Hædde, bishop [of Wessex], **4**; 12
Hagona, *presbiter*, abbot, **2**
Hamgils (-gyls), abbot [of Glastonbury], **4**; 12
Harold, earl of Wessex, xlix, lvi
Harthacnut, king, 76
Heahmund (Eah-), *presbiter*, **3A, 6A, 6B, 10**; 24
Heca, father of Hunewine, **17**
Helmstan, bishop of Winchester, **5**; 9
— bishop [of Winchester], **3B**
Hemele, [*praefectus*], **2**; 5
Hengthe, father of Ælfgeat, **14**
Henry I, king, xvii, xxxv, lxi, lxii; 71
— abbot of Sherborne, xvi, xvii
Heortric *see* Byrhtric
Heoteman, *presbiter*, **6B**
Herewulf, *minister*, **3B, 6B**
Hermann, bishop of Sherborne and Ramsbury, xiii, xx, xxi, xxxi
Honorius II, pope, xxxii, xxxiii
Hugg, *princeps*, **1**; 2
Hunewine, son of Heca, **17**
Hunfrith, abbot, **4**; 12
Hunred, *minister*, **6A, 10**
Hwita (Huita), *praepositus*, **6A, 10**

Ine, king, App. 1; xli, xlvi–xlviii; 2

Joscelin, bishop of Salisbury, xv–xviii
Juthwara, St, xxi

Kenulf *see* Cenwulf
Kola *see* Cola
Kyma *see* Cyma

Laurentius, archbishop [of Canterbury], **1**; 2
Leofnoth, *minister*, **19**
Leofric, bishop of Exeter, xlvii
— abbot [of Muchelney], **11**
— *dux*, **16, 20, 21**
— *minister*, **19, 20**
Leofsuna, abbot of Cerne, **14**
Leofwine (Leowine, Lof-), *dux*, **15, 19**
— *minister*, **11, 19** bis
— *disc thegn*, **14**
— of Exeter, **17**; 60
Leutherius, bishop of Wessex, 2
Luhha (? for Lulla), *minister*, **6B**
Lullede, *dux*, **3A**
Lulling, *minister*, **5**; 17
Lullric, *minister*, **3A**

INDEX OF PERSONAL NAMES

Lutsige of Wight, **17**; 60
Lutting, 60
Lyfing, bishop *be northan* [of Worcester], **17, 21**; 60
— bishop [of Wells], **14, 15, 19, 20**; 50, 54

Milred (-ræd), *minister*, **3A**, 5
Monnel, *minister*, **6A**, 10
Mucel, *minister*, **6B**

Nithmund, *minister*, **3A**

Oda, archbishop [of Canterbury], **9, 18**
— bishop [of Ramsbury], **7, 8**
Odda, *minister*, **7, 8, 15, 16, 20, 21**
— brother of Ælfric, **17**
Offa, king, App. 1; xlii, xlv, li
Ordbyrht, bishop [of Selsey], **19**
Ordgar I, ealdorman, lx; 77
— II, *minister*, **16, 20, 21**; lx, lxi; 76, 77
— brother of Ælfgar and Æscbeorn, **17**
Ordulf, *minister*, **11, 19**; lx, lxi; 68
Oscytel, bishop [of Dorchester], **18**
Osferth, *dux*, **7, 8**
Osgod, *minister*, **16, 20**
Osmær, *minister*, **21**; 77
— **17**
Osmund, St, bishop of Salisbury, li
— *minister*, **3A, 5, 6A, 6B**, 10
Osræd, *minister*, **3B**
Osric (Osirich), abbot of Horton, lxi
— abbot, **3B**
— *princeps*, **3B**
— *dux*, **3A, 4, 5**; 12
Oswald, archbishop of York and bishop of Worcester, 41, 46, 79
Oswulf (Osulf, Oswuulf), bishop [of Ramsbury], **18**
— *presbiter*, **6B**

Peter, prior of Farley and abbot of Sherborne, xvi
Plegmund, archbishop of Canterbury, li, lv
Probus, St, xliii; 84–6, 88
Propus, 84

Rædnoth, *presbiter*, **6B**
Ralph, archbishop of Canberbury, lxii
Roger, bishop of Salisbury, xvii; 32
— abbot of Sherborne, xvi
Romanus, abbot, **1**; 2

Scilling, *praefectus*, **2**; 5
Scirwold, *minister*, **16, 20**
Sigeberht, king, App. 1; xli, xlix
Sigeferth, *minister*, **15**
Sigehelm, ? bishop of Sherborne, xxxix and n. 52
Sigeweard (Seward, Sigweard, -werd, Siwærd, Siwerd), bishop, 48
— abbot [of Abingdon], **21**; 76

— *dux*, **21**
— *minister*, **16, 19, 20**
— **14**
Sihtric, abbot of Tavistoke, **17**; lx, lxi; 60
Smelt, *presbiter*, **16**; 58
Stigand, *presbiter*, **16, 20**
Swithun, bishop [of Winchester], **3A**; 9

Theobald, archbishop of Canterbury, xvii
Theodred, bishop [of London], **7, 8, 9**
Thored, *minister*, **16, 20**
Thurstin, prior and abbot of Sherborne, xv, xvi, xxxii, lxii
Toki (Tokie, Toky), *minister*, **21**
— father of Care, **17**; 59, 60
Torhthelm, *diaconus, praepositus*, **6B**
Tovi (Toui), *minister*, **16, 20, 21**

Uhtred, *dux*, **7, 15**
Ulf, **17**; 59, 60
Ulfcytel (-kytel), *minister*, **15, 19**
Ulfred, *minister*, **3A, 3B**
Urki, *minister*, **16, 20**

Wærferth, abbot, **3A**
Warelwast, William, bishop of Exeter, xxxix n. 51
Wharton, Henry, xix, xx
Wigferth, [*praefectus*], **2**; 5
Wihtgar, *minister*, **5, 7, 8**
Wihthelm, abbot, **3B**
Wihtnoth, *minister*, **20**
Wiking, **17**
William I, king, xviii
— bishop of Exeter, xxxix
— of Malmesbury, xxx, xxxi, xxxix n. 52, xlvi n. 63, lx, lxi; 18
Wine, bishop of Winchester, 83, 87
Winus, *minister*, **16, 20**
Wistan (for Wigstan), *presbiter*, **6B**
— *minister*, **6A**, 10
Wulfbold, *minister*, **7**
Wulfgar (Wulgar, Wlf-), abbot [of Abingdon], **11, 15, 19**; 43
— *famulus monasterii*, **15**; xxviii; 53
— *minister*, **7, 8, 15, 19**
Wulfgeat (-get), *minister*, **11, 19**; 67
Wulfheah, *minister*, **6B, 19**; 67
Wulfheard (-hard), *minister*, **3B, 6B**
Wulfhelm, archbishop of Canterbury, **7, 8**
— bishop [? of Hereford], **7, 8**; 31
— bishop [of Wells], **9**
— *minister*, **6A, 7, 8**, 10
— father of Byrhtwyn, lviii
Wulfhere (Wlfherio, Wlfhere), king of Mercia, **1**; 2
— *dux*, **3A**
— *minister*, **3B, 5, 6A**, 10
Wulfhild, St, abbess of Barking, lviii–lx
— abbess of Horton, lviii–lx

INDEX OF PERSONAL NAMES

Wulflaf (Wulflauus), abbot, **3A, 3B**, 5
Wulfmær, *minister*, **7, 8**
Wulfnoth (Wul-), *presbiter*, **20**
— *minister*, **7** *bis*, **8** *bis*, **11, 16, 20**; 31
Wulfred, *minister*, **6A, 7, 8, 10**
Wulfric, *preost*, **14**
— *minister*, **6B, 9, 18**
Wulfsige (Wlfsin, Wlsin, Wulsin), bishop of Cornwall, lvi
— abbot of Westminster and bishop of Sherborne III, xiii, xviii–xxi, xxviii, xxxii, xxxv; 36, 41–6, 58
— bishop [of Sherborne I], **9**; xxvii
— bishop [of Sherborne II or Cornwall], **10**; 38
— bishop [of Sherborne III], **11, 12**
— *minister*, **7, 8**
— *famulus*, **15**
Wulfstan (Wlstan), archbishop of York [I], **7, 8**
— archbishop of York II and bishop of Worcester, xix, xxxiii; 44, 48, 50, 67
— archbishop [of York II], **14, 15**
— bishop [of London II], **11**
— *minister*, **9**
Wulfthryth (Wolfrida), St, abbess of Wilton, lix, lx
Wulfweard (-werd), *minister*, **15**
— of Winsham, **17**; 60
Wynsige, *minister*, **6A, 10**

2 INDEX OF PLACE-NAMES

Abbamburh see Albambruth
Abbotskerswell, Devon (*Cærswellan, -wylle, Carswell, -wylle*), **18**; xxxvii, xxxix, lxii; 63, 64
Abingdon, Berks., 16, 43, 53
Acforde, xlii, l
Æscantun, **3**; 9
Albambruth, App. 1; xlii, l
Algerstoke *see* Halstock
Allen, river, *see* Wimborne
Alton Pancras, Dorset (Aueltune, Aulton, Awultune), **13**, App. 1; xlii, xliv, xlv, xlix, lvii, lviii
Antony, Cornwall, lxi
Archet *see* West Orchard
Ascan, xlii, xlix
Ash Priors, Somerset (*Æsce*), l
Atforde (? for *Acforde*), App. 1; xliii, l
Athelney, Somerset, xxii, xxx, xxxi; 54, 57, 58
Axe, river, Devon, Dorset (*Axan*), **19**; l

Banwell, Somerset, xlvi
Barking, Essex, lix
Barnstaple, Devon, xlviii
Bath, Somerset, xiv; 15
Beaminster, Dorset (*Bega monasterium*), lvii, lviii; 47
Bedeslean, xl, xlii, xlix
Beer, Devon (Bere), 68
Beerham, Devon (Berham, -hamme), **19**
Benville, Dorset, 54
Berner(h), Cornwall, lvi
Bibbern Brook, Dorset (Bydeburnan), **8**
Binegar, Somerset, xlvi
Bishop's Lydeard, Somerset (*Lidgeard*), liv
Bishop's Tawton, Devon, xlviii
Bittleford, Devon (*Bitelanwyrthe*), **18**; lxii; 64
Bleadney, Somerset, liv
Boselingtone, App. 1; xli, xlix
Bovey Tracey, Devon, 64
Bradford Abbas, Dorset (*Bradanford, Bradanforda, Bradeford, Bradenford*), **7, 11**, App. 1; xxxiii, xxxvii, xl, xlii, xliii; 29, 31, 36, 44, 84, 86
Bredon, Worcs., 23
Brimley, Devon (*Bromleage*), **18**; lxii; 64
Bubbancumbe, Dorset, **13**
Buchæmatune, Dorset, **13**
Buckfast, Devon (*Bucfæsten*), **17**
Buckland, West, Somerset, liv
Bury, Suffolk, xviii, xix; 44

Cællincg, Cællwic see Kelly
Cærswylle see Abbotskerswell
Calne, Wilts. (*Cauna*), l, lviii
Cann, Devon, Dorset, l
Canterbury, Kent (*Cantwarubyri*), **10**; xviii, xxvi n. 31, xxxvi n. 48; 16, 17, 50
Castleton, Dorset, 31, 84
Catsley, Dorset (*Catesclive*), xxxv n. 46
Cerdel (? Chard, Somerset, or Chardstock, Devon), App. 1; xlii, xlvii, xlix
Cerne, river, Dorset (*iuxta Cernel*), App. 1; xlii, xliv, xlv
Chard, Somerset, xlii, xlvii
Chardstock, Devon, xlvii
Charminster, Dorset, xliv, xlv, lviii
Chester, Ches., xiv
Chesterblade, Somerset (*Chesterbled*), App. 1; xlii, xlvii, l
Chichester, Sussex, xiv
Chippenham, Wilts. (*Cippanham*), **7, 8**; 30
Cleihangre, Clethangre (? Clayhanger, Clinger), App. 1; xliii, l
Clifton Maybank, Dorset (*Cliftune, -tun*), **13**

INDEX OF PLACE-NAMES

Closworth, Somerset, 10
Coly, river, Devon (*Cullig*), **19**
Colyton, Devon, 67
Compton, Over and Nether, Dorset (*Comptone, Comtona, Contonam, Contone, Cumbtun, Cuncton*), **11**, App. 1; xxxii, xxxiii, xxxvi, xxxvii, xl, xlii, xliii; 31, 44
Congresbury, Somerset (*Conbusburie, Cungresbury*), App. 1; xli, xlvi, xlvii
Corscombe, Dorset (*Choriscumbam, Chorscumb, Corescumbam, Corigescumb, Corscumbe, Coruscumbe*), **15, 16**; App. 1; xvii, xxiii, xxviii, xxxii, xxxiii, xxxv, xxxvi, xxxix–xli, xliii; 10, 44, 53, 54, 57, 58
Crane, river, Dorset, 73, 74
Crediton, Somerset (*Cridianton, -tune*), **17**; xiii, xiv, xxxi, xlii, xlvi–xlviii, l, lii–lv; 2, 16, 60
Crutecoune see Erute-
Culmstock, Devon, xlvii
Cumtun bricgge, Dorset, **9**
Curndunam, ? Dorset, xxxvi

Easton, Somerset, xlvi
Edington, Wilts. (*Ethandun*), **3**; 9
Ernlege, 63
Erutecoune (? Yarcombe, Devon), App. 1; xlii, xlvii
Est Canne, App. 1; xlii, xlix, l
Ethelbaldingham, App. 1; xlii, xlix
Exeter, Devon (*Excestre, Exon*), **17**; xiv, xlvi, xlvii, l; 87
Exmouth, Devon (*Exan muthan*), **21**

Fleet *see* Seaton

Getemynst' see Yetminster
Glastonbury, Somerset, xxi, xxx, liv; 2, 3, 41, 87
Gloucester, Gloucs., 16
G'ncric, xl, xlii, xlix

Halstock, Dorset (*Algerstoke, Halgan stoc, -stoke, Halgastoc, -stoke*), **3, 11**, App. 1; xxxii n. 44, xxxiii, xxxvi, xxxvii, xl, xlii, xliii; 8, 10, 44
Hampton, Gloucs., lix
Hamptone (? *for* Southampton, Hants.), lix; 9
Haydon, Dorset (*Hægdune*), **17**
in Henangre, App. 1; xlii, xlvii
Henegar in Culmstock, Dorset, xlvii
Holcombe Rogus, Devon (*Holancumb, -cumbe*), **11, 13, 14, 17**; xxiv, xxxii, xxxiii, xxxv, xli, lvii; 44, 47–9, 59, 60
Hooke, river, Dorset, xlv
Horriford, Devon (*Horegan ford*), **19**
Horton Abbey, Dorset (*Hortune*), archives of, xv, xxxvi, lviii–lxii; charters of, xvii, xxi–xxxii, xxxvii; 54, 58; early history of, xiii, lviii–lxii
Huish, Dorset, Somerset (*Hiwisce*), **13**

Ipplepen, Devon (*Ipelanpænne, Iplanpen, -penne*), **18**; lxii; 63, 64
Iscan, xlii, xlix

Kelly, Cornwall (*Cællincg, Cællwic*), lv, lvi
Kilkhampton, Cornwall (*Kelk*), App. 1; xlii, xlviii, xlix
Kingston, Dorset, xxxvi

Lanprobi (? in Sherborne, Dorset), App. 1; xli, xliii, xlix; 2, 83–8
Lawhitton, Cornwall (*Landuuithan, -withan*), lv, lvi
Launceston, Cornwall, lvi
Laurestocam (? Dorset), xxxvi
Lichfield, Staffs., xiv
Lidden, river, Dorset, xlix
Lincoln, Lincs., xiv
Littleham, Devon (*Littlanhamme, lytlan-*), **21**; lx, lxi; 77
London, Middx, **12**; xix; 44, 46
Loscombe, Dorset, xxxvi
Luttes crundele, Somerset, 60
in Lydene, App. 1; xli, xlix
Lydlinch, Dorset, xlix
Lyme, Dorset (*Lim, Lym*), **2, 11**, App. 1; xxvi n. 32, xxxiii, xxxv, xl, xlii, xliii; 5, 44
Lyme Regis, Dorset, 5
Lyminge, Kent, 2

Maddacombe, Devon (*Mædercumbe*), **18**; 64
Maiden Newton, Dorset, 48
Maker, Cornwall (*Macor, Macuir*), App. 1; xli, xlii, xlviii, xlix
Malmesbury, Wilts., xxi, xxv, xxx–xxxii; 2, 3, 8, 15, 17, 18, 35
Mangerton, river, Dorset, xlv
Mannington, Dorset, 73
Matterley, Dorset (*mapoldor lea*), **20**
Mendips, range of hills, Somerset (*apud Menedip*), App. 1; xli, xlvi
Minehead, Somerset (*Mynheafdon*), **17**
Montebourg, abbey, France, xlv

Netherbury, Dorset (*Nutherburie*), App. 1; xlii, xliv, xlv, xlix, lviii
Netherstoke, Dorset (*Nitherstocam, -stoce*), **3**; xxxvi
Newton (*Niw[antun]*), **13**; 47, 48

Oakford, Devon, l
Oborne, Dorset (*Woborna, Woburnam, Woburnham, Wocburne, Womburnan, Wonburna*), **10, 11**, App. 1; xxxiii, xl, xli, xliii; 38, 39, 44, 86

INDEX OF PLACE-NAMES

Ogwell, Devon (*Woggan wille*), **18**; 64
Okeford, Dorset, l
Orchard, West, Dorset (*Archet*), lvii, lviii
Osanstoke (*Osanstoc*), **4**, **11**; xxii, xxxii, xxxiii, xl; 12, 44

Parret, river, Dorset, Somerset (*iuxta Pedridun, Pedrian*), App. 1; xli, xlii, xliv
Pawton, Cornwall (*Polltun*), xlix n. 80, lv, lvi
Peder . . ., **13**
Perrott, North, Somerset, xliv
Perrott, South, Dorset (*Pedret*), xxxv and n. 46, xliv, xlv
Peterborough, Northants., 35
Pidel (on river Piddle, Dorset), App. 1; xlii, xliv, xlv
Plympton, Devon, xlviii, liii n. 91, liv
Potterne, Wilts. (*Poterne*), App. 1; xlii, xlv and n. 63, lviii
Powerstock, Dorset (*Ponner, Porstock, -stoke, Power*), App. 1; xlii, xliv, xlv
Priddy, Somerset (*Prediau*), App. 1; xli, xlvi
Propeschirche, Dorset, xliii; 44, 85, 86

Rame peninsula, Cornwall, xlii, xlix
Ramsbury, Wilts., xiv, xxxi, xlv
Rochester, Kent, xxxvi n. 48
Ros (? Rame, Cornwall), App. 1; xlii, xlviii, xlix
Roseland, Cornwall, xlviii, xlix

St Germans, Cornwall, lii, liii, lvi
Salisbury, Wilts., xiii–xvi, xxii, xxiv, xxvi, xxxii, xxxv, xxxvi, xliv, xlv, li, lii, lvii; 2, 12, 36, 43, 46, 47, 58, 86
Sandford, Devon, liii
Seaton, Devon (*Fleet, Fleote*), **19**; xxxix; 67, 68, 77
Selsey, Sussex, xiv
Shaftesbury, Dorset, lviii, lix; 16, 30
Sherborne, Dorset (*Scireburnan, -burnensis*), archives of, xiii–xxi; castle, xxii; 30, 33; charters of, xxi–xxxii; dedication of, lix; estates of bishopric, xxxvii–lviii; estates of monastery, xxxii–xxxvi
Sherborne Wyke, Dorset (*Wica, Wycam*), xli, xliii, xliv; 31, 84
Snarstok, App. 1; xlii, xlix, l
Snarstokis Treov, xlii, xlix
Southampton, Hants., lix
Stalbridge, Dorset (*Stapelbrige, -brigge, Stapilbrigg, Staplebruge, Stapulbreicge, -brige, Stawilbrycge*), **11**, App. 1; xxxii, xxxiii, xxxvi, xxxvii, xlii, xliii
Stalbridge Weston, Dorset, xl; 33, *and see* Weston
Stocland, Dorset (*Stoc-*), **11**; xxxiii; 44, 85, 86

Stoke Abbott, Dorset (*Abbatistocam, Stocas, Stoce, Stoche, Stoches*), xxii, xxxii, xxxiii, xxxvi, xxxvii, xl, xlii, xliii; 44, 84
Sturminster Newton, Dorset, 48

Tamar, river, Cornwall (*iuxta Thamar*), App. 1; xli; 88
Tauistoke (? Tavistock or Tawstock), App. 1; xlii, xlviii
Tavistock, Devon (*Tæfingstoce*), **17**; xlviii, xlix, lx, lxi; 42
Tawstock, Devon, xlviii
Thorney, Middx, 42
Thornford, Dorset (*Thorford, Torneford*), **9**, **11**; xxii, xxvii, xxxiii, xli; 32, 36, 44, 86
Toller, river, Dorset (*Talre, in Tolra, Tollor*), **16**, App. 1; xlii, xlv, xlix
Toller Whelme, Dorset, xlv; 54, 58
Tregear, Cornwall, xlviii n. 79
Trigel, Cornwall, xlviii n. 79
Trill, Dorset (*Tril*), **13**

Up Cerne, Dorset (*Upcerle*), **13**; xlv, lvii

Wallingford, Berks., 32
Wareham, Dorset, lix, lxi
Wegentesfunte, App. 1; xlii, xlix
Wellington, Somerset, liv
Wellow, river, Somerset (*Wlueue, Wluue*), App. 1; xlii, xlvii
Wells, Somerset, xiii, xiv, xlvi, xlvii, xlix–lii; 15, 87
Westminster, Middx, xix; 2, 41, 42
Weston, Dorset (*Westona, -one, Westtune, Westum, -un*), **8**, **11**; xli; 30, 32, 33, 44, *and see* Stalbridge Weston
Weston in Corscombe, Dorset, 33
Whitby, Yorks., 2, 83
Wight, Isle of (*Wiht*), **17**
Willam (? Wells, Somerset), xl, xlii, xlix
Wilton, Wilts., lix; 9
Wimborne, Dorset, lxi
Wimborne, river, *now* r. Allen, Dorset (*Winborne, -burnan*), **20**, **20A**
Winchester, Hants. (*Wentanea, Wintancastrensis*), **5**; xxxvi n. 48, xlv n. 63; 9, 16, 17, 32, 85
— New Minster, li, lviii
— Old Minster, xxxi; 15, 18, 63
Winford, Somerset, l
Winfrith Newburgh, Dorset, l
Winsham, Somerset (*Winesham*), **17**
Winurod, App. 1; xlii, l
Woch, river, Dorset (*Woth*), App. 1; xlii, xlv
Wookey, Somerset, xlvi
Womburna see Oborne
Worcester, Worcs., xix, xxxiii; 35, 44
Writhlington, Somerset, lviii

Wulfheardigstoke, 11; xxxiii, xli; 44
Wycam see Sherborne Wyke
Wyllon, Dorset, 13
Wynford Eagle, Dorset, l
Wytecumbe, App. 1; xlii, l

Yarcombe, Devon (*Ercecombe, Erticoma*), xlviii
Yeo, river, Dorset (*Gifle*), 7, 9; 36
Yetminster, Dorset (*Getemynst'*), App. 1; xlii, xliv, xlv, xlix, lvii, lviii; 47

3 WORDS AND PERSONAL NAMES USED IN BOUNDARY MARKS

āc 'oak tree'. *greatan ac* **8**; *acs hirste* (interlin.) **20**; *okhurste, okstub* **20A**
adūne 'down', downward'. *adune pænne on cumbweg, adune on strem* **19**; *adun ponne andlang pæs broces* **21**
æcer 'field, plot of land'. *bydel æcer* **19**
Ælla or **Ælle** (pers. n.) ? *ellewurðie* **21**
æsc 'ash tree'. *on pone esc, æsc leage, æsc* **3A**; *æsc leage, on ðone æsc* **3B**; *æsc leage, of pam æsce* **8**
Ætta (pers. n.) *ættan wylles heafde, ættan dene, ættan wylle* **7**
ǣwielm 'river-source'. *tollor æwylman* **16**; *of pone æwylm* **21**
Afa (pers. n.) ? *on auan ford* **21**
ān 'one'. *ane dic* **3A**; *anne mapulder, anne stan* **8**; *an hiwisce* (*bis*) **18**; *anre higde* **19**
apuldor, apuldre 'apple tree'. *hara apolþore* (interlin.), *haran apoldran* **20**; *hore apeldore* (*bis*) **20A**
Axa (river n.) see index 2

Ballard (ME surname) or **Bealdheard** (OE pers. n.) *ballardesham* **20A**
*****Bealtūn** (? place-n.) *bealtunes ersc* **8**
bearu 'wood, grove'. *suð beara, ciddes beara* **20**; *suth beare, cheddes bere* **20A**
beneoðan 'under, beneath'. *beniðan dic* **19**
beorg 'barrow, tumulus, hill'. *beorh leage* **8**; *hornes beorh* **15**; *hornes beorg, ruwan beorge* **16**; *to pam beorge* **18**; *on pa beorgas* **20**; *gorbuerge, on pe buereges* **20A**; *fugelis beorh dune, fuhgeles beorhge* **21**
Beorhtrǣd (pers. n.) ? *beorreding mæd* **8**
Beornrǣd (pers. n.) ? *beorreding mæd* **8**
bere 'barley'. *berhamme* **8**
besūðan 'south of'. *besuðan dyrnan leage* **19**
betwēonan 'between'. *betweonan cealdan lace ҃ cullig* **19**
bilig, obscure, ?adj. *bilian wyrpe* **8**
biric, byric 'birch tree'. *bisic* [for *biric*] *garan* **20**; *Burches gore* **20A**
Biss (British river n.) ? *byssan broc* **15**
Bita (pers. n.) ? *bitun liege* **19**
Bitelanwyrðe see index 2
bitun, obscure. *bitun liege* **19**

blæc 'black'. *blacan dune, blacan dune ecge* **20**; *blake dune, blake dun egge* **20A**
Breguweald (pers. n.) *browoldesham* **3B**; *breowoldesham* **15**; *browoldes heal* **16**
brōc 'brook'. *holan broc, hlosbroc* **3A**; *stanbroc* **8**; *byssan broc* **15**; *cealdan broc, holan broc* **20**; *chealde brok, hole broc* **20A**; *to pan broce* **21**
brōm 'broom'. *brum dun* **16**
brōmlēage see index 2
brycg 'bridge'. *cumtun bricgge* (see index 2) **9**
burna 'stream'. *mylenburnan* **7**; *bydeburnan* **8**; *mylenburnna* **9**
Bȳd (river n.) ? *bydeburnan* (see index 2) **8**
bydel 'beadle, herald, warrant officer'. *bydel æcer* **19**
byden 'barrel, tub'. ? *bydeburnan* (see index 2) **8**
Byssa (pers. n.) ? *byssan broc* **15**

ceald 'cold'. *cealdan lace* **19**; *cealdan broc* **20**; *chealde brok* **20A**
Cidd (pers. n.) *ciddes beara* **20**; *cheddes bere* **20A**
cirice 'church'. ? *cirichylle* **8**. See also **crȳg**
coccel 'cockle, tares'. *coccelmæres dene* **16**
col 'charcoal'. *colpytte* **16**
corf 'cut, gap'. *miclan corf* **15**; *corf get* **16**
Cotta (pers. n.) *cotte dene* **16**
croft 'small enclosed field'. *kinges crofte, walerondes crofte, hwite croftes dich* **20A**
crūg (O. Welsh) 'hill, barrow'. *on cric* **3A**; *cric* **3B**; ? *ciric hylle* **8**; *miclan cruc* **15**; *on cruc* **16**
crundel 'quarry, chalk-pit'. *focgan crundel* **15**; *fogga crundel* **16**
crymel 'small piece'. *crymelhamme* **19**
cullig (river n.) see index 2 under Coly
cumb 'valley'. *tymbercumb, wibbelescumb* **3A**; *hloscumbes heafud* **7**; *rigcumb* **16**; *mæscumbe, mædercumbe* **18**; *scypcumb, cumbweges heafod, cumbweg* **19**
cumtun see index 2
cyning 'king'. *kinges crofte, kinges hei3es hurne* **20A**

denu 'valley, dean'. *ættan dene, andlang dene* **7**; *ærne dene* **15**; *cotte dene, coccelmæres dene, earne dene* **16**; *langan dene* **18**

dīc 'dyke, ditch'. *ane dic, liuedic* **3A**; *lyfdic ad aliam lyfdic* **3B**; *ealdan dic, andlang dic* (*bis*), *oþ þa dic* **7**; *lyfdic* **15**; *on þa dic, beniðan dic* **19**; *in to þare dich, trockes dich, hwite croftes dich* **20A**; *ealdan dic* **21**

dierne 'hidden, obscure'. *dyrnan leage* **19**

dūn 'down, hill, moor'. *brum dun* **16**; *blacan dune, blacan dune ecge* **20**; *blake dune, blake dun egge* **20A**; *fugelis beorh dune* **21**

eald 'old'. *ealdan herpað* **3A**; *ealdan dic* **7**; *ealdan weg, ealdan hagan* **8**; *ealdan dic* **21**

earn 'eagle'. ? *ærne dene, earne leawege* **15**; *earne dene, earna dene* **16**

ēast adj. 'east, eastern'. *east healfe* **7**; *east healfe* **9**; *east lea* **20**; *east lea* **20A**
— adv. 'eastwards'. *þanon east* **7**; *east andlang weges* **8**; *þanone east* (*bis*), *east andlang þære dic, east up andlang þæs slædes* **21**

ēastmest 'easternmost'. *eastemestan holan weg* **9**

ēasteweard 'east side of'. *on lyngærstun eastewerdne* **9**; *on fogga crundel eastweardne* **16**

ecg 'edge'. *on ecge, andlang ecge* **7**; *be ecge* **9**; *norh ecge, blacan dune ecge* **20**; *norþh egge, blake dun egge* **20A**

Ecgwulf (pers. n.) *ecgulfes treow* **7**

ellen 'elder tree'. ? *ellewurðie* **21**

ende 'end, limit'. *leas ende* **15**; *leas ende* **16**; *weggeleawe norþ ende* **20A**

Enna (pers. n.) *ennan pol* **7**

eoþ, obscure. *oþ eoþ* **18**

ersc 'stubble field'. *bealtunes ersc* **8**

Exe (river n.) *Exan muðan* (see index 2) **21**

fal(o)d 'fold, pen'. *faldhege* **3A**

feld 'open land'. *ut on feld* **8**

***filde** 'dwellers in the open land'. *fildena wylle* **8**

***Focga** (pers. n.) ? *focgan crundel* **15**; ? *fogga crundel* **16**

***fogga** '? a type of grass'. ? *focgan crundel* **15**; ? *fogga crundel* **16**

ford 'ford'. *ford, horsford, fyres hylleford* **3A**; *syres* [for *fyres*] *ford* **15**; *fyrs ford, staford* **16**; *horegan ford, nyðeran stanford* **19**; ? *wiþehlakeuorde,* ? *sondieuord* **20A**; *auan ford* **21**

fōt 'foot'. *yrþlandes foton* **19**

fugol 'bird, fowl'. *fugelis beorh dune, fuhgeles beorhge* **21**

fūl 'dirty, foul'. *fulan slo* **16**; *fulan landa* **21**

fyrs 'furse, gorse, bramble'. *fyres hylleford* **3A**; *syres* [for *fyres*] *ford* **15**; *fyrs ford* **16**

gærstūn 'paddock, grass enclosure'. *lyngærstun* **9**

gāra 'gore, point of land, triangular plot'. *bisic garan* **20**; *Burches gore, gorbuerge* **20A**

geat 'gate, opening'. *corf get, þam gete, hlype gete* **16**; *ruwan leges gete* **20**; *ruan leges ʒete* **20A**

gelǣte 'junction of roads'. ? *weggeleawe* **20A**; *wega gelæto* **21**

(ge)mǣre 'boundary'. *Wulfrices gemære* **20**; *mer haʒan, wluriches imere* **20A**

gemearcode 'marked'. *gemearcodan lindan* **20**; *imerekede linde* **20A**

gerihte 'straight on'. *on gerihte* **8**; *on gerihte* (*ter*) **19**

gierd 'twig, rod'. *gyrd lea* **16**

Gifle (early n. of r. Yeo, see index 2) *oþ gifle* **7**; *on gifle* **9**

grēat 'massive, thick'. *greatan ac* **8**

grēne 'green'. *grenan weg* **15**; *grenan weg* (*bis*) **21**

hafoc 'hawk'. *hafocys setle* **21**

haga 'hedge, fence, enclosure'. *on hagan* (*ter*), *ealdan hagan* **8**; *on þone hagan, lyc hagan* **15**; *mearc hagan* **20**; *mer haʒan* **20A**

hamm 'enclosure, meadow, water-meadow'. *browoldesham* **3B**; *breowoldesham* **15**; *berhamme, crymelhamme* **19**; *ballardesham* **20A**

hār 'hoary, grey, old', possible secondary meaning 'boundary'. *haran stanas, hara apolþore* (interlin.), *haran apoldran, haran wiðig,* ? *heara Wulfrices gemære* **20**; *hore stones* (*bis*), *hore apeldore* (*bis*), *hore wiþeh, hore wluriches imere* **20A**

hēafod (i) 'head, upper end'. *hloscumbes heafud* **7**; *cumbweges heafod* **19**; *wiþehlake heafde* **20A**
(ii) 'source'. *ættan wylles heafde* **7**

hēah 'high, lofty'. *hean wifeles hylle* **8**

healf (i) 'side'. *east healfe* **7**; *east healfe* **9**
(ii) 'half'. *healfan treowe* **16**; *healfan hide* **21**

healh 'nook, corner'. *browoldes heal* **16**; *norþ heal, suþ heal* **20**; *north heale, sut heal* **20A**

hege 'hedge'. *wiþighege, faldhege* **3A**; *kinges heiʒes hurne* **20A**

her(e)paδ 'military path, highway'. *ealdan herpað* **3A**; *andlanges herpaðes* **15**; *on herepað, on herpað* (*bis*) **18**; *on ðone herpoð* **19**; *to þan herpaðe* **21**

hīd 'hide of land'. *anre higde* **19**; *healfan hide* **21**

hīwisc 'hide of land'. *an hiwisce* (*bis*) **18**

hlīep geat 'leap-gate'. *hlype gete* **16**

hlōse 'pigsty'. *hlosbroc* **3A**; *hloscumbes heafud* **7**; *litegan hlosstede* **19**

WORDS AND NAMES USED IN BOUNDARY MARKS

hlȳde 'noisy brook'. *on hlidan* **3A**; *hlydan pol* **15**; *hlyda pol* **16**
hol 'hollow, lying in a hollow'. *holan broc* **3A**; *holan weg* **9**; *holan broc* **20**; *hole wei, hole broc* **20A**
horig 'foul, dirty'. *horgan sloh* **8**; *horegan ford* **19**
Horn (pers. n.) ? *hornes beorh* **15**; ? *hornes beorg* **16**
horn 'pinnacle, gable, horn'. ? *hornes beorh* **15**; ? *hornes beorg* **16**
hors 'horse'. *horsford* **3A**; *horsa tor* **18**
hrēod 'reed, rush'. *hreodmæde lace* **19**
hrycg 'ridge'. *up to hricgge, andlang hrigcges* **9**; *andlang hricges* **15**; *smalan hricg* **16**; *andlang hricges* **19**
hrycgweg 'ridgeway'. *on þæne hricgweg, of þam hricgwege* **19**; *hricgwege* **21**
hūne 'hoar-hound' (a plant). *huna lege* **3A**
hund 'dog'. *hunda troh* **3A**
hwīt 'white'. *hwite croftes dich* **20A**
hyll 'hill'. *fyres hylleford* **3A**; *cirichylle, hean wifeles hylle* **8**; *stocchylle* **16**
hyran 'to belong'. *þa wic þe þar to hyrþ* **18**
hyrne 'angle, corner, curving valley'. *on hyrn, up andlang hyrn* **20**; *kinges hei3es hurne, on hurn* **20A**
hyrst 'hillock, copse'. *andlang readan hyrstes* **16**; *acs hirste* (interlin.) **20**; *okhurste* **20A**
-ing- (connective particle) *beorreding mæd* **8**; *odding torre* **18**

lacu 'stream'. *andlang lace* (*bis*) **7**; *on þa lace* **9**; *on þa lace, oþ þa laca* **18**; *hreodmæde lace, cealdan lace* **19**; *wiþehlake heafde, wiþehlakeuorde* **20A**
land 'ground, piece of land'. *þæs landes* **3A**; *fulan landa* **21**
landgemǣre 'boundary'. *landgemære* **3A**; *landgemæru* **9**; *landgemæra* **18**; *landgemæro* **19**; *landgemære* **20**; *londimere* **20A**; *landgemæro* **21**
landscaru 'boundary'. *landscore* (*quin*) **18**
lang 'long, tall'. *langan dene* **18**; *lange þorne* **20A**
lēah 'wood, clearing, meadow'. *preosta lege, huna lege, æsc lege* **3A**; *æsc leage* **3B**; *beorh leage, æsc leage* **8**; *leas ende, trynd leawege, earna leawege* **15**; *leas ende, gyrd lea* **16**; *dyrnan leage, bitun liege* **19**; *mapoldor lea, east lea, linlæge mor* (interlin.), *linleage mor, ruwan leges gete* **20**; *mapeldure lea, east lea, linlege mor, linle3e mor,* ? *weggeleawe, ruan leges 3ete* **20A**
Lidwiccas 'people of Brittany'. ? *lydewicnæsse* **21**
līn 'flax'. *lyngærstun* **9**; ? *linlæge mor* (interlin.), ? *linleaga mor* **20**; ? *linlege mor* (*bis*) **20A**

lind 'lime tree'. *þære linde* **18**; ? *linlæge mor* (interlin.), ? *linleaga mor, gemearcodan lindan* **20**; ? *linlege mor (bis), imerekede linde* **20A**
liteg, obscure, ?adj. *litegan hlosstede* **19**
lycce 'enclosure'. ? *lyc hagan* **15**
Lyfdic (? river n.; v. *dīc*, first element obscure) *on liuedic* **3A**; *de amne lyfdic, ad aliam lyfdic* **3B**; *on lyfdic* **15**
lȳtel 'little'. *lyttlan tor* **18**

mǣd 'meadow'. *west mæd, beorreding mæd* **8**; *hreodmæde lace* **19**
mǣddre 'madder'. *mædercumbe* **18**
mǣdrǣden 'piece of mown grassland'. *seo mædrædon* **19**
mæst 'mast, food for swine'. ? *mæscumbe* **18**
mapulder 'maple'. *anne mapulder* **8**; *mapoldor lea* **20**; *mapeldure lea* **20A**
mearc 'boundary'. *on merc* **9**; *mearc hagan* **20**; *mer hagan* **20A**
mere 'pool'. ? *coccelmæres dene* **16**; *on þone mere* **20**; *on þane mere* **20A**; *norþran mere* **21**
micel 'big'. *miclan corf, miclan cruc* **15**
middeweard 'middle of'. *to ættan dene middeweardre* **7**; *on miclan cruc middewearne* **15**; *on cruc middeweardne, on brum dun middewearne, on rig cumb middeweardne, on gyrd lea middeweardne* **16**; *on mapoldor lea middeweardne* **20**; *on mapeldure lea midewarde* **20A**
mōr 'marshland, moor'. *linlæge mor* (interlin.), *linleaga mor* **20**; *linlege mor* (*bis*) **20A**
murt, obscure. *murtes wyll* **16**
mūða 'mouth'. *Exan muðan* **21**
mylen 'mill'. *mylenburnan* **7**; *mylenburnna* **9**

næss 'promontory'. *lydewicnæsse* **21**
niðera 'lower'. *niþerstoce* (see index 2) **3A**; *nyðeran stanford* **19**
niðeweard 'bottom of'. *on bealtunes ersc nyþeweardne* **19**
norð, norðera adj. 'north, northern'. *norh ecge, norþ heal* **20**; *norþh egge, north heale, weggeleawe norþ ende* **20A**; *norþran mere* **21**
— adv. 'northwards'. *norþ on readan weg, norþ andlang hricges, norð on þæs yrþlandes foton* **19**; *norþ on þa haran apoldran* **20**; *north on þe hore apeldore* **20A**; *norð on þone grenan weg* (*bis*) **21**
norðan 'north of'. *be norðan lydewicnæsse, be norðan þam fulan landa* **21**
norðeweard 'north part of'. *on beorreding mæd norþewearde* **8**

Odda (pers. n.) *odding torre* **18**
ok see **āc**

WORDS AND NAMES USED IN BOUNDARY MARKS

on, obscure. *ones þorne* **20A**
ongēan 'against'. *upp ongean stream, ongean stream* **16**

penn 'fold, pen'. *on pen, of pænne* **18**
pleging stōw (variant of **pleg stōw**) 'place for sports'. *plegin stowe* **21**
pōl 'pool'. *ennan pol* **7**; *hlydan pol* **15**; *hlyda pol* **16**
prēost 'priest'. *preosta lege* **3A**
pytt 'pit, hollow'. *colpytte,* ~ *pette, wæter pytt* **16**

rā 'roe, roebuck'. *ran wylle* **9**
rēad 'red'. *readan weg* **3A**; *readan hyrstes* **16**; *readan weg* **19**; *readan weg* **20**; *rede wei* **20A**
riht adj. 'straight, correct'. *on riht landscore* **18**
rihte, rihtes adv. 'straight, directly'. *forðrihtes on browoldes heal* **16**; *rihte to hafocys setle, rihte to þan hricgwege* **21**
rīð 'stream'. *andlang riðan* **21**
***rod, *rodu** 'clearing'. *on þa rode* **18**
rūh 'rough'. *ruwan beorge* **16**; *ruwan leges gete* **20**; *ruan leges ʒete* **20A**
ryge 'rye'. *rigcumb* **16**

sǣ 'sea'. *up of þære sæ, ut on sæ* **19**; *ut on Sæ* **21**
sandig 'sandy'. *sondieuord* **20A**
scēotan 'to run, rush, flow'. *cealdan broc scyt on winburnan* **20**; *chealden brok scyt on Winborne* **20A**
scȳp (W. Saxon) 'sheep'. *scypcumb* **19**
sele 'hall, dwelling'. *on þone sele* **21**
setl 'dwelling, place'. *hafocys setle* **21**
slæd 'valley'. *on þæt slæd* **19**; *þat slad* **20A**; *to þam slæde* **21**
slǣget 'sheep pasture'. *on þæt slæget* **20**; *on þat sleaʒet* **20A**
slǣp 'slippery, muddy place'. *on slæp* **9**
slōh 'slough, mire'. *horgan sloh* **8**; *fulan slo* **16**
sluth (? river n.) *in to sluth, andlang sluth* **20A**
smæl 'small, narrow'. *smalan hricg* **16**
sondieuord see **sandig**
stān 'stone'. *stanbroc, on anne stan* **8**; ? *staford* **16**; *swiþredes stan* **18**; *nyðeran stanford* **19**; *haran stanas* **20**; *hore stones* (*bis*) **20A**
stānig 'stony'. *stanigan weg* **16**
stede 'place, site'. *litegan hlosstede* **19**
stigol 'stile'. *on stigele* **3A**
stoc 'place, dwelling'. *niþerstoce* (see index 2) **3A**
stocc 'stump, stake'. *stocchylle* **16**
stōw see **pleging stow**

strēam 'stream, current'. *andlang streames* (*bis*) **7**; *andlang streames, up on stream* **9**; *andlang streames, upp ongean stream* (*bis*) **16**; *on streame, up be streame* **18**; *adune on strem* **19**; *andlang streames* **20**; *an lang streames* **20A**; *up on stryem, up andlang stryemes* **21**
strōd 'marshy land'. *strode* **20A**
stubb 'tree-stump'. *okstub* **20A**
sūð adj. 'southern'. *suð beara, sup heal* **20**; *suth beare, sutheal* **20A**
— adv. 'southward'. *sup on þone mere* **20**; *suth on þane mere, Sutþe to weggeleawe, suthe in to þare dich, sutþe under gorbuerge, suthe anlang sluth, suthe þane hole wei, sutþe to þan lange þorne, suthe in þane okstub, suth in þe hwite croftesdich, suthe to ones þorne* **20A**; *suð to ellewurðie* **21**
sūðeweard 'south part of'. *bydel æcer suþeweardne, berham suðeweardne* **19**; *suð beara suþeweardne, sup heal supeweardne* **20**; *sut heal suthward* **20A**
sūðweard 'southwards'. *suthward on þe wiþeʒes* **20A**
Swīðrǣd (pers. n.) *swiþredes stan* **18**
syres see **fyres**

þorn 'thorn tree'. *lange þorne, ones þorne* **20A**
thwert-over (ME) 'transversely'. *þwrthouer to walerondes crofte* **20A**
timber 'timber'. *tymbercumb* **3A**
Tollor (British river n.) *tollor æwylman* **16**
torr 'rock, tor'. *horsa tor, lyttlan tor, odding torre* **18**
trēow 'tree'. *ecgulfes treow* **7**; *healfan treowe* **16**
trind '? round'. *trynd leawege* **15**
trock, obscure. *trockes dich* **20A**
trog 'trough, trough-like valley'. *hunda troh* **3A**

ufeweard 'upper part of'. *on west mæd ufewearde* **8**; *on readan weg ufeweardne* **19**
ūtscyt 'outlet'. *mylenburnna ut scyt* **9**

Wæneca (pers. n.) *wænecan wyrþ* **20**; *wenecan wwrþe* **20A**
wæter 'water'. *wæter pytt* **16**; *in þat water* (*bis*) **20A**
Walerond (ME pers. n.) *walerondes crofte* **20A**
weg 'way, path'. *readan weg* **3A**; *ealdan weg, andlang weges* (*bis*) **8**; *holan weg* **9**; *grenan weg, trynd leawege, earna leawege* **15**; *stanigan weg* **16**; *readan weg, andlang weges, cumbweges heafod, cumbweg* **19**; *readan weg* **20**; *weggeleawe, hole wei, rede wei* **20A**; *wega gelæto, grenan weg* (*bis*) **21**. See *hrycgweg*

west adj. 'western'. *west mæd* 8
—adv. 'westwards'. *west be ecge* 9; *west andlang weges, west þonne on herpoð* 19; *west on wænecan wyrþ* 20; *west on wiþehlake heafde* 20A
***Wibbel** (pers. n.) ? *wibbelescumb* 3A
wīc 'dwelling, house, village'. *on þa wic* 18
Wifel (pers. n.) ? *hean wifeles hylle* 8
Winburna (river n.) see index 2
wīðig 'willow'. *wiþighege* 3A; *in þa wiþgas* (interlin.), *haran wiðig* 20; *on þe wiþeʒes, hore wiþeh, wiþehlake heafde, wiþehlakeuorde* 20A
woggan wylle see index 2

worð, wyrð 'farm, homestead'. *bilian wyrþe* 8; *wænecan wyrþ* 20; *wenecan wwrþe* 20A
worðig 'farm, homestead'. *ellewurðie* 21
Wulfric (pers. n.) *heara Wulfrices gemære* 20; *hore wluriches imere* 20A
wyll, wylle (W. Saxon) 'spring'. *ættan wylles heafde,* ~*wylle* 7; *fildena wylle* 8; *ran wylle* 9; *murtes wyll* 16
wyrtruma 'root, ? edge of wood'. *be wyrtruman (bis)* 16

yrðland 'arable, ploughed land'. *yrþlandes foton* 19

4 LATIN GLOSSARY

The following abbreviations are used: n. = noun; v. = verb; adj. = adjective; adv. = adverb; p.p. = past participle.

acumen (n.) [16]: point, *hence* uppermost part *uel. sim.*
adnichilatio (n.) [15]: nullification
agellus (n.) [2, 3, 11]: field
agius (adj., from Greek ἅγιος) [19, 21]: holy
Albion (n.) [8, 11, 15]: Britain
amminiculum (n.) [15]: aid, support
anathema (n.) [8]: curse, excommunication
anathematizatus (p.p., from Greek ἀναθεματίζειν) [5, 9]: cursed, excommunicated
angligenus (adj.) [19]: English
antedictus (adj.) [7]: aforesaid
apicellus (n.) [8]: letter, character
archipresul (n.) [12, 19]: archbishop

barathrum (n.) [16]: Hell
basileus (n., from Greek βασιλεύς) [11, 18]: king
brauium (n., from Greek βραβεῖον) [11]: prize, reward
breuicula (n.) [7, 15]: a brief document
breuiuncula (n.) [15, 20]: a brief document
Bryttania, Britania (n.) [7, 19]: Britain

caraxo, craxo, karaxo (v., from Greek χαράσσω) [8, 15, 19, 20]: to write, endorse
carisma (n., from Greek χάρισμα) [18]: favour, bounty, grace
caruca (n.) [12]: cart (*in the phrase* carucarum onera, cart-loads)
cassabundus (adj.) [3]: tottering (*a phrase whose currency among draftsmen of charters is probably owed to Aldhelm*)
cassata, -um, -us (n.) [3, 4, 7, 9, 11]: a measure of land, a hide

cautio (n.) [1]: a written undertaking
cenobialis (adj.) [15, 16]: pertaining to a monastery
centupliciter (adv.) [1]: a hundredfold
circumgiro, -gyro (v.) [15, 16, 20]: to enclose, bound
circumseptus (p.p.) [7]: enclosed, bounded
cleronomus (n., from Greek κληρονόμος) [20]: heir
clito, clyto (n., ultimately from Greek κλυτός) [15, 19]: prince
condono (v.) [2]: to grant
confinium (n.) [16]: bounds
cosmus (n., from Greek κόσμος) [19]: the world, universe
cyrographum (n., from Greek χειρόγραφον) [19]: a hand-written document, charter

dapsilitas (n.) [7]: bounty, generosity
decima (n.) [12]: tithe
deifice (adv.) [15]: divinely

eiulo (v.) [1]: to bewail, lament
elimosina (n.) [2, 3, 16]: alms
exenium (n., ultimately from Greek ξείνια) [19]: gift, donation

familia (n.) [8]: unit of land (?); *see above,* p. 32
fiscus (n.) [1, 5]: tax
flosculus (n.) [15]: a little flower

grauedo (n.) [16, 21]: burden
grauitudo (n.) [1]: burden, oppression
gyrus (n.) [18]: circuit

ierarchia (n., from Greek ἱεραρχία) [**8, 16**]: holy office
indeclinabiliter (adv.) [**18**]: unalterably, unceasingly
indesinenter (adv.) [**8**]: incessantly
indicibilis (adj.) [**7**]: unspeakable, indescribable
indiculus (n.) [**8, 16**]: document, charter
ineffabilis (adj.) [**15**]: indescribable
inenarrabilis (adj.) [**15**]: indescribable
inmarcescibiliter (adv.) [**1**]: unfadingly

leuigo (v.) [**5**]: to lighten, alleviate
literula (n.) [**7, 8**]: letter, character

mancusa (n.) [**19**]: mancus (a gold coin, or its equivalent in gold or silver, with a value of 30 silver pence)
mansa (n.) [**16, 18, 19, 20, 21**]: a unit of land, a hide (*in* **11** *the word is erroneously spelled* massa)
mansio (n.) [**1, 2**]: a dwelling, a unit of land
mansiuncula (n.) [**15**]: a little dwelling, a unit of land
minula (n.) [**7**]: a small letter (?) (*from* minium?)
misericorditer (adv.) [**1**]: mercifully
monarchus (n., from Greek μόναρχος) [**15, 19, 21**]: king, monarch
monasteriunculum (n.) [**3**]: a small monastery
multipliciter (adv.) [**2**]: in manifold ways

omnipatrans (adj.) [**8**]: all-accomplishing, almighty
omnitonans (adj.) [**7**]: all-thundering, almighty
optimas (n.) [**3, 7**]: magnate, prominent man in the realm

patricius (n.) [**2**]: important man

patricius (adj.) [**1**]: pertaining to a *patricius*
peccamen (n.) [**2**]: sin
perdono (v.) [**5**]: to grant
pergamenum (*par-*) (n.) [**15, 20**]: parchment
peripsema (n., from Greek περίψημα) [**7, 8**]: off-scouring, rubbish (*a word which owes its currency among draftsmen of charters to Aldhelm*)
philargiria (n., from Greek φιλαργυρία) [**11**]: love of silver, avarice
protomartyr (n.) [**3**]: the first martyr, St Stephen
protoplastus (n.) [**15**]: the first-created man, Adam

quisquilia (n.) [**7, 8**]: waste, rubbish (*a word which owes its currency among draftsmen of charters to Aldhelm*)

reboans (adj.) [**7**]: resounding, echoing

satrapa (n.) [**5**]: *probably a latinization of* OE thegn
scedula (n.) [**3, 7, 8, 15, 20**]: document, charter
singrapha (n., from Greek συγγραφή) [**4, 8, 16, 19**]: charter, document
solicola (n.) [**7, 8, 15, 20**]: inhabitant (of the land)
soma (n., from Greek σῶμα) [**8**]: body

tartareus (adj.) [**1**]: hellish
tartara (n.) [**15, 18**]: Hell
tauma (n., ultimately from the Greek letter *tau*) [**19, 21**]: +, the sign of the cross
taxatio (n.) [**5**]: assessment for taxation, fine
tenor (n.) [**7**]: condition
totillo (v.) [**7, 8**]: to totter

uocamen (n.) [**15, 19**]: name
uulgariter (adv.) [**16, 18**]: commonly

DIPLOMATIC INDEX

An index of *sanctio* clauses is regretfully omitted because it would involve extensive quotation from the texts.

1 VERBAL INVOCATIONS AND PROEMS

(a) *Invocations*
Annuente dei patris ineffabili humanae proli clementia **15**
In nomine cosmi saluatoris … immortale **19**
In nomine Dei nostri saluatoris **4**
In nomine Domini **12**
In nomine domini Iesu Christi **10**
In nomine domini nostri Iesu Christi **1, 18, 21**
Regnante Domino nostro inperpetuum **5**
Regnante imperpetuum Deo et domino nostro Iesu Christo **20**
Regnante imperpetuum domino nostro Iesu Christo **2, 3, 6, 22**

(b) *Proems*
Cum cuius imperio hic labentis seculi prosperitas **20**
Dum in nostris temporibus bellorum incendia **5**
Flebilia fortiter detestanda totillantis saeculi piacula **7, 8**
Et hoc saeculum iusto moderamine dispensanti **2**
Igitur apostolicis dictis nos congrue parere oportet **18**
Omnia quae uidentur temporalia sunt—et quae non uidentur aeterna sunt **4**
Omnis quidem susceptio et datio passionum terrarum **21**
Omnia qui hic humanis considerantur obtutibus **16**
Omnia speciosa regna huius labentis uitae **3**
Oportet nos ergo fratres karissimi istum contempnere mundum **9**
Ðæm hiehstan ðæm untosprecendlican ealra ðinga **6, 22**

2 DISPOSITIVE WORDS

(a) *Past tense*
annotare mandaui **15**
annui **11**
ic habba … agifen **10**
impendere curaui **21**
liberaui **3**
perdonare diiudicaui **5**

(b) *Present tense*
annotari censeo **11**
concedo **16, 18, 19**

condonare dignatus sum **2**
confirmo **20**
constituo **1**
constituo et ordino **12**
do atque concedo **9**
forgyfe, -gyfo **6, 22**
libenter tribuo **7**

(c) *Future tense*
dabo **4**

DIPLOMATIC INDEX

3 ROYAL STYLES

(A) *Dispositive clause*   (B) *Subscription*

Cenwalch
regnante Deo rex **1**   rex **1**

Cynewulf
rex **2**   rex **2**

Æthelwulf
occidentalium Saxonum rex **3**
rex occidentalium Saxonum **4, 5**   rex **3, 4, 5**

Æthelberht
West Saxna kyning **6**   cyning, rex **6**

Æthelstan
rex Anglorum per omnitonantis dexteram totius Britannie regni solio sullimatus **7**   totius florentis Bryttannie rex **7**
rex Anglorum per omnipatrantis dexteram apice totius Albionis dullimatus **8**   singularis priuilegii ierarchia preditus rex **8**

Eadred
occidentalium Saxonum rex **9**   rex **9**

Eadwig
gentis Anglorum ceterarumque per gyrum nationum basileus **18**   rex Anglorum **18**

Edgar
cing **10**   cyning **10**

Æthelred
totius Albionis Dei gubernante moderamine basileus **11**   rex Anglorum **11**
gratia Dei sullimatus rex et monarchus totius Albionis **15**   gubernator sceptri huius insulae **15**

diuina dispositione gentis Angligenae et diuersarum nationum industrius rex **19**   totius Britannie monarchus **19**

Cnut
rex Anglorum **16**   singularis priuilegii ierarchia preditus rex **16**

rex Anglorum ceterarumque gentium in circuitu persistentium gubernator et rector **20**   gubernator sceptri huius insulae **20**

Edward the Confessor
rex regali dignitate **21**   rex Britanniae totius Anglorum monarchus **21**

Englalandes cynge mid Godes gyfe **22**